PRAISE FOR *SPRINTING THROUGH NO MAN'S LAND*

"Astonishing. With beautiful prose, compelling narrative, and meticulous research, Adin Dobkin does far more than just record the history of a race—he conjures an entire world reeling in the aftermath of World War I."

—Phil Klay, National Book Award winner and author of *Missionaries*

"Beautifully written, compellingly told. Adin Dobkin weaves together a masterful narrative of war, returning, and the resilience of the human spirit."

—Elliot Ackerman, National Book Award finalist and coauthor of *2034: A Novel of the Next World War*

"A moving and deeply researched book documenting the Tour de France's rebirth after the Great War. Dobkin's prose is lyric and at turns intricate and sweeping. He brilliantly captures Europe's collective longing to rebuild through a competition whose epic terms and improbable cast of characters speak to the hope and uncertainty that defined a generation devastated by violence. More than a chronicle of sport, this is an incredible story of how the mind and body reckon with the scars of war."

—Jen Percy, author of *Demon Camp: The Strange and Terrible Saga of a Soldier's Return from War*

"Vivid and inspiring. A century ago, in a brutal race like no other, cyclists faced war-torn roads and their own demons, and Dobkin spins through their tale in a sweet gear, showing the power of sport and the resilience of the heart."

—Jason Fagone, author of the bestselling *The Woman Who Smashed Codes: A True Story of Love, Spies, and the Unlikely Heroine Who Outwitted America's Enemies*

SPRINTING THROUGH NO MAN'S LAND

SPRINTING THROUGH NO MAN'S LAND

ENDURANCE, TRAGEDY, AND REBIRTH IN THE 1919 TOUR DE FRANCE

ADIN DOBKIN

Published by Little A, New York

www.apub.com

Amazon, the Amazon logo, and Little A are trademarks of Amazon.com, Inc., or its
affiliates.

ISBN-13: 9781542018821 (hardcover)
ISBN-10: 154201882X (hardcover)

ISBN-13: 9781542018838 (paperback)
ISBN-10: 1542018838 (paperback)

Cover design by Edward Bettison

Cover Photo: 1912 Tour de France by Maurice-Louis Branger/Roger Viollet/
Getty Images

Printed in the United States of America

First edition

To Jeff and Julie

For whom left am I first?

—Lucie Brock-Broido, "You Have Harnessed Yourself
Ridiculously to This World"

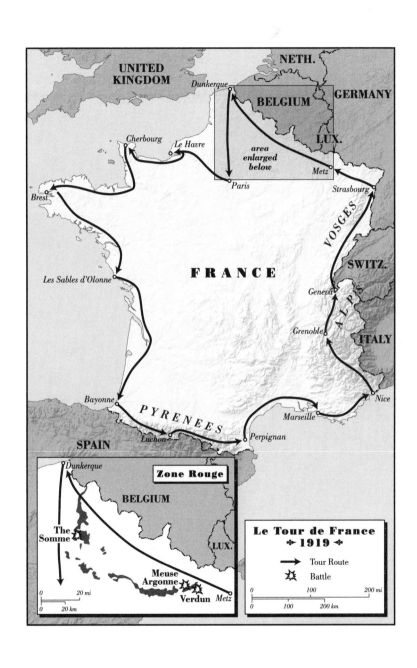

UNITED
KINGDOM

NETH.

Dunkerque

BELGIUM

GERMANY

LUX.

Cherbourg *Le Havre*

*area
enlarged
below*

Metz

Paris

Strasbourg

Brest

V O S G E S

SWITZ.

F R A N C E

Les Sables d'Olonne

Geneva

A L P S

Grenoble

ITALY

Bayonne

Nice

P Y R E N E E S

Marseille

SPAIN

Luchon

Perpignan

Dunkerque

Zone Rouge

BELGIUM

**The
Somme**

LUX.

**Meuse
Argonne**

Verdun *Metz*

0	20 mi
0	20 km

**Le Tour de France
✠ 1919 ✠**

→ Tour Route

✵ Battle

0	100	200 mi
0	100	200 km

LIST OF CHARACTERS

Jean Alavoine—Thirty-one-year-old from Roubaix, France. Sprinter. Placed third in 1914 Tour de France. Served with the Twenty-seventh Dragoon Regiment and the Nineteenth Train Squadron.

Marguerite Alibert—Twenty-eight-year-old courtesan and socialite from Paris, France. Past lover of Edward, Prince of Wales.

Honoré Barthélémy—Twenty-seven-year-old from Paris, France. Climber. Turned professional in 1918. The 1919 edition was his first Tour de France. Served with the Sixth Dragoon Regiment.

Eugene Bullard—Twenty-three-year-old from Columbus, Georgia. Former boxer. Served with the 170th Infantry Regiment and the Ninety-third Squadron as a legionnaire.

Joseph Caillaux—Fifty-six-year-old from Le Mans, France. Former prime minister.

Eugène Christophe—Thirty-four-year-old from Paris, France. National Cyclo-cross Champion 1909 through 1914. Placed second in 1912 Tour de France and eleventh in 1914 Tour de France. Served with the First Cyclist Group and the Twenty-fourth Section of Clerks and Workers.

Jacques Coomans—Thirty-year-old from Magnée, Belgium. Placed nineteenth in 1914 Tour de France.

Henri Desgrange—Fifty-four-year-old from Paris, France. Editor-in-chief of *l'Auto*. Served in the 150th Infantry Regiment.

Paul Duboc—Thirty-five-year-old from Rouen, France. Placed first in 1909 Tour de Belgique and thirty-first in 1914 Tour de France.

Firmin Lambot—Thirty-three-year-old from Florennes, Belgium. Placed fourth in 1913 Tour de France and eighth in 1914 Tour de France.

Luigi Lucotti—Twenty-five-year-old from Voghera, Italy. Sprinter. Placed third in 1914 Giro d'Italia. The 1919 edition was his first Tour de France.

Alice Milliat—Thirty-five-year-old from Nantes, France. President of Fédération des sociétés féminines sportives de France.

Jules Nempon—Twenty-nine-year-old from Armbouts-Cappel, France. Amateur cyclist. Placed twenty-seventh in 1914 Tour de France.

Francis Pélissier—Twenty-five-year-old from Paris, France. Turned professional in 1919. The 1919 edition was his first Tour de France. Younger brother of Henri Pélissier. Served with the Twenty-fourth Infantry Regiment and the Eleventh Artillery Regiment.

Henri Pélissier—Thirty-year-old from Paris, France. Placed first in 1919 Paris–Roubaix and second in 1914 Tour de France. Elder brother of Francis Pélissier. Served with the Twentieth Section of Secretaries and the First Aviation Group.

Léon Scieur—Thirty-one-year-old from Florennes, Belgium. Placed fourth in 1913 Tour de Belgique and fourteenth in 1914 Tour de France.

Alfred Steux—Twenty-seven-year-old from Dottignies, Belgium. The 1919 edition was his first Tour de France.

Philippe Thys—Twenty-nine-year-old from Anderlecht, Belgium. Winner of the 1913 and 1914 Tour de France.

Joseph Van Daele—Twenty-nine-year-old from Wattrelos, France. Placed third in the 1914 Paris–Bruxelles.

Les Grands Boulevards of Paris on November 11, 1918.

1.

The end is in the colors hanging from Paris homes and restaurants, in the windows of apartments and department stores, in countless children's outstretched arms. The Allied countries' patterns trip down the boulevards, carried on a pent-up current: red and black and blue and white and yellow. The end is in the sharp waft drifting across hôtel national les Invalides' courtyard following the cannons' report and in the a cappella symphony, voices clambering over one another in celebration: the Belgian "La Brabançonne," the American "Over There," the British "Tipperary," and the French "Quand Madelon." It is in the strained brass band on the Palais de Tuileries balcony, whose instruments glint, cast light onto two captured Rumpler C.III airplanes, and in old men and women's joyous weeping at the foot of the Strasbourg statue. Since 1871 it had been draped in mourning's black crepe, but earlier its veil had been lifted, and it now floats on a flower bed cast by the passing crowds. The end is in the delicate bursting champagne bubbles whose green glass bottles are emptied as soon as they're uncorked in bistros across the city. The end is in the crowds who jostle and kiss and tell each other stories on rue des Martyrs and quai de Jemmapes, Champs-Élysées and rue Saint-Dominique, cour du Commerce-Saint-André, quai Branly—almost every street in Paris. Can it be? *they ask each other.* Is the war really over?

◆ ◆ ◆

Henri Desgrange watched the celebrations pass by on rue du Faubourg Montmartre. Crowds renewed themselves along the blister of a road through Paris's ninth arrondissement, on the Seine's right bank. The editor stood, stiff. His soldier's posture had not yet left him. When he'd held his unit's colors, his face set for the army photographer, it had taken effort to stay as rigid as his soldiers, three decades younger than Desgrange. Anyone who knew him would say he thought nothing of the gap in their ages. Stasis didn't suit him. Desgrange always appeared in constant motion: his white hair swept back over his still dark, wayward brows, his chin cocked out, his eagle nose just barely upturned, as if to focus on some prey.

He had watched his neighborhood dim in the preceding years, though that day it was, for at least a moment, reborn. The powder-blue dressing rooms and gilt mansions of les Grands Boulevards, their extravagant rose gardens concealed behind modest steel fences, all remained a short walk away, but the artists who had once made their homes nearby had moved to the city's left bank and carried Paris's cultural mass with them. The occasional salon and cabaret still opened its doors on fall evenings like this one, however, and new jazz clubs had moved into the shuttered spaces between, buoyed by the unending tide of the city. Desgrange, the editor-in-chief of the sports daily *l'Auto*, could look out his office window and see the corridor that led to Bouillon Chartier's entrance where waiters scribbled out customers' receipts on unfussy paper tablecloths. He'd sometimes take his journalists to the restaurant after editorial meetings, when a walk to boulevard Montmartre felt too far with the evening's deadlines. If he turned his head to the left, he could just make out the second-story awning of Gaumontcolor. The cinema's neon lights cast a faint glow on the opposite wall; geometric shapes snapped in and out of existence on the pavement underfoot.

Anyone waiting outside the theater that day was subsumed by the passing bodies who crowded the Faubourg Montmartre street. Few were willing to miss the celebrations that continued into the late afternoon. For the first time in years, the streetlights remained lit as the evening aged but did not wane; they cast a glow on the people's newly freed movements well into the night.

Parisians, Americans, British, Belgians—most anyone who found themselves in the French capital—amassed on the streets that day to celebrate the armistice signed between the Allied countries and Germany. They arrived knowing the fighting on the western front had ended at 11:00 a.m., though most who crowded onto the avenues had not yet heard what the document's terms were. Whatever clauses and subclauses had been agreed on by their leaders and those on the table's opposite side mattered little to the people's immediate celebrations: it was enough that the thing was through.

No matter the conditions of the armistice, no matter how much Germany paid for those four years, the document couldn't make up for the war's cost. Like the rest of France, Desgrange had been consumed with the war. It had stamped his existence, left no corner un-inked. And his country? The war had threatened to tear it from its foundation, to cart off its remains, to expand Germany's excision of territories and to break apart the alliance France had formed with Great Britain. The country's borders had not collapsed any further in the war—they'd expanded—but the conflict had succeeded in its first aim: to uproot the ground in tracts of land to Paris's northeast. In doing so it shattered those young men, and plenty of old ones, too. Men who had been sent away in those first days of fighting with spirit in excess. Their stamina hadn't lasted as long as the war did. Those men couldn't be blamed; they had volunteered for a tragedy few had expected or prepared for, even those who led the aggressors. A few saw how war had changed in the sixty years before 1914, in the cast artillery guns and industrial train tracks that ran like roots behind units in the Crimean War and in Vicksburg's trench networks in the American Civil War. The Great War revealed those logistical and engineering lessons as ruinous, if inevitable, advances to warfare. Little could have protected the men on the front, short of killing every last German who had stepped onto their country's trampled ground. Underfoot, the land carried each side. It held as they advanced and retreated, back and forth, but after four years it was broken: its roads dredged up and its farmlands and forests fallow. Negotiating with German generals and politicians might have spared lives, but after the war had slowed, burrowed into the clay, no conversation could have brought back those poilus Desgrange had funneled through *l'Auto*'s offices.

In a corner of *l'Auto*, Desgrange helped establish the headquarters of a government-sponsored physical fitness program for soldiers. In one visit, young Parisians could enlist and begin their physical training before being sent to military schools outside the capital, nearer to the front. Desgrange watched over them as an instructor in the first years of the war, as the young men sprinted the length of Parc des Princes velodrome and marched along the public trails of bois de Boulogne. The editor had advocated for fitness as a means to a healthier and more meaningful life with colleagues like Pierre de Coubertin, the head of the International Olympic Committee. With the war, it had become a means of surviving, to better fight against the larger and more-well-trained German military. The preparations, which had once been running, lifting weights, and crawling through obstacle courses as an end in itself, became a way to sprint more quickly across flare-lit no man's land, the strength to carry an ammunition crate to a machine gun nest in the moments before a counterassault, the ability to flatten one's frame as artillery shells whistled and grew silent in the fresh craters around one's dugout. In other years, a soldier who couldn't carry his own equipment or could only run halfway across the emptiness of no man's land would never reach the front, better to just place him elsewhere, but this war didn't hold such standards.

Then there were those soldiers Desgrange had led when he himself volunteered, three years into the war. His family had persuaded him not to join at its outset: he had served before, continued to do more for his country than anyone had asked of him. Then there was the matter of his asthma—he should leave the fighting to younger men. He volunteered and only told them once he was gone from the house. When he did, the first days of cavalry charges and parade marches—relics from past wars—had already been realized as useless. The Great War had not paid mind to traditions or symbols, to the degree any war does. It instead asked for more at each turn—another village to consume, leaving only a foundation stone or two; two more months of curfews and forced relocations; one's mail arriving opened and resealed. It bound an entire country—entire countries—with each fiber of their individual and collective beings. The poilus who fell next to Desgrange on the Argonne's muddy ground were dead and nothing could be done for them, but the editor thought about the people they'd left behind, too: wives and children who'd relied on them for food; France, who needed their labor and political service and their mere existence. No terms could bring them back.

A blank page lay in front of Desgrange. His fingers draped over the typewriter's keys and his frame hunched over his desk, fifty-three years of rigorous use not weathering it. Almost from the day the war broke out, he had used his editorial position at *l'Auto* to share his opinions about the Germans and the ongoing war in the newspaper's pages. The sentiments of his next column, to appear on the front page of the following day's issue, had sat in his mind for months. He only needed to gather up the words. "Listen!" he typed.

Just four months before, German soldiers had been sixty kilometers from Paris, sending artillery shells down onto the city's streets and flying over Parisian rooftops in twin-seat bombers. The intrusions were imprecise, but their presence, even their suggestion, had been threatening enough to cause people to pick up their pace when walking back home from the neighborhood épicerie. In October, Desgrange had returned home from the forests of Champagne, after his unit, the 150th Infantry Regiment, had fought in the Lorraine. His unit had left the trenches. They were temporarily removed from the lice bites and the wind that stormed through their open roofs but were still subject to the daily rhythms and training that constituted life near the front. Desgrange had been reassigned from the 150th to serve as a consultant to the national committee responsible for physical rehabilitation and fitness. It would be a comfortable role for him, though he had served well as an old poilu. On October 19th, he boarded a train, destined for his home.

The city that welcomed him was more or less as he had left it in 1917. The war had continued its chaotic erosion, but the people there had, by then, settled into their new routine. Streetlights were promptly extinguished at 10:00 p.m. each night. Men, wearing black morning suits, gathered in lines at Gare de Lyon, shuffling toward makeshift enlistment booths set up at the train station, each stand bearing a "Bureau Militaire" sign and a French flag. Desgrange returned to life with his mistress, Jeanne Deley, in the western part of the city. He checked in on his daughter, Denise, who lived at his mailing address, where he officially lived with his wife, Marie Dulaurens. He kept his distance from them and preferred to communicate by letter, but took care of them both, sending *l'Auto* employees to check in on them and making sure they didn't have any financial worries. He would occasionally visit Denise there on rue Deschanel, just next to Champ de Mars and the Eiffel Tower, while picking up the mail that had been sent to him. Both Desgrange and Marie had their lovers and were comfortable maintaining the façade of their half-empty apartment.

How many people stood between their homes now, hundreds of thousands? The cares, worries they had—all of it over.

"I know it, feel it; it angers me, warms my heart," Desgrange continued.

The reports had started a few days before. On November 6th, just after midnight, a radio telegram arrived at the Eiffel Tower monitoring station—a tiny cement room embedded in the base of the monument's south pillar. The message held the names of four German officials aboard a train car that had left Berlin that morning: Matthias Erzberger, the recently appointed secretary of state; Count Alfred von Oberndorff, a commissioner responsible for foreign policy; Major General Detlof von Winterfeldt, the military representative of the chancellor; and Captain Ernst Vanselow, a naval representative. The four were headed to a set of tracks outside Compiègne, to the northeast of Paris. The new German government had directed them to negotiate a peace with the Allied countries. Once there, they would meet with the supreme Allied commander, Ferdinand Foch, and Rosslyn Wemyss, first sea lord of the British navy, who were aboard Foch's personal train car, waiting for the delegates. The four would hear the Allied countries' demands and do their part to end the war.

Bulgaria, the Ottoman Republic, and the newly formed Austria and Hungary had already signed agreements with the Allies, ending the hostilities between them. Germany had opened negotiations on October 3rd but had continued fighting until a similar agreement was signed. The German Empire faltered then fell, and negotiations continued. German soldiers saw the end of the war and their orders to continue fighting. Some of these soldiers, most of them conscripted, rejected the risks they were being asked to take; a few mutinies arose along the front. They understood the nature of the war's end without needing someone's signature.

In the early morning of November 11th, the armistice remained unsigned. Seventy-two hours were left before the deadline would pass.

With it, the hope for an immediate peace would be lost, even if the war's condition were otherwise unchanged. The Allies' terms were harsh, a few impossible, like their request that Germany decommission more submarines than it possessed at that moment. Privately, the German representatives had been told to push for every concession they could but ultimately sign the armistice regardless of its final details.

That morning in Paris, the newspapers had been printed with the latest news from the front. French soldiers had been fighting Germans at the border for 1,561 days. The French had made progress near Avesnes and north of Charleville according to the daily edition of *Le Figaro*, but Germans had pushed back fiercely to the north. A few lesser commanders still wanted another opportunity to distinguish themselves, even if the war's end had been determined. Few papers made any predictions about what would come of the negotiations, as if discussing it would only undermine whatever chance peace had.

Paris woke, people began their daily routines: teachers made last-minute adjustments to lesson plans, conductors started up the Nord-Sud rail lines, factory workers clocked in to vast buildings on the city's outer edge that had been repurposed to manufacture wartime needs: 75mm artillery shells, Renault FT light tanks, industrial lathes and crucibles, small pieces of the endless supply chain leading toward the front.

Until 10:00 a.m., when the telephones rang at *Le Matin* and *L'Echo de Paris*'s offices, no one outside the Rethondes Forest had heard the news. The editors who answered the phones had been told the Germans had signed their names to the document that would determine the peace that followed. Even after the news broke, only pedestrians who walked past the newspapers' offices on rue des Panoramas and place de l'Opéra could see the hastily tacked signs declaring the war's end. Those who passed by began to spread the news. The sound of the cannons reverberated from hôtel national les Invalides' walls at 11:00 a.m. For a moment, Paris was a negative imprint of the front. The sound—once constant, now an echo, painless waves crashing through the front's foul air—began and ended in that second. Then Paris fully woke.

Desgrange paused. His fingers hovered over the keys. The paper's founding message, written by him and published in *l'Auto*'s first issue on October 16, 1900—nineteen years ago—said the newspaper would avoid political issues, in contrast to its many competing sports dailies. He and *l'Auto*'s advertisers had seen an opportunity to differentiate themselves from *Le Vélo*, their widest-circulating opponent, whose writers and editors regularly waded into domestic political conversations. *Le Vélo*'s editor-in-chief, Pierre Giffard, had come to the defense of Alfred Dreyfus in its pages, to the chagrin of *Le Vélo*'s conservative advertisers. Dreyfus, a Jewish officer in the French army, had been convicted of selling military secrets to the Germans. At the time of Giffard's defense, those who supported Dreyfus hoped to reopen his case and overturn the conviction, while anti-Dreyfusards thought that doing so would weaken people's faith in France and its government. An antisemitic undercurrent ran throughout. At the time of the affair, Desgrange was a public relations representative of Clément-Bayard automobiles, itself a *Le Vélo* advertiser. He had already left his days as a professional cyclist behind. He had not broken from the sport entirely, though. Only a few years before he had become the director of Parc des Princes, an arena with a cycling track in the city's western suburb of Boulogne-sur-Seine. Desgrange wrote articles and opinion pieces about physical education and sports for *Le Vélo* and other publications outside his regular public relations duties. As the Dreyfus Affair continued, he remained publicly mute, a quality that appealed to his employer, Adolphe Clément-Bayard.

Soon after Giffard declared his support of Dreyfus in his newspaper's green-tinted pages, Clément-Bayard, the founder of the company bearing his name, brought Desgrange into discussions between *Le Vélo*'s advertisers. Clément, like the other corporations who advertised in the paper, had publicly disagreed with Giffard's slant in *Le Vélo*'s coverage. Clément and the others had pulled their advertisements in protest. They had little desire to return that money to *Le Vélo* anytime soon. Instead, they hoped to create a competing sports daily that would sate the public's interest in athletics without the political coverage that had fragmented readership. Clément believed Desgrange could be an ideal editor for the new paper: he was a cyclist who had achieved some public acclaim after setting records in the hour, the fifty and hundred kilometers, and the hundred-mile lengths on bicycles. He had written columns and books on his own experiences. As a public relations manager, he knew how to deal with journalists, even if he wasn't one himself. The advertisers didn't want to consider anyone else for the job; they offered the editor-in-chief position to Desgrange. He accepted.

L'Auto's founding message well represented its early stance toward politics, even before the war broke out. "What we wanted to say is said," Henri wrote to *l'Auto*'s readers of the Dreyfus Affair, though the paper had said nothing until that point. He didn't comment on Dreyfus again. The advertisers of the new sports daily, yellow tinted in contrast with *Le Vélo*'s green, were satisfied with their investment.

L'Auto's founding and the Dreyfus Affair were far from Desgrange's mind that November evening. His enemies, those his readers and advertisers shared, weren't fellow Frenchmen but foreigners. He saw little chance a civil war would erupt between his fellow citizens who hated the Germans and those who thought they were being treated too harshly in their defeat. The few who believed that were in the minority and most were smart enough to recognize it and watch their own language. *Le Vélo* had shuttered in 1904 and the war had created a common enemy, one all of Paris could agree upon—Desgrange was free to write as he pleased. Given the celebrations on most every Paris street, in countless small towns on the city's outskirts, and in trenches that had been rendered worthless, l'Auto's major advertisers like Jacques Braunstein at Zig-Zag and the Palmer Tire executives wouldn't mind their ads abutting another of Desgrange's political columns. They had remained loyal to the editor over the years. They had trusted him to expand the newspaper's circulation in its first years as it competed directly with Le Vélo, and had stuck by him once Le Vélo had closed, quotas on materials had restricted l'Auto's coverage, and its reporters—fighting-age men—had been called to the front. The newspaper's readers had more pressing concerns than what l'Auto covered, cycling and gymnastics, running and yachting. But the sporting events Desgrange and his correspondents wrote about, those that continued in the wartime years, provided those readers with a release from the events that filled the pages of other newspapers: the movements of battleships, the arrest of foreign spies not far from where they lived, the deployment of units filled with sons, husbands, and fathers.

In l'Auto's early days, Desgrange worked to live up to his advertisers' initial confidence. His public relations experience, however, hadn't carried him far in the newsroom. He had few ideas for stories and didn't have much knowledge on how to manage a team of journalists. He only followed what others in the industry did and hoped the absence of something—political coverage—would be enough to drive readers to l'Auto. His brash writing hid a caution in business manners: whenever possible, he preferred others take risks in developing new projects while he waited to see whether their ventures would pay off. Given that plenty of other sports dailies were still in the market, even after Le Vélo faltered, l'Auto's circulation stalled in those first years. The newspaper's future had been uncertain enough that Desgrange's job had been threatened. The advertisers expressed their hope he would turn things around, a sign that anyone without his relationships would have already been fired from the job. The threat wasn't enough to change Desgrange's nature, but it at least opened him to others' ideas.

Desgrange held an editorial meeting in response. He asked the journalists who worked under him and those administrators on the business side of the paper for their ideas on how *l'Auto* could grow its subscription base. Géo Lefèvre, a twenty-six-year-old cycling and rugby correspondent whom Desgrange had hired away from *Le Vélo*, spoke up. Lefèvre's previous employer had sponsored sporting competitions and provided exclusive coverage of the results: Paris–Roubaix, Bordeaux–Paris, Paris–Brest–Paris. The three were one-day cycling events that *Le Vélo* helped organize and run. By offering readers exclusive interviews with the contestants and by following the cyclists on each section of road, *Le Vélo* encouraged nonsubscribers to pick up the paper on race days. Some, they hoped, would even subscribe after seeing the surrounding reporting. The one-day cycling races worked well for the newspaper's aims: the races didn't require much in the way of logistics and took place on regular roads instead of in stadiums—for-profit companies themselves that would have their own ideas about coverage. The events appealed to competitive cyclists but also attracted amateurs. Races any longer than one day would be difficult for cyclists who didn't train for endurance. On a longer race, registrants would flag, but the sponsoring newspaper could extend the days it offered in-depth coverage. More adventurous than Desgrange, with less to lose, Lefèvre suggested a cycling race longer than anyone before had considered, one spanning France's entire border. "A Tour de France," Desgrange clarified.

The Tour had existed as part of French life even if it had never been a cycling race. Kings went on tour to inspect their more distant lands, to let those with tenuous allegiances know that they remembered them; craftsmen left their hometowns for tours to learn how others in regions not their own built cathedrals, baked pastries. *Le Tour de la France par deux enfants*, a book French children read in primary school, described two children's journey around their country to find their uncle. A Tour de France race on bikes had never been considered, but it could be imagined. It was enough for Desgrange to not dismiss Lefèvre's idea immediately.

The editor took the journalist to a café after the meeting and discussed the proposed race further. The pair decided Desgrange would bring the idea to *l'Auto*'s business director and cofounder, Victor Goddet, for his input. If Goddet thought it impossible, that was easy enough: the idea wouldn't go any farther. When Desgrange went to him, however, Goddet thought it was just what *l'Auto* needed.

The Tour de France's first years surpassed Desgrange's guarded expectations. People left their homes to watch the cyclists on the 1903 Tour's six stages. In time, the Tour route extended, hewed closer to France's borders. The cyclists beat the bounds of their country. They marked France's borders and every town they rode through, in each new clime they reached. As the cyclists biked through some of the same small towns in subsequent years, the association between that town and the Tour grew. The towns formed the Tour, and the Tour formed the towns as well as the country.

Many cyclists didn't find the Tour appealing at first. It was unquestionably more difficult than one-day events with relatively large purses for the cyclists' investment of time and training. The Tour was a challenge as much as a race. The average professional didn't know whether they could finish until they rode back to Paris. Sponsors still promised cyclists' salaries for the competition, however, and with the smaller prizes along the way, racers could justify the effort. *L'Auto* and Desgrange's job were saved. Near the Tour's end, *l'Auto*'s circulation ballooned, multiples of *Le Vélo*'s on its best days. The competing paper shuttered in 1904. Desgrange even became comfortable with the race he had once considered a gamble. He had made it part of his image: the father of the Tour de France. It was his foresight, after all, that let it occur those first years, before its concept had been proven. Géo Lefèvre—who had conceived of the race—was transferred to writing about boxing and aviation while Desgrange stayed involved with the Tour's administration, covering it in regular dispatches as he followed its route.

On the day of the twelfth Tour's start, June 28, 1914, the archduke of Austria, Franz Ferdinand, was assassinated in Sarajevo. The cyclists were already on the road to Le Havre when Gavrilo Princip fired two shots into the archduke's car. They rode on even after they heard the news. The race ended on its scheduled day of July 26th. On August 3rd, France entered the war; Tour winner Philippe Thys's Belgium had already been invaded by that time. With the news, plans for the thirteenth Tour—the event that had saved *l'Auto* from failure—halted. The race couldn't hope to cycle along the country's borders.

Desgrange and the paper couldn't afford to stagnate until the war had ended, even if the Tour couldn't take place. *L'Auto* continued to cover life and sport during the wartime years, even as one after another major sporting event was canceled or held with smaller crowds and diminished competitors. In his columns, *H. Desgrange* was replaced by *H. Desgrenier*, a thin pseudonymous veil. The paper's founding promise of reporting unaffected by politics fell away with the other vestiges of the prewar landscape.

Desgrange's columns darkened. "This is our work!" he began in his August 15th column, just before Desgrange had turned into Desgrenier. German politicians "alone are amazed to see France draw up against the German brute, they who haven't bothered to study, for twenty years before the war began, our moral and physical evolution." He barely distinguished between German leaders and German men who had been conscripted in the fight against France. He continued writing columns supporting France's decision to fight as the war went on, when his country's prospects were dim and plenty of other Frenchmen were supporting politicians' few attempts to resolve the war quickly and peacefully. He continued after he volunteered for the military in April of 1917, at the age of fifty-two, sending his columns back by post. He only let a few close friends and his mistress know his decision. He privately hoped to carry out the mission he had been writing about since the war's start, to do his part in reclaiming the French lands that had been lost after the Franco-Prussian War and to fight the Germans who would have his country reduced even further.

L'Auto's front page was at times a small altar to former Tour competitors. The name of a cyclist from the 1914 edition of the race would appear. "Lapize falls on the field of honor," "Death of Lucien Petit-Breton: the end of a great champion—the accident—his main victories." In the editor's bold pen, cyclists who had died in the war were memorialized. Those reading the obituaries were safe behind the lines, celebrating in Paris while their country's heroes had been brought down in the war. They should remember them, Desgrange wrote in his columns, celebrate them, do anything but forget them.

He ended the obituary of Octave Lapize, the 1910 Tour champion, who had been shot down eight kilometers behind French lines in a dogfight, with one last proclamation: "Hourlier, Comès, Faber, Bouin, Engel! And now Lapize!" he wrote, listing the cyclists killed in the war. "O heroic dead, victims of this Teutonic barbarism, receive splendidly this beautiful son of superb France. He will be, like you, worthily avenged!" Three winners of the Tour had been killed in the war; others had been maimed. Countless not-yet professionals and aspirants who might have someday competed in the race died in the front's churn.

But the war had ended, and the crowd outside *l'Auto's* office flocked past. The people of France, or at least those who read him, had come to expect something from Desgrange: a salve for those preceding years, someone who recognized the hardships they had gone through, would continue to go through, who wasn't afraid to place blame for those hardships. He was a voice of confidence who could direct their attention, someone who recognized, knew personally, the costs they had endured and the spirit that had stayed with them despite the war's toll. He couldn't disappoint them by letting its end pass without comment.

"Ah! My dear country, what suffering we've paid to purchase your resurrection," Desgrange typed. "And what funeral hours next! What grief! The despair we had when the German brute took advantage of us with his methodical planning!" Desgrange drew his conviction from the same source he had found those years back, at the war's outset, when he'd told French boys to not take mercy on the German soldiers but to shoot them where they stood. "Let us draw a line. Let us live." He paused once more. "Goodbye to the Boche, and hello to your home!"

Desgrange knew some towns along the front would need to be rebuilt entirely. The land around them might never be useful again. Local politicians and whoever chose to return home might find new uses for the fallow ground—more factories, perhaps, like those that had sprung up far from the trenches, supplying the battle lines with all they needed. Bricks or cement could pave over the cratered landscape. People might be able to turn those onetime towns into bustling cities that could supply new factories with the workers they would need. Or the land might stay as it was that day, a memorial spanning hundreds of kilometers where visiting crowds could look in from its edges, few desiring to intrude any farther. Some towns—Ailles and Courtecon, Moussy-sur-Aisne and Allemant, Hurlus and Ripont and Nauroy and others—were given to the war as martyrs. The government had already deemed them irreplaceable, at least in physical terms. Next to nothing stood where streets once ran through their center. The towns, politicians decided, could be moved elsewhere; they could be re-created with old plans and local memories—whose house stood next to the butcher, which town hall features should be preserved and which were always complained about, and so on—but they couldn't exist where they once had been. At the Meuse–Argonne, Desgrange had witnessed that putty knife of the war, flattening the landscape and whatever features had once existed. The people wouldn't leave the war behind; nothing could cause them to do that, not entirely. But maybe their eyes could be directed elsewhere, at least for a time. Let them see that the scarred country still had its strength, its élan, even if that sinew was not what generals thought it to be in the war's first days.

Nine days had passed since the armistice's signing. The November 20th edition of *Le Temps* arrived on newsstands in the morning fog. Headlines said that on Thursday, the German naval fleet would likely be surrendered to the Allies, barring any delays. On the newspaper's final page, between advertisements for the bookstore Berger-Leverault and Vin de Vial tonic, the editors noted small events not worthy of including on the front page. In two days, poet Jean Richepin would hold a lecture on American life at the Sorbonne; the Société de Auteurs held their general assembly the evening before; the Maisons Laffitte horse track on Paris's outskirts would enter the final week of its annual season. Small bits of lifelike grass on tilled ground broke through. These scraps were marginal, but they at least existed. Pronouncements and congratulations from liberated towns decorated its borders. Proclamations from foreign leaders, congratulating the French for all they'd done for the world, filled whatever space remained.

Paperboys unbundled and stacked the daily edition of *l'Auto* at newsstands. An article discussed how Henry Farman, a French airplane designer, had revealed plans for an aircraft that could transport twenty people in its hollow fuselage. The Six Days of New York bicycle race—scheduled to take place in Madison Square Garden December 2nd to 7th—would return after being canceled in the preceding years. Organizers hoped this year's race could reclaim just some of its previous glory. Robert Dieudonné penned a new short story, "Pot of Varnish," which Desgrange published. The editor-in-chief's column appeared on the center of the front page. It still carried the byline *H. Desgrenier.* The article concerned the project Desgrange had worked on during the war, before he had volunteered for the front: national physical fitness. An announcement, written in fine print to accommodate its lengthy contents, took up the two rightmost columns of the front page and extended four more onto the second. It described plans for an upcoming race, what documents interested cyclists would need to register, their arrival locations in various cities, and the itinerary of what had already been an ambitious race, in what was bound to be, according to Desgrange, its most ambitious edition.

THE CYCLING TOUR DE FRANCE: 13TH EDITION—From June 22 to July 21, 1919.

The winner of the first Tour de France, Maurice Garin, right, at the race's finish line in Paris, 1903.

2.

Desgrange and *l'Auto* would host the thirteenth Tour less than eight months after the armistice's declaration. Desgrange had placed himself and the whole publication on precarious ground with his decision. Once his choice to host the Tour that year had been made, however, the only hope the race had of succeeding was if its founder spoke about its inevitability, its continued and unequaled scale in a year when no one would have expected its return at all. *L'Auto*'s yellow pages were littered with updates on the upcoming race in the months before it began: an explanation of the rules that would govern the cyclists as they rode in the race that year, that competitors who abandoned would be responsible for how they returned home, that the only advertisements allowed were tire and bicycle brand acknowledgments at the race's end. Desgrange hoped with enough news about the Tour, cyclists would have no choice but to register. He hoped his readers would feel like they were part of the Tour by knowing every one of its functions. He also reminded them that a *l'Auto* subscription for the Tour's length was just four francs if they lived in France, five for international subscribers, and two and a half per month for poilus. If the cyclists didn't arrive in *l'Auto*'s offices for registration, if *l'Auto*'s near-daily updates could only name a single new competitor or two every week—an amateur who hoped to compete in the Tour's B classification, or an older cyclist who would have otherwise ended his competitive years—Desgrange's and *l'Auto*'s reputations would suffer.

L'Auto's circulation had waned in the war. Paper had been rationed like wool, wood, steel, and food. The quotas reduced *l'Auto*'s daily pages from six, or eight on news-heavy days like the Tour's start, to four, not that the newspaper had an abundance of stories or advertisers to fill even those remaining pages. Sports sections at general-interest newspapers shrunk or disappeared. *L'Auto* journalists, like those at most every other paper, were called up to fight. They left the newspaper's offices one last time before heading to the front in the first waves of 1914. A few were replaced, but the diminished role of sports, and the question of who would spend their money on a newspaper dedicated to the remaining sports competitions, prevented *l'Auto* from continuing business as is.

The newspaper could survive a year without the Tour. Desgrange didn't know, however, whether someone else would attempt hosting a race like the Tour if he did not. He held no dominion over the roads the racers biked over. In January, *Le Petit Journal*, a general-interest daily, announced the Circuit des Champs de Bataille, a seven-stage event through the northeast regions most directly affected by the war. Without the Tour, *l'Auto* still provided readers with sports coverage, but little would then separate it from another newspaper that could do the same, that had correspondents who could attend those same events, where they could interview the same athletes *l'Auto* correspondents could. Even general-interest dailies, which gave less attention to individual competitors and didn't report on each track-cycling event or negotiations between sports unions and national administrators, printed race results. Sports were a luxury, no doubt, though at least the average Frenchman paid little for the privilege—just ten centimes for a copy of *l'Auto*, which held within it all the coverage of the preceding day's stage during the Tour. If readers were lucky enough, on the day the race passed through their town, they wouldn't even need a copy of the paper to tell them what had happened, at least for that single moment. All they would need was to rise early enough to watch the cyclists pass through their town's center. If they did, they could maybe witness a Tour rider—mud coated, unnoticing of the world around him, until a passerby gave him a few francs or some food for his effort—stop for a moment or two if his tire blew or if he lived in one of the towns where a checkpoint took place. The Tour cyclist was either super- or subhuman depending on who watched him, an automaton of the road. At the checkpoints, spectators jostled to find space close enough to the clearing where judges stood so they could shout at the racers while the judges inspected their bikes for tampering before the cyclists again left for the road, continuing their path around the country.

Some inhabitants who had watched the Tour ride through their towns for years, pass by their family homes, would not do so this year. He knew cities like Belfort, normally a Tour stop, were broken, too caught up in the war to accommodate the cyclists for even a single night. The town's fortifications had been incapable against German artillery strikes' violent geometries. Few hotels remained where the cyclists could stay. That year's competitors would ride through Belfort, but they wouldn't celebrate with its inhabitants, wouldn't wake up in the town for a day of rest before again starting on the race. Towns where the Tour had once made its home were gone, and Desgrange could only express his fondness for their memory; their connection with the Tour was severed. Some of the towns Desgrange remembered in *l'Auto* columns, but others were never large enough for the cyclists to do anything except pass through. For the inhabitants of the town, it had been a moment of pride, even if they'd barely appeared in *l'Auto*'s pages. In the Tour's route that beat against France's borders, it defined the land; it represented, in real terms, regions once abstract to French people who rarely ventured far from their hometowns. The country was only as healthy as those towns along the front. The race couldn't do much for the towns that remained along its frayed edge, besides providing them a brief distraction, but that limit was enough for Desgrange to continue the Tour's path.

If *l'Auto* was to host the Tour, the race needed to exist as it did in those years before the war, not a dilute version through the country's safe interior, but stretching up against the new and old borders as it had done before. Anything less wouldn't be a tour. If it could avoid the worst scandals of its first years—when competitors' cheating had been so complete and intricate that race officials didn't know if they could use any of the results. If *l'Auto* could gather up enough cyclists willing and able to race around that new hexagon with little notice. If the cyclists could be pushed, ordered to revisit those areas planted with millions of boot prints, with motorized tracks that chipped away at dirt roads once only used for the occasional market trip. If Desgrange could do all that, the Tour could be more to France than it had ever been.

The country's victory in the Great War gave way to a tempered, steely outpouring of national pride. The Franco-Prussian War—the event whose end draped the Strasbourg statue in black—was behind them: the Alsace region had been returned. The grief over its cost would last as long as the pride over the returned land, would perhaps extend beyond it. Still, the French people celebrated for what they and the Allied countries had accomplished, what they had secured. It was the least they could do for those soldiers who had paid for their success.

◆ ◆ ◆

Desgrange hadn't discussed the possibility of that year's Tour with its would-be cyclists when he announced the race. It would have been difficult to reach most of them in that first week after the war's end. French cyclists had been drafted into the war like any other men of age. Those who were competitive in a race like the Tour could fight, and the war held laxer standards than the Tour's strains. Desgrange would have had to locate their units still spread along the western front, or in garrisons that could have been anywhere in the country to see whether their commanding officers would give them leave for a month. If the officers did, he'd have to ask the cyclists whether they even wanted to join the Tour, whether they'd accept diminished conditions from earlier race years, whether they'd want to spend that time racing instead of back home. Even those who had finished their three years of active service before the war began had been called up as part of their twenty-five years of reserve duties, which, amid the Great War, amounted to service that would have been active in any other year. The war and its appetite had wiped away those distinctions. The only cyclists whose ability to race Desgrange knew for sure were those who could no longer ride.

Desgrange did manage to contact a cyclist stationed at the Second Aviation Group's depot in Lyon-Bron. Eugène Christophe's time in the Second hadn't been like his earlier service as a First Cycling Group mechanic. He had moved from unit to unit in the war, but at least in the First he'd been stationed with a friend, Georges Perrin, a fellow cyclist whom Eugène spent most evenings with, competing in one-on-one races around the nearby airfield. Eugène knew few other cyclists had the opportunity to ride their bikes at all, so he'd made a point of keeping up his otherwise stalled training on those nighttime circuits. They weren't much of a replacement for the actual races Eugène would be competing in during any other year, but there was little alternative. Plenty of others had to cross the muddied ground on foot, the sunken duckboards difficult to navigate any other way for cyclists who had joined infantry units. With only months before the thousands of kilometers between the Tour's start and its finish, Eugène knew those men would have even fewer opportunities to reacquaint themselves with their bikes.

At thirty-four years old, Eugène had already passed the average Tour competitor's age, or at least those most competitive for its general classification prize. He was two years older than Maurice Garin had been when he won the first Tour in 1903, the oldest winner of the Tour de France to that point. Each year he had competed in the race, his eyes had grown heavier, held those past races within them, none more so than the 1913 race. His sagging brows and the dark bags underneath framed them. Eugène had been a contender for the Tour's top prize for years and had competed in the race since 1906. In 1912, he'd placed second. Only an accident on the sixth stage had prevented him from beating Odile Defraye, a Belgian he'd battled for first place. In 1913, it had looked like he would win the general classification after seven attempts, but then that attempt failed, too.

Eugène had always managed to find time to cycle as other competitors gave up their bikes and training regimens while they fought in the war. He had first served in the military for the then-mandatory two years, starting in 1906, with the 119th Infantry Regiment. When he'd arrived at his post, in a time of relative peace for mainland France, he quickly grew despondent over the limited mobility offered to him as he sat around the unit's headquarters, drilling and training but doing little else. His commanding officers noticed his morale and said a position he might be interested in had opened up. He applied and was given the job of messenger between Trou d'Enfer, where his company was stationed, and the unit's headquarters at Courbevoie.

He left active service and joined a reserve infantry regiment near his home. He lived alone just outside the city, not far from Parc des Princes velodrome where he would compete on occasion. He started to race more frequently, and the bicycle company Alcyon began to give him a salary for racing in national events, with a bonus for top finishes, but like most other cyclists, it wasn't enough for him to get by at one hundred francs a month, particularly in the winter when races slowed. It was a regular French cyclist's existence, proud of the fact that they worked when they didn't compete. In those cold, static months, he worked as a mechanic, tinkering with machines more complex than the one he rode on.

His first major win was the 1912 Milan–San Remo. The others called him l'Homme de Bronze. Eugène stood around the other competitors in the hours before the race began. He spoke with them and with the race officials, gaining their favor as someone who, in those hours before a race started, seemed to lack the competitive drive that forced the others to distance themselves from those who understood their lives better than most. He was far from intimidating while off his bike and was built more like a wrestler than a cyclist, which only further blinded the others to his abilities. Once the race began, they watched as the young, laughing competitor took off at its start and barely slowed along the nearly three hundred kilometers between the two northwest Italian cities, gritting his teeth and tensing his body's length, a coiled spring.

Eugène had been called back to service in August of 1914, during the first general mobilization of the Great War. He'd been in his late twenties then, only six years removed from active duty, and not so far along in his mandated twenty-five reserve years. He was a desirable soldier still, one who had already gone through training and who hadn't lost his physical abilities by the time he was called up.

He had been given certain conveniences, as a soldier who had already served once. The army saw his technical proficiency as more important than whatever physical attributes he could bring to the fight. He had even received approval to compete in the occasional race, leaving his unit for a few days or a week to compete against the older cyclists who'd been granted the same accommodations. When the 1917 Paris–Tours was brought back after a two-year hiatus, Eugène competed and placed third behind Philippe Thys and Marcel Godivier.

The occasional short race Eugène had competed in during the war was the same sort that would kick off l'Auto's 1919 race schedule. The single-day races couldn't compare to months of training leading up to a race like the Tour, but at least he would have a chance to size up his competitors, see what efforts would be required of him to match their times on the different Tour settings. He would ride along the same trails he had competed in before the war, see how the war had changed them, whether the ground he now covered required a different sort of resilience.

In January, Desgrange had decided that, in addition to the Tour de France, *l'Auto* would host Paris–Roubaix in April. The last edition of the single-day race had taken place in the spring of 1914. Unlike some other single-day races whose destinations and routes had been protected from the front, Roubaix was an industrial city of 120,000 on the Belgian border. In the war, no one except those with orders to would have cycled so close to the fight. Before the race could occur, however, Desgrange decided that a team would be dispatched to survey the route and chart a new course if any stretch of road used before was now untraversable. Victor Breyer, a *l'Auto* journalist, was selected to lead the surveyors. Desgrange also wanted to include a cyclist, someone who had competed in the race before, knew its intricacies and unique challenges, and who might be able to offer suggestions to Victor along the way. A cyclist who had a good relationship with officials would make the job easier. Desgrange reasoned that even if the cyclist who helped chart the route eventually entered the competition, his advantage would still be limited by his own athleticism and that of his competitors. His knowledge of the route, whose conditions would surely change in the month between the survey and the race, would be small. The editor believed that Eugène, with his ability to traverse a variety of road conditions and fix bikes that would inevitably break down across any unpleasant stretches, was ideally suited to the job.

When Eugène met Desgrange in Paris before the cyclist left with Victor, he appeared more serious than he had been before the war began. His gray eyes had always stood out from a pack of cyclists, even after racers had crashed through mud and rain, rendering all their other features close to indistinguishable. His face was sunken. It wasn't that Eugène's eyes were mute, dead—he always had a keen awareness about him—but he had lost weight from his cheekbones. Something hard and heavy was suggested in them, a dark thought never far from his mind. His smile rarely reached his eyes. In past years, he had kept a long mustache, one that hung past his jawline. It had earned him the nickname the "Old Gaul." But he had shaved it before the war began, and to that day he had kept his face closely cropped.

Desgrange knew from his time watching Eugène compete that his severe appearance belied his easy nature. Peers and organizers thought him affable, quick to joke, even taking severe setbacks in stride. As much as Eugène enjoyed the base thrill of racing, he seemed to care most about the fact he was simply being paid to cycle, but he was also serious about the sport, committed to it. He once broke off a marriage engagement in 1912 shortly after winning Milan–San Remo when his fiancée's father told Eugène he'd have to find a new profession to secure her hand. He'd left their home forever, destined for the Circuit de Brescia he was registered to compete in.

At just over five foot three inches, Eugène's frame was smaller than many of his competitors, particularly those who excelled on the flat track of the velodrome or across longer routes like Paris–Tours. His muscled thighs didn't power him across flat ground with the same acceleration as those with longer limbs. Instead, his strength became apparent on varied terrain, when drag drew itself across a racer's body for hours on end, when the air from a cyclist immediately in front wasn't enough to make up for the incline they both climbed. Sprints allow a cyclist to gain an edge over a pack, but they are difficult to sustain. Rather than changing a cyclist's position across hundreds of kilometers, sprints create an edge at an opportune moment in a race. Eugène always hoped to be well in front of the others by the time they lifted themselves from their seats, careening toward the finish line.

Fortunately for Eugène, Desgrange noted in *l'Auto* that the cyclist who would win the Tour de France would be someone who didn't view the race as fifteen individual stages, where one last burst of speed might make the difference between a first- and a second-place finish. Instead, the race favored cyclists who approached it as a single length of endurance, spread out over a near-continuous month of cycling. In the 1913 Tour, and in every Tour since, *l'Auto* reinforced this belief by shifting the Tour's scoring from a model based on points a cyclist received for their position in a stage to a model that measured cyclists' times on each stage and aggregated the results.

In climbs and descents, Eugène faced little competition. He had trained for endurance as a cyclo-cross racer, a discipline held in cold winter months, where each competitor rode and hiked across an obstacle-laden dirt course. If any cyclist had built their career to best handle the varied ground and independence required by the Tour, it was him.

The two-man team surveying the Paris–Roubaix route spent days traversing roads that would take the competitors less than one, reaching dead ends in rubble-strewn roads, only to backtrack to find a more manageable path. Eugène and Victor left Paris in March, two months after Desgrange announced Paris–Roubaix in *l'Auto* and one month before the race would begin. They began their trip northeast, using past race routes and maps as well as their own perception of the road in front of them to chart a course. They noted the potholes too large for a pack of cyclists to cross, which trees threatened to collapse on the road before the race day, which towns still had enough structures and inhabitants to serve as checkpoints for the cyclists. Every aspect of the race had to be reconsidered.

A stretch of land between Albert and Vimy was of greatest concern to Eugène and Victor. The destruction centered on Arras, a Baroque-style town built on a chalk plateau. In the Great War, Arras had been just shy of ten kilometers from the front. German soldiers had approached the town at the end of August 1914, threatening to occupy it soon after the war began in earnest. Trenches were built around the city, which became a staging ground for attacks and for a defense against those attacks. The fields surrounding the town were cut and sterilized. Germans shelled Arras to keep the French aware of their presence, and the buildings within its border began to crumble and burn. Underneath Arras, the old chalk quarries had been fortified and expanded to house tens of thousands of Allied soldiers, so the foundation of the town had been chipped away. What remained was an eggshell. By the war's end, Arras had seen several major battles and was more destroyed than not. Efforts were underway to rebuild what could be rebuilt. Desgrange had decided, before sending Eugène and Victor, that the new path of Paris–Roubaix, if there was one at all, would have to avoid the city. The cyclists simply wouldn't be able to cross the ground running through it.

The end of the race was relocated, too, since the former site—a velodrome—had been pillaged for materials during the war, its wooden track uprooted from the ground. The road around them was new, one whose geological formations could be measured in months and years: the Battle of Arras in 1914 and 1917, the Second Battle of the Somme in 1918. As the pair surveyed the land, Victor recorded Eugène's impression: "Here, this really is the hell of the north."

Eighty cyclists lined up on the morning of April 20th, a little more than half the number that had competed in the 1914 Paris–Roubaix. Those who now found their stride on the route north, after years away, were older than the cyclists of that race by about four years. They had spent the years before the war on similar routes, had kept their sense for when energy needed to be spent or conserved, some small measure of the training they had once undergone to prepare for the race, while the younger cyclists were fresh from the military's ranks, if not only on leave, and had spent little if any time competing as professionals.

It was a slower and more strenuous route than Desgrange had predicted in *l'Auto*, where he'd informed fans they should expect the cyclists to start arriving in Roubaix at 3:00 p.m. The first cyclist to approach the finish line of Paris–Roubaix on April 20th did so after more than twelve hours of cycling. The last time the race had taken place, the first seven riders had come in one after another at just over nine hours flat. It was 5:00 p.m., after a day of rain, when the cyclists eventually arrived at the new finish line along avenue de Jussieu.

A cyclist named Henri Pélissier won the race. Henri cast an opposite image of Eugène, who finished ninth. He was slim and tall at five foot eight inches. He had blue-gray eyes and had held on to his mustache through the Great War. A fan could pick both him and his brother Francis out from the crowd with ease, if not by their appearance than by their behavior. The brothers were both distant while they raced. They didn't spend much time speaking to organizers or their competitors. In return, their competitors saw them as standoffish, or at least aloof, particularly Henri, the older and more accomplished of the two. It wasn't the brothers' intention, not that they cared much: they simply wanted to concentrate on their performance, the other parts of the race mattering little to them.

While Eugène took pains to ingratiate himself with the others, the Pélissiers saw the zero-sum nature of the race. Anyone who thought otherwise, in the brothers' minds, was a professional only in name. The brothers shied away from heavy food and drink before and after race stages while others took advantage of local hospitality. The Pélissiers didn't want to be weighed down while others came up to speed. They barely saw a need for alcohol's temporary salve from the competition's pains. They recognized accomplishment in others when it arrived but thought little of those who didn't perform to their standards. Perhaps no one rankled them more than the organizer of the Tour de France.

Henri was vocal in his opinion that Desgrange's strict rules and long stages, day after day, wore riders down, advantaging not those who were the best cyclists but those who were most willing to stand up to the Tour's punishment. Where Desgrange saw opportunity for strategy, Henri saw the need to follow rules over performance. The Tour's move to time-based scoring only reflected this fact, in Henri's mind: a cyclist who never came in first but simply performed consistently could easily wind up winning the Tour de France. A cyclist who pushed himself, who bore down on his competitors in a final sprint, only to injure himself—or falter—was more worthy of a race prize than a cyclist who played it safe but who performed consistently. Still, the brothers joined Desgrange's race. Both registered for the 1919 Tour ten days before it began. The prize money was good, though not as good as it had been in past years—what was five thousand francs for first place in the general classification had become only two thousand—and the Tour was undoubtedly popular across the country. Whole towns would come out to watch them pass. In the month leading up to the competition, as the cyclists raced along its path, and in the months that followed, *l'Auto* spoke to hundreds of thousands who hung on each corresponded word about how the Tour advanced.

For Henri's efforts during Paris–Roubaix, he only beat the second- and third-place finishers by less than seconds, just one then two lengths behind him. Philippe Thys, the second-place cyclist, had competed in the race since 1912. He won the Tour de France in the two years leading up to the war. Philippe was just nine months younger than Henri, not yet thirty, older than the average Tour winner and not exactly in his prime, but at least younger than Eugène. The third-place cyclist, Honoré Barthélémy, was of the new generation, those cyclists whom the Tour veterans would compete against. Honoré, like the others of his age, had only competed as an amateur cyclist before the war began. A few had just started racing as members of professional teams. He had been called up for his years of active service around when the war had begun, had joined others like him in the ranks of line infantry units— fodder for the generals who hoped to claw back whatever terrain they could.

Honoré's red hair stood out once he took off his cycling cap, plastered to his oval forehead. He looked not so distant from an overgrown schoolboy, though he was twenty-seven at the time. He'd grown up close to the Tour's departure point, in the thirteenth arrondissement. Desgrange had watched him after he came in first in the 1912 National Road Championships for Independents and now hoped he would show the older cyclists that there were others who were ready to take their places.

In 1913, the year after he won the National Road Championships, Honoré left Paris to serve. He was assigned to the Twentieth Batterie Chasseurs a Pied, a light infantry unit. When the war broke out in August, it was almost his one-year anniversary in uniform. His unit had been moved east to take part in those first battles of the war, before the fighting ground to a halt and entered the trenches. Honoré had survived those early years. His three years were up but his time in uniform extended. In January of 1919, he had been able to leave his unit and return to his bike before the races began. He went back to Paris and its roads, cycling up and down the tree-lined thoroughfares that led from the capital before he'd do so once more as part of a pack leading their competitors.

Alongside the cyclists' final positions in the race, Desgrange named their sponsors. Not all of the cyclists were backed by a company or two—typically one who provided their bike and one who provided their tires—but among those who spent months away from their homes racing, most had at least one corporate supporter who provided their salaries in the time away from their jobs. The sponsors organized the cyclists who rode for them under a single banner, with a manager and with support for their racing needs, though in the Tour, the sponsors only provided assistance for those hours the cyclists weren't racing. Once they were riding, the cyclists didn't compete as a unit. The sponsors supported them when the small, concentrated purses did not. They paid them bonuses when they placed well, softening the work and increasing the amount of training they could accomplish in the winter months, and they made sure broken-down steel frames and blown-out tires would not end a cyclist's race, though what happened on the roads between the start and finish was up to the cyclists to fix.

Of the top twelve cyclists who rode in Paris–Roubaix for a team, all wore new gray-and-blue woolen jerseys from La Sportive. A new team, one not bearing the recognizable logo of a brand, was an odd feature in any year. After the war and with the strikes and material shortages that brought into question every economic segment of France, it seemed particularly strange that a company would invest advertising funds to sponsor a new cycling team.

Most companies had rearranged their factories to accommodate government contracts, only to see those contracts dry up at the end of the war. Few were left without debts. Peugeot, a regular team sponsor, had retooled its factories to manufacture armored cars, shells, and bicycles, which were then routed to the front. Other sponsors like Alcyon had continued making similar products—motorcycles for Alcyon—to the ones they always had but shifted to fill contracts for the government instead of providing products to mailmen and delivery boys. The war had been an industrial boon for the economy. It brought factories and manufacturing jobs to previously rural areas. At the same time, it had also sapped the national GDP. Only loans from other Allied countries kept the economy running at all. In the absence of that continued support, it was not clear how France would adjust. Retooled factories became artillery targets, and physical reconstruction would be necessary anyway. French consumers—who had been limited by wartime quotas and shortages—had yet to adjust their spending to postwar deregulation.

La Sportive, which sponsored both Philippe and Honoré, had been a creation of the war. In the economic whiplash that followed the forcible molding of the economy, eleven bicycle companies had agreed to band together under a single banner, with a single manager, instead of competing against one another: Alcyon, Armor, Automoto, Clément, La Française, Gladiator, Griffon, Labor, Liberator, Peugeot, and Thomann.

The companies—many of whom had sponsored their own teams before the war—pooled their advertising money to support a team. The cyclists would receive salaries, but with less competition to drive up sums, their offers were diminished. It was still better than nothing for the cyclists, whose job prospects, like countless other returning men, were unclear. Without a sponsor's salary, few could afford to compete for a month.

For that year's Tour, La Sportive had agreed to sponsor a team as well as the prize that would be awarded to the winner of the general classification. The La Sportive roster grew as the Tour neared, picking up other riders who had placed well, like Henri after Paris–Roubaix had ended.

◆ ◆ ◆

The Brasier 15A automobile left the offices of *l'Auto* at 10 rue du Faubourg Montmartre at the witching hour, carrying the race officials who would follow and lead the cyclists over the next month as they traversed the country, even on those roads that were scarcely roads, before returning to the place where they would start in just a few hours. The old moon had left the sky; a new one had just replaced it. The headlamps of the touring car lit the road in front of it, where the pavement had become weathered over the past year. Municipal attentions had been drawn elsewhere. The men in the car bristled: for all their confidence, the upcoming endeavor would determine the future of their employer— the business and the man—and most of it was out of their hands. They weren't sure what would greet them on the city's western edge, along the Seine, at rue de la Tourelle. Plenty of cyclists had signed up for the competition, and, assuming everyone showed, there would be some semblance of a race, but they were less certain what the public would make of it, and what the racers themselves would think. Their boss believed the Tour was needed, for him and for their newspaper—for the people, too, if they were willing to see it that way, as a national cultural exit from the wartime years—but he could only do so much to make others view it the same way he did. And if the people didn't agree, if they weren't receptive to Desgrange's message, it might as well be the end of his career. The paper, well, who knew; other publications were willing to take their place. Desgrange had christened himself the father of the race, but if that race went away, he'd be nothing.

The car passed by place de la Concorde and Jardin des Champs-Élysées. The Eiffel Tower stood along the river's edge. Few strolled through its gardens at that late hour. Paris was at its most beautiful in that moment, when the structures built for the humans who inhabited it were standing but free from the daily commotion that distracted from their beauty. It was as if the people had been raptured, taken away to somewhere else, and the city—for however brief a moment—looked as though it would stand that way forever, that no force could weather it, however untrue that might have been. They crossed the Seine and entered the even quieter outskirts of the city. There, a trickle of people were out on the streets.

The crowd grew as they neared the wooden stands. Hundreds of shadows mingled in the bleachers that surrounded a simple oblong track, itself around an unkempt patch of grass. An unrecognizable sight from its days as a royal hunting ground, though its newer name still called to those past inhabitants: Parc des Princes.

The officials decamped from the car and prepared for the cyclists' entrance to the stadium. There, the contestants would sign in for the first time before the 3:00 a.m. start. They'd repeat the procedure before and after each stage of the race, as they beat around the country's new border as if they were kings or crusaders inspecting the new lands, just one of the many checks the officials had put in place to ensure the race—for all its peculiarities—had a deserving winner.

The first to enter the stadium was Maurice Borel, a B classification cyclist from Clermont-Ferrand. Émile Masson arrived, the first A classification cyclist. He signed into the book laid out for him on the table.

Desgrange watched as Émile signed his name then stood back, his bike resting beneath his hand, taking a spot where he'd wait for the moment when the pack would ride down rue de la Tourelle, out of the city.

It was fortuitous that Émile was the first A classification cyclist to sign his name. A few days ago, Desgrange had published his predictions for the 1919 winner of the Tour de France. Of the veteran cyclists, his top picks were Henri—who had, only two days earlier, officially received thirty-days' leave from his commanding officer to enter the race—Philippe, Eugène, Jean Alavoine, and Louis Heusghem. Of the younger crowd, he thought Émile, Alexis Michiels, Hector Tiberghien, Francis Pélissier, and Honoré Barthélémy would lead the others. Of those ten, those two generations of cyclists, Eugène and Jean Alavoine were too old for Desgrange. The thirty-one-year-old cyclist who now lived in Versailles looked like a private-school boy with his glossy middle part and with a mouth too small on his face, but he couldn't compete with those younger cyclists. Louis, Desgrange reasoned, was too heavy to sustain his pace on the road's more difficult terrain. Francis was still too young, and Honoré didn't yet have a mind for strategy; Desgrange believed Honoré's only plan was to attempt to ride as fast as possible for as long as he could. No, it would come down to Henri, Philippe, Émile, and Hector. And of the first two, Desgrange had a hunch they wouldn't cut it: a race as difficult as the Tour needed young talent, with just a bit of experience, who were in their best shape.

Émile and Hector had only just left military service, but Desgrange believed the training they did accomplish and their resolve would sustain their efforts over the pitted ground of the northeast, and provide the grit needed for stages that stretched nearly five hundred kilometers. He also saw something beyond training that would separate the pair, something unnamable and undefined. If anyone made it through the unbearable course, Desgrange thought, it would be Émile.

Not long after Émile's entry, the rest of the cyclists arrived: the Pélissiers, quiet, who rode in together on their bikes; Jean, his burly hands looked ready to crush his steel bike's handlebars; Eugène, buoyant.

Outside, cheers from the crowd along rue de la Tourelle signaled the impending entrance of another racer. Whatever doubts the officials still harbored about the race's existence were extinguished. Philippe signed in at 2:45 a.m. The roar quieted, and a hush took its place. Those who couldn't see inside the velodrome's interior waited for the racers' exit. Charles Rauvaud, the journalist from *l'Auto* who was driving the Brasier, checked the clock once more before he released the car's brake and pressed it into gear. Then they were off, Jean and Eugène, Henri and Francis, Philippe, and sixty-two others, to a roar that built alongside them with those first few turns of their pedals.

A French infantry regiment marches between Amiens and Montdidier in 1918.

3.

The steel frames creaked as the bikes were brought to speed. The cyclists stood, each pedal bearing their weight in turn as the other lifted, momentarily released with its corresponding leg. The grease-slaked bike chains tugged against the gears, one ridged metal ring on either side of the bikes' back wheels. The racers and their bikes were synchronous, a movement in one resulting in a reaction from the other: a man leaned to the right, and his bike veered into the oncoming turn; if he jumped at the far end of a ditch, spectators could see his seat springs lift. The cyclists had adjusted their mechanics for the flat terrain between Paris and Le Havre, sewn fresh pneumatic tubes into their tires, tightened each nut until the bike felt like a single object instead of hundreds of parts held together, each straining independently along the roads. On the unengaged side of the wheel, a larger gear turned, disconnected from the force of the cyclists' bodies. They felt the pebbled road underneath their tires. Paris's streets had been well maintained for a century; even the Americans, when they visited, thought those flat surfaces that ran through the capital and the main arteries of the country were nothing short of enviable, feats of engineering and administration. That day, each imperfection transmitted its dimensions through the bikes' frames. The cyclists first felt it in their pedals, squarely underneath their weight. The roads made their wheel hubs shudder. The vibrations moved to their fork ends and passed through the racer's body, up the seat post and to the top of their heads. They rode as a pack through Paris, past crowds who lined the sidewalks and cheered for their favorite cyclists. They were teammates—once part of small cliques, now a single gray-and-blue pack. They were neighbors; Philippe and two other cyclists, Firmin Lambot and Léon Scieur, had all spent time in the small town of Florennes. Some had seen each other in that year's earlier single-day races, but others hadn't heard from their competitors in four years. They were, for that moment, both collectively and individually, some of the most popular people in the French capital, which was, at that same time, the world's capital. Just beyond Parc des Princes, the Treaty of Versailles had been signed one day before. It was not too much to think some of the representatives who had spent their days at the palace, who had made Paris a temporary home during the peace conference, were now up early to watch them. They would have seen Luigi Lucotti, the only Italian in the race. The twenty-five-year-old had continued cycling while the others were deployed. His freshly buzzed head and gaunt, almost haunted face passed by rows of people waving flags, hats in hand. Unlike the others, he continued to wear the sky blue of the Bianchi-Pirelli cycling team. Jules Nempon, a B classification cyclist, unsponsored, had friends watching him even if few others would have recognized his unlogoed jersey. They saw their cycling partner leave the city on his third Tour: his first attempt aborted, the next behind twenty-six others, the third to be determined. His friends supposed he would have a story, at least, no matter how long he lasted, but with only two months to train since he had been detached from his unit, they figured it would be a short one. Both the cyclists and those who watched them ride along the Parisian roads were surprised at the other's existence. Surprised that the race could continue so soon after the war, that men were willing or able to ride in it, even those who were paid for their effort. Those men had still willingly set down their regained lives to ride through a terrain most would do anything to avoid, that they had been unable to avoid not so long ago. Even along those first 388 kilometers between Paris and Le Havre—mostly undamaged except for parts of the Somme department—that spectators would leave their homes to watch them despite all the country had gone through, that ordinary men and women would find time to support an event like this one while their city was still shrouded by scaffolding, had not been clear when the cyclists were registering. Whatever vanity was delivered by the Tour, more so than the average cycling event, may not have come for them that year.

The tires' cadence changed as the cyclists crossed pont de Saint-Cloud. One thrum turned to another then back again as they rode over the bridge that had connected Paris with its western neighbor for more than one thousand years: built and rebuilt to accommodate a growing city and the men and women who used the bridge to traverse the Seine. To their left, trees ascended along the far riverbank, on the grounds of a former imperial estate that had been turned into a park. To their right, the town of Saint-Cloud and their route out of the city. The cyclists turned after crossing the bridge and followed the river. In the Tour's first stage, as close to a warm-up as existed in the race, they stayed together as a tidy pack. They conserved their energy. Those farther back siphoned speed from the cyclist in front of them, while the privileged leader confronted the wind's drag pushing past his shoulders. When he was tired, he let another take his place. In the early morning darkness, they crossed the Seine again at pont de Puteaux, pont de Neuilly, and once more at pont de la Jatte, moving to one side of the river and then back again, as if to satisfy a traveler's superstition. They didn't reenter Paris. They only traced a fleeting rim around its northwest edge.

Henri Pélissier paid close attention to the ground underneath his wheels. Signs of neglect dotted its surface: patches where the pebbled surface had been scraped clean and only the hard-packed dirt underneath remained, acute dips and ridges from unnamed events. The route was intact, at least, a road, even if the integrity of each new stretch couldn't be taken for granted. He rode near the front of the pack, comfortable in his position, but behind the first few cyclists. His secondary place allowed him to conserve a measure of his energy before the morning's tendrils released them. He watched the leaders' ungainly frames, not as controlled as they'd been in past years. They blocked Henri from the buffeting air; he kept his eyes open while others resorted to goggles or looked down toward the road. Louis Engel, a French cyclist, led him. Four years older than Henri, Louis was already past his prime, like so many of the others. He stood little chance of holding on to his position long enough to threaten the elder Pélissier. Even Desgrange had admitted that Henri was a likely contender for the general classification title, despite his age. Henri knew the editor's prediction that Émile Masson would win had been mindless speculation, an effort to rouse him and the others. Desgrange liked to think of himself as holding the keys to the Tour—he did while planning the cyclists' path and in specifying their conduct on the roads—but he had little sense for what went into the cyclists' efforts while they rode. He had never competed in his own creation, hadn't raced on a bike at all in decades. Like Luigi, Henri had continued training and cycling in events when others hadn't been able. Even if he wasn't an obvious choice according to his age, his recent results—first in Paris–Roubaix and Paris–Bordeaux, then the French Road National Championships just days before—should make up for whatever penalty his age incurred. In front of Louis, Desgrange rode in the Brasier with Charles Rauvaud, the other race officials, and the *l'Auto* correspondents. The passengers watched the cyclists as they continued along boulevard de Courbevoie, the car jostling over the same road they traversed. The pack passed underneath a regional railway bridge that turned the dark night nearly pitch black for a second.

The Pélissiers had been raised in the city they had just passed through. Henri was the second of five, born after his older sister, Augustine. Then came Jean Jr., then his riding partner, Francis, and finally the baby, Charles. As the oldest son, Henri had been privileged among the rest, as much as his parents, Jean and Elisa-Augustine, could afford. Jean Sr. had set out on his own as a cattle farmer just a few years before Henri was born, and Elisa-Augustine had left a waitressing job to marry Jean Sr. and move in with him. They weren't wealthy, but they found the means to give Henri his first bicycle when he was eleven—barely big enough to ride it. Most people in their neighborhood, in the eighteenth arrondissement, wouldn't have dreamed of owning their own bike like he did, unless their work necessitated it, but the young Henri would ride down the streets with Jean alongside him, back and forth down the block, with the scaffolded Sacré-Cœur standing tall atop the hill behind them.

Jean Sr. didn't tell Henri he could use his bike to compete against others. In Jean Sr.'s mind, the bike was a novelty, a practical means of conveying his son from place to place, not that Henri was going very far when Jean Sr. first bought the bike for him. He ran his household firmly. His own strong sense of morality guided him as he led Henri and the others to follow the path he had taken, a simple life. Henri was a proud child already, though: haughty for his age, unafraid of testing his father or anyone else above him. He did so in the open, unlike his other siblings, when they tested Jean at all. Henri and his father fought regularly. Eventually, Henri left his family home after working for his father for a few years. He remained in Paris and stayed in touch with his family, except for his father. He worked in construction and began competing in local cycling races as an amateur.

Henri began his two years of active service in 1910, serving with the Third Engineer Regiment. His commanding officers at the time noted that he suffered from a weak constitution. It wasn't a tense time for the unit, though there was always the chance they would be sent to a French colony to tamp down uprisings, as they had done in Morocco and Madagascar not so long ago. He had suffered from pulmonary edema the year before and had returned to his bike only months earlier. Whatever the case, Henri—by his own choice or in actuality—couldn't perform the duties ordered of him. By the time the Great War broke out, his records informed officials to pass over him in all but the most unexacting drafts.

Francis and Henri's brother Jean, born between the two cyclists in 1892, left for the front while Henri remained in Paris. Francis continued serving in the Twenty-fourth Infantry Regiment while Jean lived in the trenches with his fellow soldiers of the 150th Infantry Regiment: the same unit he'd been assigned to before the outbreak of the war and the one Henri Desgrange would eventually join as a lieutenant.

In March 1915, a shell burst near Jean. A metal splinter, or rocks buried in the ground it impacted, sprung out and sliced through Jean's carotid artery. He was taken to the nearby auxiliary hospital set up at Sainte-Menehould, where he died. There had been nothing anyone could do. These things just happened. It was fate. He was buried at the Marne with other soldiers who had died in the battle; eleven days later le ministère de la Guerre notified his family. After Jean's death, Henri considered traveling to one of the military's review boards so his exemption could be lifted, but his father, who had already lost one son and who saw Henri's luck for what it was, persuaded him not to.

The following year, in May, Henri married Léonie Jenin. That same month, her brother, Henri's childhood friend and now his brother-in-law, was killed in Verdun, stabbed with a German bayonet. On November 30th, Henri arrived at the central recruitment bureau in the city, determined to enlist. The military acceded. They first assigned him to the Twentieth Section of Secretaries, where he served as a cyclist for the unit of Paris recruiters. Eventually, he was transferred to reserve status at the beginning of 1917 and joined the First Aviation Group.

He was always close with Francis, though Francis was the more loyal of the two, as younger brothers are wont to do. After the war, they became closer. As he had with his father, Henri butted heads with race organizers and other cyclists. It helped that he had someone on his side. Those who competed against him after the war thought his temper had become quicker; he would argue about his times or complain about the race conditions without cause.

Francis had started to compete in races, too, to their father's chagrin. The Pélissier brothers' postures while cycling were complementary. Henri, nicknamed "ficelle," or string, was tall and lean. Francis cast a larger image. He was even taller than Henri and most other cyclists at just under five foot ten, had the same steely eyes as his brother, and a distinctive scar underneath his left eye. He was also more solidly built than Henri. His racing style was subtler. He was more pragmatic, despite his younger age, more calculating and strategic when fighting for position in the pack and while communicating with others along the route. Henri used other cyclists. He couldn't stop them from drafting behind him, but it mattered little: he was unconcerned by their performance much of the time. It was enough that he had their distant respect.

Henri still preferred almost any of his competitors to the officials who rode in front of them in the Brasier. In his mind, Desgrange and the others who put on the Tour had done little except profit from his and the other cyclists' previous performances, and if Desgrange had his way, Henri and the rest of them would only be paid enough to leave their jobs for a time. Better yet, they would be wealthy enough to compete in the race as amateurs, asking almost nothing from administrators except to make sure they didn't cheat. As long as their performances didn't suffer. Desgrange thought the glory of winning the race was worth more than any money, though he recognized he'd have few competitors that way. Day after day, Desgrange would write his dispatches from the latest town the cyclists arrived in, lifting the competitors in his race as if they were immortal, then doing his best to test that fact, past any point of reason.

It was still more night than day when the calls from the crowds faded. The cyclists exited the country's center; all that remained were the words they exchanged with one another and with the officials in front of them. One cyclist, they learned, had already crashed. Those who had seen the accident thought the bike would need repairs. They didn't know if it would be worth it for their unfortunate competitor to continue, whoever it was. Desgrange's rules mandated that a single bike frame be used for the entire race, and during a stage, only the cyclist himself could repair it. Even if that cyclist could repair the bike—no sure thing, depending on what had happened to it—an early hit to his time would require double the effort just to rejoin the other tailing cyclists. The identity of the unlucky racer was at first unclear. Then the news reached the leading riders and spread to the pack's edges. An image of Francis flashed through one racer's mind as they heard the news—he had been bucked from the bike, he had sprawled on the ground, he had gotten up slowly. It had taken only a moment's glance away from the road, or a rock kicked up by another cyclist's wheel, for him to crash less than an hour into the race. There was nothing any of them could do; they continued without him.

It was a cool summer morning. The cyclists continued their deliberate arc northwest. Henri, hovering in the fortieth position of the sixty-seven riders, rode into the town of Mouy at 5:40 a.m. Their destination that day was Le Havre, almost directly west of the town. Around him, local textile factories' looms spun with the currents of the Thérain, a tributary of the Seine. To make it to their destination, the riders would first continue north, then cut back down along the coast to the port city. Though it was not yet bright, a hint of the day's sun could be seen through the trees along rue de Colombiers. The temperature, not more than fifty-eight degrees Fahrenheit, suited their efforts. The waxed jackets they carried with them were tied to their bikes' frames, unused, but it wasn't so hot that they felt stifled underneath their gray-and-blue wool jerseys. The pack continued riding out of the city, just one of countless they'd forget in not so long. The sun had risen more fully by the time Francis bore down the same road into the town, a little less than two hours later.

Despite the ideal conditions, the cyclists already began to feel their efforts clash against their lack of training and the roads' disrepair as they left the main paths and took byways that only connected one town with another. Officials stationed in the towns and in the Brasier quickly lost track of cyclists' tire punctures. It was poor luck to have to change a tire, though the road's conditions and the questionable quality of the tires found for the cyclists would at least have to be endured by them all. A cyclist replaced the tire as quick as he was able and continued on, hoping to not lose much time. In any normal year, they would all have to endure a few flats along the Tour's route, but as more of the day passed, it looked like the flat rubber tubes crossing their torsos, scrounged up by La Sportive from the few factories that could accommodate their order, wouldn't be enough for their route.

Henri left the Seine department and entered the Somme. The Brasier spat and rumbled ahead of the pack. The journalists looked back now and then to check the leading cyclists' progress, but they were caught up in their own conversations: they joked about old races, the routes and riders who lived on in their friends' thoughts of them. The cyclists had traversed more than 100 kilometers and were nearing the first stop of the stage, in Amiens, where they'd have a moment to account for themselves and their bikes, as well as replace their depleted water bottles. Then, they'd return for another 238 kilometers before the day was over.

Henri rode on rue de Saint-Just, a flat road. At varying stretches an embankment would rise on his right then left, protecting him from the sun then backlighting the trees on either side of his path. He had worked his way toward the front of the pack as the race neared Montdidier. He was within sight of Desgrange and the other officials now. Almost all the cyclists wore identical colors, so it was difficult for the officials to identify anyone unless they asked one of the grunting cyclists. Only their numbered bibs separated them. From the side of the road, their faces jostled against one another, mussed into a cloud from the Brasier's kicked-up dirt.

Montdidier had been a small town even before the war; no more than five thousand Frenchmen lived there. In its center a statue of Antoine-Augustin Parmentier had stood, a military pharmacist and nutritionist who had advocated for the use of potatoes in soldiers' diets. It was the one detail that described the cyclists' route through the town, just enough of a symbol, a sign to grab onto as they rode through Montdidier's center. Each settlement was like one of a thousand others.

The pack veered right at the small square where Parmentier's statue once stood. His hands had been full then: one held two books, the other a potato. On the stone plinth, Parmentier stood over a prostrate figure. He handed the old man another starchy root. Only the statue's plinth remained; Parmentier's body had been hauled off elsewhere, plundered, melted down, when Germans occupied the town in the war's last spring. Few pieces of Montdidier remained around the plinth. Some of the wartime rubble had been cleared, enough so that the cobbled road reappeared from underneath the brick dust. Some piles of debris still formed berms along the road's outer edge. Behind the berms, walls stood, but little more. From above, the town's structure was clear—foundation lines were still visible, but roofs had given way and some buildings existed as not much more than short fences around a stack of bricks.

The war had held the town in its grasp for years. Montdidier had been traded back and forth between the Allies and Germans almost until the moment of armistice in 1918. It was next to the front lines in the Hundred Days Offensive, the Allies' final push, where hundreds of thousands of casualties were sustained despite the end's proximity. Each exchange of the town—from the Allies to the Germans and back again—provided barely any respite, though at least the French had no desire to plunder Montdidier.

The buildings retained some of their faces from before the war: paint unpeeled in some parts, a few scraps of wallpaper, too. The walls' edges, however, had been brutally scribed. Neat squares had turned into two-dimensional spires. The unfinished ends of bricks peeked through; carbonized remains hid the rest of the red clay. Their appearance was primeval: cousins of the stone walls that separated ancient plots. What remained was sturdy enough, but primitive. Another town like a thousand others. Between these buildings, a few people had shown up on the sides of the road—from where, the cyclists wondered to themselves—to watch them pass.

A minute ahead of schedule, at 8:44 a.m., the first group of twenty-five entered Amiens. Henri sat comfortably in third. The cyclists grumbled to each other and to the officials and journalists who mingled around them. They expressed frustration as they picked at their damaged wheels, as if scratching at mites. It was already clear their tires could barely handle the roads. A cyclist would stop to replace a deflated back tire only to make it one hundred meters more before the front tire popped with a fierceness that rattled the steel frame and rendered the bike momentarily disobedient. They made their frustrations known to the *l'Auto* editor.

The newspaper had promised them in the weeks before the Tour began that tires would be provided for each stage, but on June 27th, two days before the race began, a notice mentioned that because of shortages—itself the byproduct of labor strikes throughout the year as women and immigrants found themselves removed from their wartime jobs—a suitable tire supply hadn't been found. Tire factory workers were part of the strikes that ran throughout the country. On top of the shifting labor population, workers complained about insufficient wages given inflation after the war's end. The companies understood the workers' concerns but didn't see a clear solution: government contracts had ended, and the companies were left with retooled machines that had been producing goods the country no longer needed. Bicycle tires weren't an economic priority, so it instead fell to the cyclists and their teams to keep the riders equipped.

A *l'Auto* official visited each of the cyclists. He bent down to look underneath their bike's thin leather saddle. He picked at a uniform piece of lead the referees attached to its underside during registration. The lead was an attempt to ensure cyclists didn't alter or change their bikes along the course. They had only one frame to carry them around France's boundaries. When the riders registered, they had also provided the newspaper with relevant information about their bike and their preferred tires, not that the latter was of much use. The official then looked at the bike's drivetrain for the matching lead piece. Any cyclist whose lead was missing would be penalized.

Another official took the two emptied water bottles from each cyclist and handed them two full ones. A small but essential comfort, the least the newspaper could do. They similarly hadn't been able to agree on a price for musettes—small bags cyclists could throw over their shoulders—filled with food. *L'Auto* said they could instead fill their pockets with rolls, cheeses, fruit—whatever was within reach. If at least ten cyclists arrived at the stop at the same time, they could fill their pockets without the timekeeper's watch extending their time. The morning cold hadn't given way to the daytime heat. The crowd that had watched them ride into Amiens closed in around them as the officials finished their inspections in the order the cyclists had arrived, then broke apart to let each cyclist pass through.

The Amiens stop went by quick. The pack had little time to recover from the first stretch of the stage. Some joked and laughed despite their strains. Eugène was at ease. His weathered appearance hid his seemingly boundless energy. He was stocky and muscular compared to the others, more of an athlete, but hardly people's popular image of a cyclist. He had none of a wrestler's caution, however, no matter how many times people compared him to one. Instead, he cut cleanly through mud and mountain while taller racers flapped like wayward laundry.

The riders prepared themselves. They took one last sip of water before replacing the bottles on their bike's frames, and plucked at their tires' rims, making sure the quick, muted hum of the wheel was to their satisfaction. Each rider looked at their bike one last time, though they knew it would do little to prevent the accidents that tore others from the road.

The first half of a long stage was typically slower than the second, as the cyclists' large morning meals, eaten before they set off, settled in their stomachs. Eventually they rode until they were no longer full. They didn't yet need a second meal, or at least they didn't know when they could get one. A thin consommé at a trailer, provided by a bouillon company, was set up in some of the towns. Cyclists were free to eat when they wanted, but few allowed themselves anything more than a quick bite from a café as their bikes were inspected. For most, unscheduled stops were kept to a minimum. After a meal had settled, they would accelerate again, attempting to sustain that equilibrium for as long as possible.

Henri and Francis paid closer attention to their diets. Henri planned his attacks for those early morning hours when he had the strongest advantage against his overfed, stagnant competitors. The night before a stage, the brothers avoided drinking, unlike most everyone else who blunted the aches of the prior day with local spirits.

Henri mounted his bike and let the wheels take over from his extended leg. His dust-coated hands gripped the straight handlebar tops, and, with a kick, he advanced alongside the others as the pack swept from the town.

The cyclists continued along the Somme River westward. They passed more towns. A single road led from one to the next, connected the inhabitants of each place with those around them. Before the Tour, few French people had understood their place within the larger country.

France for them had been limited to the land they encountered each week or month, when they rode to the next town to buy groceries or to repair their farm tools. When the Tour first began, the map *l'Auto* printed each year—displaying the circuit the cyclists would trace—provided the people with a sense of place that limited educations did not. A national map was a relatively new accessory in primary school classrooms. The people in those towns, with scarcely any connection to politicians in Paris, began to feel like they were part of the race, the larger country, the route that extended from the western coast to the changing border in the east. When the Alsace was reclaimed in the Great War, people who had irregular contact with the northeast could see, in definite terms, how it changed the shape of their country even if they didn't understand the new lands' ramifications to foreign affairs or hadn't learned of its mythology. Their collective payment—the lives of their families and their friends—had gone toward reclaiming that border. They had little say over that cost, but the Tour at least gave them some ownership of that territory as part of the whole.

Even in the smallest towns, people gathered along the cobbled roads. Some had clear favorites. They called out "Cri-cri!" as Eugène passed, a bird-like call mimicking his last name. Other spectators looked on in wonder as each cyclist rode through their town. Some of them cheered wildly, seemingly without cause, celebrating the fact of the cyclists' existence. As they rode along quai Sadi Carnot in Tréport, they caught their first glimpse of the Atlantic Ocean on the port's outer edge, behind rows of small fishing boats. The water was a ruddy blue, earthy with silt and sand in the shallow waters. They could see, in the keyhole of the port's breakwater, the ocean itself: a flat expanse. Henri and the others veered away from the coast before they could spot more than that sliver.

They traced a path along coastal roads. Despite their proximity to the ocean, they were far enough from the water that the landscape looked like any other stretch of land between them and Paris. Farmland was to their right, between the road and the rocky beaches, with crinkled green cliffs overlooking the water. On occasion, however, when the road neared the water and if the land was fallow, a thin lead band could be seen splitting the brown earth and the blue gradient of the sky. To the riders' left, the farmland extended all the way to the broken ground they had passed earlier that morning.

The stage's second checkpoint was in Dieppe. Some knew the town for the scallops that fishermen pulled from the waters outside its port. The damp shellfish were transported in wooden crates to the local Saturday market, where sunbaked men split the rippled shells to reveal ecru and tangerine inside. The town was 259 kilometers from the race's start at Parc des Princes, and 129 kilometers from the end of their day in Le Havre. The cyclists sprinted into town, the distance they had already traveled forgotten.

In towns along the route, groups as small as a few men who drank together on Friday afternoons, who hoped to attach their name to a Tour winner, to have their names included in *l'Auto*'s pages, would pull together a small prize for the first man to enter their town. Dieppe gathered one such prize for that sprint's winner. Henri rode at a frenzied pace alongside Jean Rossius and Jules Masselis, two Belgian cyclists. The three rode in front of the others, biked along the port's edge, before they turned left onto Grand Rue, tracing the coastline. The steel frames held steady against the pistons of the racers' legs, the ground solid enough that their tires held against the sprint's pressure. The townspeople lined the street, cheering as the bike frames torqued back and forth, the men standing to push their bikes faster, as if trying to pry apart the earth underneath. Henri gathered the strength for one last push, but the three remained on equal footing. Both Jean and Jules edged out in front at the last second and crossed the finish line just before him. The crowd and race officials stood on the other side, greeted them, and collapsed in on the cyclists as they drifted past. It was 1:48 p.m., the first 259 kilometers had taken the first pack almost eleven hours to complete.

Officials checked the bikes, replaced the cyclists' water bottles. Jean Rossius received a winner's plaque from the mayor, which Desgrange then stored in the Brasier. The Belgian had a single permanent forehead crease across his face, as if he'd received a scar from a cycling cap. Just as soon as they had entered, the cyclists left, their times recorded by race officials for their end-of-stage scoring. They were moving again, jockeying with each other to gain any advantage that might carry them through the stage's final roads. As if to separate them, the ground they encountered thinned, became little more than capillaries. For one hundred kilometers after leaving Dieppe, they wound through towns on these roads, foliage pushing in from either side, not neatly following the edge of the country, but instead cutting a winding path between farms and the Atlantic waters. Turns gave way to tall hedges that concealed unaware cars, blind until the final moment. Still, the cyclists veered in front of one another with little regard for lanes if an opportune moment came. In these conditions, the pack fractured. Despite the flat ground and manageable distance, it became clear how difficult that year's race would be. Before Saint-Valéry-en-Caux, 295 kilometers into the leg, Jules Masselis's tire was punctured. Philippe's tire followed, then Jean Rossius's. Even Eugène, who had trained for the race, stopped on the side of the road, clutched over with hunger pains. Henri's tire popped near Veulettes. It happened to others, too, unable to stand up to the thin, diminished roads or the demands of the race. The pack rearranged itself again and again to accommodate each lost cyclist.

Jean Rossius rode alongside Philippe as the afternoon wore on. The stage pushed them both, but Philippe, who had run out of water earlier, after the stop in Dieppe, was more fatigued than his fellow Belgian.

Philippe had been able to continue cycling as the war went on, traveling from his home in Anderlecht to Brussels and even to Paris. Still, the races he had competed in were shorter than any single-day they would take part in on the Tour. His climb up the steep paths along the edge of Lake Como could only replicate a fraction of the Tour's challenge. Before the war, before the gray-and-blue jersey he now wore, Philippe had ridden for Peugeot-Wolber, and Jean for Alcyon. Jean lived in Retinne, a town along the Belgian border with Germany. It had resisted in the first days of the German invasion. Then it was clear fighting would only cause them more injury in the inevitable occupation.

They had fought against one another in more difficult Tour stages before, but Philippe told Jean he didn't think he could continue the race. Without water, he could only ride for so long, and even if his bottles were refilled, he was unprepared for the race. Jean passed Philippe one of his water bottles in response, hoping it would last him until they stopped in Le Havre. He couldn't do anything for Philippe's muscles, but he'd continue riding next to him if it would help the cyclist regain some of the energy he had lost. In other years, perhaps Jean would have felt less allegiance to the past Tour winner, but they were both riding for the same team now, in a foreign country and in a race unlike any other they had encountered.

By the time the first cyclists entered Fécamp, just fifty-three kilometers from Le Havre, Eugène and the others were fifty-five minutes behind Desgrange's proposed schedule. The small crowd Eugène passed by had waited patiently for him, for the sixty-six others, some of whom had already quit, others who would not be there for hours. With the day waning, the larger crowds left them behind just as the other cyclists did.

Eugène rode downhill into the town. He passed the local church. The hill it sat on gave way to an unobstructed ocean. Then the path collapsed into a hairpin turn. In the early evening hour, the sun still sat squarely in the sky. Another four or five hours remained before it would fall away.

The pack receded from the ocean, a reverse tide. Already the towns blurred together: their ports, their squares and statues, the people who watched along the side of the roads. After 6:00 p.m. the first cyclists entered the outskirts of Le Havre. Jean Rossius rode in front of Henri. Eugène dropped behind them. Jean was ahead by what looked to be a minute or more. Henri pushed himself but realized that catching up to the others was unlikely. On the street around him French flags waved, but also the black, yellow, and red of Belgium. Among the crowd that cheered for him were those who waved miniature versions of the flag, their support behind Jean. Down the hill to his right, in a large white converted seaside resort, the Belgian government in exile had conducted affairs of the state after the German invasion in 1914. He was in their neighborhood.

He rode along a straight road toward the port where the day's race ended. Just two blocks over was the city's rocky beach, abutted by Chantiers Normand, a military shipbuilder, and Batterie Royale, protecting the harbor from unwelcome foreign vessels. Both stood beside hôtel Frascati, a large beachside resort that held visiting guests in the wartime years.

The townspeople stood everywhere along the boulevard. They cheered for Henri despite his disappointment in his time. His second place was—in part—due to luck that he may not have later. He hadn't suffered any punctures; he simply didn't ride as fast as Jean. He'd have to improve if he hoped to compete on the alpine climbs.

Desgrange watched as Henri and the others rode through the city. The race officials had left the Brasier. The timekeeper remained at the finish line to record their times while the other officials sat in the bar at l'Hotel Moderne waiting for the cyclists to join them and sign into the logbook. Desgrange handed Henri a pen when he arrived so he could sign in, validating his place. Cyclists had already started to leave the Tour behind, to stop on the side of the road before they entered the city, not bothering to notify the officials they were no longer competing. They would simply return home on their own dime, as the Tour rules had specified. Each Tour had a winnowing in the first stages. Cyclists, particularly amateurs who competed only for themselves, realized the effort and the cost associated with competing in the race. This year the number of cyclists who abandoned the race grew as they realized they only had themselves to rely on instead of the race organizers for sustenance and support. Despite that, as he watched the people who cheered for the cyclists who remained, Desgrange saw as much of the old Tour's spirit as he had ever seen. If only one cyclist was left, it would have been enough for the crowds to show up, to wave their morning *l'Auto* editions with the hope that cyclist would remember their face from the crowd, would return after he had logged his time and sign their copy.

Just past the finish line, the rickety frames of cranes turned back and forth as they loaded and unloaded cargo from the military ships docked in the harbor. Henri reached them after fifteen hours and fifty-seven minutes. An industry's worth of ships and supplies, even months after the war's end, still filled the harbor. In a few hours the sun would set and the operation would continue, in Le Havre and in Cherbourg and Brest, the two destinations in front of the cyclists, where soldiers still arrived and left from Camp Pontanezen, a military base that had eclipsed Brest in size. There was no war left for those men to fight, only its remnants to witness and clean up.

The 813th Pioneer Infantry Regiment

July 2, 1919—Camp Pontanezen, Brest

As the cyclists witnessed the war concluding around them, the rest of France, and those who had fought in the war but had come from elsewhere, were still responsible for sewing up the scuffed sack of the country, letting as few businesses, refugees, and displeased foreign residents as possible fall through its undone weave.

On July 3rd, the cyclists would ride toward Camp Pontanezen on the outskirts of Brest. To those who passed by it, the American military base still functioned as if the soldiers stationed there hadn't received news the war was through. The population of the camp, the American soldiers who rested there for a few days or weeks, had diminished slightly from the hundreds of thousands who had waited within its confines before embarking on one of the vessels destined for England and the United States in the first waves after the war's end. Months after that initial exodus, men were still leaving the country via the port of Brest a mile and a half southwest of the camp. From the port, soldiers boarded ships that took them to New Jersey or Virginia or a handful of other states. Then, they traveled alone on journeys back to the other forty-six. With each departing group of war-weary men, another set of clean faces appeared with orders taking them east, to Paris or some other stretch of land between Pontanezen and Berlin.

The camp rested on a south-leaning slope, surrounded by farmlands that the US military had gradually requisitioned to accommodate the endless flow of soldiers. What was once a fifteen-acre plot had grown to a sprawling thousand acres to make room for the men who'd been released from France's gullet. As barracks and other facilities were constructed on the wet farmland underfoot, Pontanezen felt not so different from the living conditions on the front, the slop beneath their Pershing boots, the cold percolating through canvas and thin wood walls, though at least there hadn't been the threat of snipers or artillery. The first winter the camp opened—in 1917—soldiers filing through Pontanezen saw unrelenting rain on the days when it didn't snow. The ground turned into a thick mud, and the human waste generated from those who stayed there polluted the wells that had been bored into the ground. Water sourced at the camp had to be treated before it could be drunk. It wasn't a soothing prologue to the front, and only slightly more tolerable for those who at least had home to look forward to. Those men garrisoned at Pontanezen—their shoulder patches displaying the camp's omnipresent duckboard with its double-wide wooden strips, slatted just enough to let the wetness from their boot bottoms seep down into the mud below—had it worse.

◆ ◆ ◆

As the cyclists left Paris, the men of the 813th Pioneer Infantry Regiment camped in the muddy purgatory, recovering from an abbreviated war and preparing to leave it at least physically behind. The men of the 813th, a colored unit, clipped their entrenching tools onto their field packs, screwed together the bronze brushes of their rifle kits and slid them down through their Springfield's bore. The rifles hadn't found much use in the preceding months, but the muck of the east and of Pontanezen itself was enough to plug them up.

Each choice they had made and those that had been made for them—joining the military, shipping over to France, working in the mud among the dead, contributing in whatever way Black men from the US had been allowed—was met with distrust from their fellow enlisted soldiers and officers, not to mention they were treated as though one slip would be their downfall: a dishonorable discharge, a disciplinary board. It hadn't been enough for them to join the war effort, to volunteer for a fight that had already killed hundreds of thousands of Allied soldiers. Some of the men had gone back and forth—should they fight for a country that only treated them as partial citizens?—before eventually deciding that to do so, to join the war, was better than the alternative, and service might at least grant them the confidence of those in their community that their mere existence wouldn't. In response, their communities, the white people closest by, cautiously watched them, considered whether they would use what they had learned in training, as if fighting for their country was a precursor to fighting against their communities once they had arrived back home. Their lieutenant, Knowlton—a white man who no doubt felt the weight of his post—hoped their limited training would slip from their minds into the cold Atlantic waters as they shipped back.

The 813th's war had scarcely happened. Less than a year had passed since that first evening when Knowlton nodded in and out of consciousness as the paddleboat carrying him and his men turned lazily, holding its position in New York Bay. Knowlton had grown up in Freeport, Illinois. The 813th's enlisted soldiers—Harvey Blue, Cannady Burks, Percy Dilworth, Allen Floyd, and on—had been sent from Philadelphia, Cincinnati, St. Louis, as far as Molino, Florida, and countless places between after receiving notices from the draft board their numbers had been called. They had trained together at Camp Sherman in Ohio before being sent out to the East Coast. The training felt more like work than preparation for war: parade drills and target practice were rare instances when it didn't feel like they were slave labor for the commanding officers. They were to be deployed as a "pioneer" unit. In other circumstances, it was a title something close to storied: men tasked with keeping combat structures strong and secure, then fighting when those same structures came under attack. In other militaries, the designation came with distinct uniforms and grooming standards. For the 813th, it meant they were a labor battalion, men the army deemed incapable of serving in combat units, who would instead work and support the military while others went to fight.

The morning after the 813th had arrived in Hoboken on the paddleboat, they boarded the USS *Pocahontas* with scarcely a formal goodbye from the city. The *Pocahontas* was a ship that had once run passenger routes between Germany and Yokohama, until it had been seized by US forces. In the early hours, they set sail for France on that papered-over enemy ship.

Knowlton stayed with the other Company F officers. They spoke among themselves and let the men in their units mostly do as they pleased on the passage over, which was fine for both parties.

Knowlton hadn't taken them seriously as soldiers. In his estimation, his platoon saw whatever danger or obstacle was right in front of them, but didn't look much further, a quality that troubled him as the one who'd lead them in battle, if it ever came to that. As the 813th rode across the Atlantic Ocean on the former German liner, Knowlton got the impression that they believed everything was fine; the war was in the distance, not there aboard the ship. He saw little need to counsel them and instead watched from a distance. He was pleased they didn't cause much excitement, at least on the first half of the voyage. The only complaint Knowlton received came after one soldier's patrol cap had gone missing, stolen by another man.

During the second half of their three-month crossing, an influenza outbreak swept through the ship. Before it docked in Brest, several men were confined to their beds, wondering whether they would make it to the battlefield. Knowlton had come down with a mild form of the illness late in the voyage, as they neared the port. The USS *Pocahontas* docked and the lieutenant was promptly sent to a hospital in town for a week of recovery. By the time he was released, his men had been sent east without him. He was told the men were in Le Mans, a little over halfway between Brest and Paris. He received updated travel orders and left Brest for his unit's new post. He arrived in Le Mans, only to find the unit wasn't there. They were, instead, he was told, in Bricon, receiving trench warfare training. It took Knowlton another three days to join them.

Bricon was halfway between Paris and Switzerland. There, the 813th was supposed to receive the standard training for infantry units, more practical than their schooling back at Camp Sherman. It was the schooling each unit who would approach the front was given. As a pioneer unit, Knowlton's men would be responsible for building and rebuilding trenches and dugouts, maintaining lines of communication, roads that had been taken over for the war that would now carry returning civilians and a bike race that would traverse the country.

Instead of the full training, his men had only received three cursory weeks of basic firearms handling and a primer on life in the trenches, a fraction of the time allotted to white infantry units who sometimes received months of specialized training before being sent to quiet parts of the front in preparation for larger battles. The military didn't think the 813th needed to be fully prepared to work on Allied roads. At the end of the three weeks, they received orders to move closer to the front. They traveled to Dompierre in the Meuse. There, the 813th were to help rebuild the damaged roads leading into and out of the town.

Black men received hostile treatment from the army. Stories had gone around about a Catholic group, the Knights of Columbus, who erected a tent at Camp Romagne for the exclusive use of the white soldiers who clerked there, while Black men who served on mortuary duty were excluded from the structure. Within days, the tent had been razed by the disgruntled Black soldiers. At Base Hospital 56 in Argonne, a wounded Black soldier had been refused treatment for almost seventy-two hours before being seen by an army doctor, and then only begrudgingly. Secretaries on ships had attempted to relegate Black soldiers to steerage, or the lower deck otherwise reserved for cargo.

The 813th was no exception. They had stayed at Dompierre for a month, far enough from the front that they had little danger of being targeted, but near enough they could still hear the battle's rumble from their position: the tympanic thrum, the low kazoo slide, like air released from a charged vessel. On November 10, 1918, at around 3:00 a.m., an orderly woke Knowlton as he slept in his dugout. The battalion had orders to move. Around the town, well-sourced rumors had been circulating that the armistice would be signed within a day. It was unclear what good would be served by having his men move closer to the front in those final hours. Half of Company F, including Knowlton and his men, as well as all those in Company E began marching to Hannonville, toward the front. As they did, the shelling began.

The sound began as a compression against the men's eyes and skin. Then shockwaves of air sucked the breath from their lungs and sapped blood from their extremities, sending it toward the brain. If a man was close enough, he'd encounter the blast and the molten metal, as well as bone and dirt and noxious foreign substances clambering for his open wounds. Heat followed the initial shock, if the blast didn't destroy the body. In some of the worst battles of the war, the shells had rolled in, more than one per second, for hours if not days on end.

The men of the 813th faced shelling far from the worst seen in the war. The Germans had no assault planned on their position. Instead, the bombs had been a promise that they would continue to fight, that an Allied assault would still exact a cost even if the war was over but for a set of signatures. The men of the 813th hadn't yet seen battles up close, however—not even a quieter stretch of the front—and they scrambled into the bomb proofs like rabbits, Knowlton later wrote, waiting for the whistling to cease. They spent the rest of the early morning in hiding.

Later, as if a curtain had been drawn, the sounds that had once reached their ears—some far, others much closer—receded from their position like footsteps. At 11:00 a.m. a collective tension released itself from their ranks: their conversations grew louder, soldiers ventured out from the trenches, one at a time, then in small groups. All exhaled. One army left, the other remained.

For the 813th, given their late arrival, it felt like the war had only just begun. They still had their orders, even if any small hope they held about fighting in the war was gone. They would finish the work the army had tasked them with; there would be no more artillery strikes to undo it. Plenty of rebuilding remained across those miles of the front.

Throughout no man's land, men were lying where they'd fallen. When a soldier was injured, efforts were sometimes made to retrieve him under the cover of darkness, when possible, but many times, it wasn't worth the danger. During the fighting, the sounds of dying men were constant, like crickets in the night, faint beneath the distant boom of artillery thunder. Once a soldier had died, recovery lost its importance. If the line was pushed forward, and what was once no man's land became a safe zone for one of the armies, then those who lay there were buried in shallow, undistinguished graves—a temporary solution to clear the ground and save the remaining soldiers from unnecessary trauma, at least until more permanent structures could be erected. When the battlefield tides were slow to shift, however, bodies lay atop the ground for days or weeks.

The men of the 813th began their postwar days in this landscape. As they watched other units retreat from the front, heading to nearby towns or back to Paris, before leaving from Brest or one of the other embarkation ports, the 813th remained along the dormant battle lines and carried out their orders. They began collecting bodies that had settled in the mud and the craters. They gathered what was left of the men, the drab fabric scraps, the unclasped pendants, the oil-stained, dog-eared pocket notes, however much or little remained. They began to bury the dead. There were no graveyards yet, but the 813th did their best to inter the soldiers neatly, where they might be found at a later date. It had taken a morbid week to clear their surrounding area, working long days.

Once they had finished, the unit moved back to Dompierre. Until they set off for Brest in July, they spent their days working on the roads and structures in the surrounding areas, the checkpoints and barracks from where soldiers would keep the peace as the land repopulated.

After a few months of labor, they left for Pontanezen. Once they arrived at the camp, the soldiers there treated them as they had been treated by the rest of the American military: no better or worse after they'd finished their orders, completed the job few would willingly take on. Casual neglect was their most common, satisfactory interaction with the white men, but on rare occasions, they were surprised by compassionate assistance. Otherwise, outright hostility defined soldiers' reactions to them. Most of Camp Pontanezen itself, the duckboards crossing muddy ground, the ramshackle wooden huts for the mass of soldiers, had been erected by Black men, including the 813th's sibling, the 803rd. Without them, the wet farmland would have been uninhabitable for even a small group of soldiers, to say nothing of the countless ones who flowed through it on the way to and from the front.

Pontanezen's commander, Brigadier General Smedley Butler, had at least recognized the colored units for their efforts, though he had little desire for anything more than basic courtesy. Butler had done away with his most outright appearances of racism as the commander of the Gendarmerie d'Haïti. Instead, he traded them for a paternalistic attitude toward the units under his command. More broadly, Butler had built a name for himself as something close to egalitarian and was the first one to cart a duckboard from the Brest wharf—work well beneath his rank. After that first board was delivered, the labor battalions went to work, eventually turning those wooden slats into a logistical master-piece. Pontanezen appeared from the muddy depths, like a buried city.

It had been less than a year since the unit had formed in New York. Knowlton watched as his men left from the camp. They headed south-west toward the Brest port, the same place where they once started their journey. There, they'd board the USS *Cap Finisterre*, another German boat that had changed hands as part of the country's repara-tions. They would scale the ramps onto her deck and run along her sides, spill out onto whatever sunlit space they could find. Some of those men would stay in uniform after they got back.

Any hopes the men felt were reserved. Most would leave the ser-vice and reenter a hostile society. Their sacrifice wouldn't be enough to change many folks' views of them, no matter what Harvey, Cannady, Percy, and the others had endured.

The men looked to the port beneath them, the streets that had been laid down by hands like theirs, where the Tour de France cyclists would pass by later that day. Maybe they'd even catch a glimpse of the rid-ers cycling through the town before the ship that held them departed.

Le Havre's monument to the war dead in Gambetta Square.

4.

Henri woke to a wind-chapped Le Havre on the morning of June 30th. The salty breeze swept the stevedores along the promenade and toward the start of their week. Coil, oil, and coffee sat aboard cargo ships in one of the port's industrial canals, the gut of the city. Before the war, hotels had grown, brought travelers from the rest of the country. The tourists spent their late afternoons and nights along the pebbly beach while the port churned. The tourism had slowed once the fighting started. The workers continued to move to the area, though, eclipsing them in the months after the war ended.

Henri and the others had the day to themselves. *L'Auto*'s editor asked only that they walk back to the bar where they had signed in the night before so that they could have drinks with members of the local cycling club in the late afternoon. "Les géants de la route," as Desgrange called the cyclists, were as much the diplomats—the visiting ambassadors—as *l'Auto*'s editor. After they finished greeting and speaking to the local club, they could have a few more hours to themselves, if they wished, before leaving for the second stage.

In the hours before the meeting, the cyclists rested, some together, others alone. A group of Belgian soldiers stationed in the town were invited to Jean Rossius's room for a chance to meet the cyclist who had led the others into Le Havre. Jules Nempon, the B classification cyclist, sat outside with a few French and Belgian competitors and ate a roast beef lunch to compensate for the previous day's fast. Though they were distant, even the brothers attended the meeting with the local sports-men. The Havrais complimented Francis on his performance. Even if his chance at winning had been ruined by his early bad luck, at least he could continue to perform on individual stages.

Henri was in better spirits than he had been when he'd entered Le Havre. That day, he learned he wouldn't need to claw back time from Jean Rossius's lead; the Belgian cyclist had earned himself a thirty-minute penalty for breaking Desgrange's rules in the first stage.

Race officials had seen who they thought was Jules Masselis pass Philippe Thys a water bottle on the pair's way to Fécamp during the stage. Article One of the Tour rules, the first section penned by Desgrange, outlined the consequences for offering assistance to another rider, no matter the reason. If the offender was among the top ten competitors in the general classification standings at the time of the penalty, an hour would be added to his time. If he was outside the top ten, he would be penalized two hundred francs. If he offered assistance to another cyclist again, race officials would move him behind the last-place finisher that stage. At the third instance, he'd be disqualified from that year's Tour. The cyclist who received assistance would first face a two-hour penalty, then would receive penalties equal to the cyclist who helped him.

Desgrange believed that the cyclists' independence, as much as the Tour's length and the regions they rode through, were central to its spirit. The race tested a cyclist's athleticism, and their endurance even more, but also the more practical interactions that would similarly determine whether they could survive the race for an entire month, whether they fit Desgrange's model of a Tour winner, as that still-pliable form became clearer in his mind after each year the race was run. The independence imposed on the cyclists defined most every interaction they had, from the time they left Paris to the time they returned one month later. They paid for the meals they received along the road, apart from what they could stuff in their pockets at checkpoints, though plenty of shop owners wouldn't dream of asking them for any francs. Even filling up one's water bottle at a pump necessitated the exchange of a few centimes. Any damage their bike suffered between that day's start and end could only be repaired by the cyclist. Peugeot, Alcyon, and the other bicycle companies had mechanics at the start and end of a stage, but once the cyclist was pressured for time, only they could make sure their bikes continued to function. While they were riding, no cars set their pace. No cyclists served as team domestiques, competitors whose main purpose was not to win but to provide favorable conditions for those who were more likely to, straining themselves in early sections of a stage only to tire and drop behind the best sprinters as they neared a finish. Each cyclist competed for themselves alone.

The independence demanded by Desgrange's rules partly extended to those moments after a stage had ended, particularly that year. *L'Auto* provided what it could, but tires and other essential items couldn't be found in sufficient quantities. Those cyclists who wanted security would have to locate their own, or have their team assist them. Managers of those teams served the riders and helped them find accommodations in the towns where they would spend their nights, resting one day before another stage began. Desgrange couldn't promise that all the towns would have accommodations for them, not hotels at least. Like the motorcycles that *l'Auto* typically used to keep track of cyclists' progress—in short supply for that year's race—many hotels had been requisitioned by the military or were damaged in the war. Desgrange had tried to avoid those towns that were unlikely to have anything for them, but the cyclists and the race officials couldn't simultaneously follow the frontier and escape all the war's damage. Those cyclists without teams had to accept whatever accommodations officials could find and they could afford. *L'Auto* had at least managed to secure extra sugar ration cards for the cyclists, but as for more essential sustenance, there was only so much the newspaper could do.

The race committee adjusted Masselis's time—accounting for the penalty they believed the Belgian rider deserved. The night after the first stage, when Jean heard a penalty had been imposed on Jules, he went forward to Desgrange and the other officials to inform them that *he* had passed Philippe the water, not Jules.

The officials, stationed at checkpoints beside the road, with fewer motorcycles riding alongside the competitors, mistook one of the two cyclists racing past them. According to the rules, Jean should receive a one-hour penalty for providing assistance to another. Due to the circumstances, however, he received only thirty minutes: Jean had come forward without prompting, and, as he explained to the officials, he'd only given Philippe the water after his fellow Belgian told him he otherwise planned to quit.

Philippe was penalized fifty francs. Minutes tacked onto his time would have been meaningless. Just meters from the finish, suffering from cramps that tightened in the pit of his stomach after hours on the road, he had become one of twenty-six cyclists who abandoned the Tour along the road between Paris and Le Havre. Two-fifths of the men who had registered that year were no longer competitors after its first of fifteen stages. A few hadn't even bothered showing up to Parc des Princes. Their commanding officers had not given them leave, or they had decided before the race began that they weren't prepared for its lengths, weren't willing to test the road conditions that had been proven—in earlier races that year—to stall and defeat even the most seasoned cyclists. The others, those who needed confirmation of what the 1919 Tour would entail before they left it, sloughed from the dwindling pack along the first 380 kilometers. Forty-one remained, fewer than the men who had completed the entire 1914 edition of the race. Philippe, a two-time winner of the Tour and cyclist who had trained and competed during the war, had given up. No one could guess who would remain when they again rode into Parc des Princes.

◆ ◆ ◆

Henri left his and Francis's room in the middle of the night. He began walking toward l'Hôtel Moderne on boulevard de Strasbourg. The building occupied a lot just down the street from the town hall, along the northern edge of the port, sandwiched between industrial buildings and shipping offices that owned the boats floating quietly just blocks away. Local fans perched on the seats of their bikes, the hoods of their cars, waiting for the cyclists to start so that they could follow in their wake. He arrived at the race station. A crowd gathered; he saw some men from the sporting club who had been there that evening. Tour cyclists, officials, and Havrais mingled, lit only by lamps. At the station, officials examined Henri's bike and signed off on its integrity. He scrawled his name into the same logbook that had sat at Parc des Princes two days before. By 2:00 a.m. the remaining cyclists had done the same. They were clean and rested as they could be, though their faces showed signs of wear already—apparent in the way they examined the road in front of the line along boulevard de l'Amiral-Mouchez. Their interactions with one another were quieter in those first hours, unlike their boisterous entrance and exit from Parc des Princes and those at the café earlier in the day. A full-faced man stood next to the growing line of cyclists. The streetlamps gave off a soft glow that spread onto the path underneath their tires. Around them, a pattering sounded, like the quiet moments in a radio broadcast. Rain, a full rain, started. The downpour and the temperature—less than fifty degrees Fahrenheit—chilled the cyclists, pricked their fingers as they gripped their handlebars' tops.

Cyclists and pedestrians alike bundled up, attempting to avoid the cold as best as they were able. The cyclists layered wool and waxed cotton jackets over their knit jerseys. The weight from those layers was apparent even before the stage began, but it would at least prevent some of the water from soaking through to their cores; it would keep their limbs from going numb for a bit longer. Their faces were sunken, exhausted and restless. The rain woke them, but whatever novelty the cold shower brought quickly wore off. Around their bare ankles splotches of muddy water formed a thin crust that extended up their legs with each step.

In his first years as a competitive cyclist, others had told Henri he wasn't strong enough to race. He had been thin, almost sickly looking when he rode in the 1910 Tour de France des Indépendants, a multi-stage race with shorter distances than the Tour. It had been established for cyclists not affiliated with professional teams, like the Tour's B classification riders. The year before, when he had suffered from pulmonary edema, he had fallen into a days-long coma. He waited in recovery as the first races of 1910 came and went. Despite his wasted appearance before the race began, Henri had placed third, a comeback after a poor second stage had dropped him to fifth place. He'd nearly quit the race, but then he won the ninth stage and placed third then second in two more stages, which moved him into third overall. He had no sponsor to provide him with a bike and wheels, unlike the first- and second-place cyclists who were being groomed for professional teams. His limited record to that point was cushioned by his sense of self, in the seriousness with which he already approached the sport and in the potential he believed he had. In the years after leaving his family home, he had remained distant from his father after they first fought about Henri's aspirations, and it wasn't until he started regularly competing and performing in races that his father saw his cycling as something more than an idle pursuit.

Francis quietly considered similar aspirations. He had watched Henri start the Tour de France des Indépendants in 1910 and imagined the same for himself. He still worked for his father at the time, however, and trained on his own bicycle, but he didn't enter a race for another two years, in May of 1912. While Henri concentrated on single-day races, Francis took part in winter cyclo-cross events, coming in second behind Eugène in the 1914 French championship, running up and down the muddy hills in the last race of its kind before the war broke out.

◆ ◆ ◆

At 2:30 a.m. the forty-one remaining cyclists shoved off from the wet ground and began pedaling down the boulevard. The less tested and less profitable B classification cyclists, who were competing for whatever personal acclaim they could gather up along the stages, in short sprints and in small sums spectators gave them as they watched the amateurs ride through their towns, saw the upcoming weeks most clearly for what they were. Few were likely to know their names even if they set aside a few francs for them. The amateurs knew the physical and financial cost of competing in that year's race better than those who had relied on teams for support in other years. Both groups realized the 5,172 remaining kilometers stood like a stone wall in front of them. They would tear at it in chunks, but they didn't know whether they would cross over it.

Henri and the others pushed off nonetheless and continued riding down the western coast. They stopped in Honfleur, 159 kilometers in, the first group arriving at 8:51 in the morning, after they had cycled for nearly six and a half hours. All had been subject to so many punctures along the way that race officials gave up trying to count them. Cyclists were sick from the effort, from the previous stage and from the short time they had to recover, not helped by the preceding day's drinks. It didn't take long for more of them to abandon on the side of the road or in the nearest town. Those who remained cycled on to the Cotentin Peninsula.

The land appeared prehuman along stretches of their route. The roads, too, reflected the peninsula's age, as did the few dwellings stubbornly rooted along its cliffs. Not visible from the road, but around the riders were the remnants of the people who had made the land their home. Those who had first appeared there were marked by two rectangular stones that had since fallen over, one stone resting between them—a passageway now only large enough for a field mouse to scamper through. Partly buried plinths, tall and slim, ended resolutely in the ground. Where they came from and their meaning was lost on those who passed by them. Even the plants looked Jurassic, their bulbous leaves bundled close to the ground on either side of the cyclists.

By the time Henri passed the red flag marking the stage's final kilometer, it was evening, around 6:15 p.m. Between the length of the two stages and the weather that had flattened his surroundings to a single dim gray, he had already lost the rhythms that distinguished one time from another. The cold rain had continued throughout, and, as a result, the sky had not shifted in color, masking morning, afternoon, and night. The rain drove him onward and swamped his progress in equal measure. When an inevitable puncture stopped him along the side of the road, he had been forced to duck underneath whatever cover he could find to repair the tube. The temperature hadn't lifted much; it hovered around fifty degrees. The wind blew from the west, off the ocean. The salt put a tang in his mouth and left it dry. The cold reduced him to his basest movements, fingers senseless, legs strained against all but the most repetitive motions. Those who saw the cyclists as little more than machines weren't so wrong.

At the end of a two-kilometer climb, Henri rode toward the finish line in Martinvast, a town just outside Cherbourg. The line had been placed at the edge of the small commune. Gendarmes stood around with tall dark kepis on their heads and waxed hooded capes. Drops ran from their manicured, obligatory mustaches. They oversaw the crowd that had gathered around the finish line, who shouted Henri's name as he neared them, those who knew the cyclist, who had waited for him that day. Others cheered as if they did, or heard the others and learned from them. Officials from the local cycling club and *l'Auto* correspondents stood around to record the cyclists' times. Henri passed by the timekeeper, who checked his watch. Just one second behind him, Francis crossed, too. The journalists and crowds ignored Francis for the moment. They gathered around Henri with their notepads and pens, hoping to collect a few words from him to run in tomorrow's *l'Auto*. "If the rules weren't the rules," he said, "I'd love to have let Francis win. And if Desgrange wasn't who he is."

Henri returned to his bike after responding to their questions. The sign-in sheet and the other race officials were waiting for him at café de Paris in Cherbourg, a short distance away, along the east side of the city's port. As Henri rode from the finish line down into Cherbourg, some of the crowd followed behind him: a few on foot, others on their own bikes. They joined a crowd that had already gathered in front of the café, waiting for the first cyclists to appear. Cherbourgeois sat on the café patio. The restaurant was filled with bodies. Those who couldn't find seats had gathered outside, pressed against each other from both sides of the road and around the table where the race officials sat with the opened logbook. A few spectators sat on the edge of the promenade. They turned around to watch the cyclists ride in, their legs dipping toward the port underneath them. Henri signed his name in the book and stepped away before the crowd was sated. Many of the supporters showed up to drink and mingle with the cyclists who'd brought the Tour to their town. A few of the racers lingered at the café, accepting whatever glasses were offered to them, soaking in the attention. Henri and Francis, characteristically, did not. Henri retired to his hotel room for the night to shake the cold that had been racking him since the morning's first hours. He would not walk back to the café following his bath to watch the others arrive well into the night, after the road had broken down some bikes more than others, at least one cyclist walking the stage's last three kilometers after his chain fell apart.

Their next day was set aside for rest. The cyclists breakfasted at their respective hotels, a string of which had been found for them by La Sportive. Eugène spoke quickly with a correspondent from *l'Auto* who asked him how he felt: better than some of the other cyclists, like Jean Rossius, who had been plagued by a stomachache after he arrived in Cherbourg. A trainer from La Sportive visited each of them in turn, making sure they were as well prepared for the following day's stage as could be expected. They sat and spoke in small groups in their individual hotels. The Pélissiers kept to themselves in their single room, instead choosing to recover alone.

The next day, they were to leave Cherbourg for Brest. The city was another peninsula away, back down the Cotentin and on to Brittany. It was the first actual stage of that year's Tour, according to Desgrange, though it meant little to the cyclists who'd already ridden 752 kilometers over poorly tended roads, and even less to the forty-two who'd already abandoned the Tour.

The first cyclists arrived at the Cherbourg café around midnight. A crowd had been gathered there since 9:00 p.m.; that it was a Wednesday evening didn't matter much to them. The town had hosted the Tour cyclists since 1911, but they had not seen them since the start of the war. People packed the café to give a few words of support to their favored racer, while others were satisfied standing away from the scrum that had formed, instead waiting to see those first ones to leave the city on bikes.

The cyclists' fatigue had only grown despite their day of rest. The rain between Le Havre and Cherbourg had slowed them; they had accomplished each crank turn through strained muscles, resistant to the cold. They had slogged through the clutch of mud on the unpaved roads that ran between towns. They were dead-eyed. Despite seeing how the celebrations before the second stage weighed some down, a few had stayed at the café the night before to celebrate with fans until just a few hours before their start. If they weren't going to win any stages that year, they reasoned, at least they could make use of the temporary glory that accompanied them for as long as they rode, as they continued to hold on to their numbered bibs and bicycles.

In that day's newspaper, Desgrange predicted how the remaining cyclists would fare. He noted the winner of the race to Brest would at least be a cyclist capable of climbing, even if he didn't eventually hold that year's designation as the climber of the Tour. The third stage—like the preceding one—traversed land more ancient than modern, with weather-beaten coastlines. What distinguished it from the Cotentin would be the ground underneath their tires. After cycling through the town of Dinan, when they'd pass the mainland's elbow onto the mouth of Brittany, the ground would begin to roll. The hills were small in comparison to the alpine stages farther ahead, but after the second stage's bitter cold, it would be enough to strain the cyclists. Desgrange predicted the pack would thin in the second half of the stage, after about two hundred kilometers, breaking up what he thought would be a single mass, only accidents and flats fracturing it across the first half.

Any Tour cyclist could ride across flat ground and keep pace with the pack. To speed up, to sprint across level ground required physical effort and a small bit of strategy to realize the right moment in which to surge. It is an intellectual exercise, and the matter of executing it is one of training. Climbing, however, asks more of a cyclist, rewards inherent talent as much as training. Climbers are unique racers, myth and fool. Their abilities are subtle, keeping a deliberate pace across stretches of ground likely to draw only the most dedicated fans. Over kilometers, they persist and move away slowly from the pack. They are distinctive on and off the bicycle. A climber's strength comes from having disproportionate power for their weight. Height tends to be less important than build: well-muscled thighs drive them against gravity's burden. They are small, except when they are not. Their efforts aren't well rewarded in the moment. At any time, it's difficult to cheer for a climber who has gained an inch or two of ground in the amount of time it takes for them to pass by a group of fans. They barely accelerate; they cannot draft. Their specialty is instead a slow toil that only shows itself once they emerge from the elevations and in the final standings for that day.

◆ ◆ ◆

The pack—less than half of those who began in Paris—set off at 2:30 a.m. They were more restrained than on the last stage, more cognizant of the land between them and the finish. Though the sun had not yet risen, the weather was already more suited to their task. They rode back along the same path they had taken just two days before, then veered toward the western coast of the peninsula. Past the racers' eyesight, the islands of Jersey and Guernsey were just twenty-five kilometers from the rocky French beaches. In the war, Guernsey had housed an anti-U-boat squadron, and Jersey had kept POW camps for Germans, well away from any hope of returning to the fight.

After 50 kilometers, with 355 kilometers remaining, almost the entire length of the preceding stage, Desgrange's prediction bore out. Jean Rossius, the winner of the first stage, who had stood in third at the end of the second stage, rode through the town of Lessay. The French roads exerted their will on his bike's frame. In the hundreds of kilometers he had crossed to that point, the roads bore through the bike's frame as Jean weighed it down, in the sharp turns around hedgerows and as he pushed down on the frame as his wheels bumbled over exposed train tracks. Surrounded by others, Jean's bicycle frame faltered and its front fork split. Jean fell. The other riders continued past. There was little they could do to help, even if they were willing to break the rules: Jean would have encountered his second penalty. He would have lost whatever time he gained from the help. And, besides, a broken bike frame was unlike a popped tire; it couldn't be replaced on the road between two towns.

At 5:32 a.m. he arrived in Coutances, at the stage's first checkpoint. Thirty-two minutes had passed since the first cyclists had arrived there. He walked in alone. Even with the bike's fracture, he remained ahead of two other cyclists, both part of the race's B classification. The officials who manned the checkpoint could see he was carrying the bike's frame. There was little to be done—he didn't have the mechanical skill to fix such a severe break. He didn't know whether it could be fixed at all— and under Desgrange's rules, no spare would save him. He informed the officials he was abandoning the race. He couldn't see any way to continue. He'd had enough of the race. One of the two cyclists behind Jean took his cue and left the race when he entered town, as Jean recovered near the checkpoint.

Most of those who remained continued alongside one another as the kilometers ticked past. Pitiless showers came and went. They turned the unpaved ground into a sloppy mud that coated their shins and flecked their bodies. They were an indistinguishable pack, a muddy wave down the roads. The morning turned to day, and whole populations of towns, it seemed, came to the side of the road to watch them pass, to celebrate those who had survived.

Henri rode on a stretch of ground that would deliver him to Morlaix along Brittany's northern coast. The town had first been occupied by the Gauls, then the Romans. It had been inhabited continually since those first centuries. A viaduct looked down on the town; the train tracks that rested on it stretched from Brest to Paris. Around Henri, the others strained against their bikes as they crossed the Arée foothills. The flat terrain gave way to the ground Desgrange warned of. The climbs sapped their meager reserves.

Henri pushed alongside the pack. He then heard a pop. He knew what had happened at once: the drag, the strain on his already labored movements. He pulled his bike to the side of the road and examined both his tires. One had sunk flat. He pulled out his supplies, unstrapped one tube from around his torso, and set to work. A puncture wasn't fatal; it barely even required tools to repair. There was little reason to worry unless a protrusion in the wheel's frame had caused the tube's collapse. Still, repairing a puncture takes time and effort. That work didn't move him any closer to the finish. Henri pulled the flat from the bike's wheel where it had been cemented into place. The tire had been sewn around the punctured pneumatic tube, so he tore at the stitches that had kept the tire and the tube bound together. He didn't bother looking for the puncture's source; there was no point to attempting a patch—it would only waste more time. He placed the new tube into the open tire pocket and began sewing it shut again, like a surgeon reconstituting his own limb. Henri finished the replacement and taped the tire back into the wheel. The tape was a temporary fix, not as secure against the frame as cement, but a necessary time-saver: each second he would have waited for the cement to dry would have been another one where he would need to race ahead to rejoin the pack. With the tire inflated, he mounted his bike and set off on the road again. Seventy kilometers remained between him and the day's finish.

Henri picked up his pace on the soft ground. The leading pack was still far ahead, too far for him to sprint and reach, but with enough effort, he was able to join a second, smaller pack made up of Émile Masson and Jules Masselis, who had both suffered from earlier punctures and had been working to reclaim lost ground. Hundreds of meters separated the two groups as they neared the end of the peninsula. Any cyclist who attempted a sprint then, with so much ground still remaining, would burn their reserves before they reached the finish line.

Regulating energy throughout the day was a challenge on the Tour, and an ability to tap into reserved energy set apart the most successful cyclists from those who struggled to break from the pack. It was also one of the strategies most difficult to govern. Some racers had a personality that allowed them to press through the kilometers; a sense of pride, or even a feeling of superiority could drive someone forward late in the day.

Slowly, imperceptibly in any one moment, the second pack quickened its pace. Henri led the others, his eyes fixed ahead. He took on the effort of setting their speed while the others drafted behind, siphoning his excess energy, contracting their bodies as much as they could to avoid the drag he instead bore. The Brasier's exhaust remained off in the distance. Only the *l'Auto* correspondents positioned along the course knew of their progress. The kilometers did not breeze past them; the roads were still difficult. Each cyclist traveled slow, slow for the pace of the average Tour, and slower than they had in past stages. Each drew deeper on their reserves; they pressed on.

By the time they were eight kilometers from the finish, the second pack had merged with the first. They were exhausted from maintaining their pace over tens of kilometers. As he joined the leading cyclists, Henri found a deeper source still. It was not from his training, or in his ascetic lifestyle the day before a stage began. It was not that he thought himself better than his competitors, or that he needed to show Desgrange he was not so old that he couldn't win the editor's Tour. Those desires were perhaps necessary but not sufficient. His brother Francis was near the front of the pack. Seeing him there spurred Henri on. *Francis! He knew he had it in him.* Beyond Francis, in the Brasier, were the officials who would talk about his efforts that day as if only the Tour could have brought them out. Anger was a deeper source, too.

Henri continued to push himself, standing on his bike, torqueing back and forth along its latitude. He passed one rider, then another. As the bikes and cyclists slipped behind him, each took on a newfound urgency. They sensed there were others who might try the same. As a cold breeze buffeted his face, Henri managed to accelerate past a few others until no one separated him from the journalists riding in the car, who had sped up to maintain a distance between themselves and the leader. Henri pushed further, until he was in a full sprint. With kilometers separating him from the finish, he continued but couldn't quite break past a rider who clung to him like a shadow. His brother Francis mirrored his movements, kept his pace. They raced down rue du Pont-Neuf into Brest, making their way over one last hill, into the port city where military ships flowed in and out of its harbor. The brothers neared the finish together. The Brasier had stopped, the officials were on foot, and the gendarmes tended to the crowd. Soldiers, still wearing scraps of their uniforms, joined with the locals who had shown up. A platform behind them had been constructed to lift the race officials up so they could view the cyclists as they approached.

It was Thursday evening, about the time families were preparing their dinners before heading off to sleep, but Brest was out in its streets, pushing against the officers in the hopes that they would break through and see the cyclists unencumbered. Hats in hand, they waved as Henri and Francis crested the hill, as if swept by a common tide. Francis passed the finish line first. This time, it was Francis whom the journalists crowded around, asking for comments on the stage, requesting every detail: when he saw his chance to win, when he'd conserved his energy and when he'd spent it, how it felt to ride alongside his brother. And Henri cheered with the crowd who shouted his brother's name.

The American military camp Pontanezen near Brest in 1919.

5.

After receiving their times, the twenty-five cyclists were told their standing in the race so far at Brest's Grand Café du Commerce. The cyclists behind Jean Rossius moved up, occupying the abandoned Belgian's onetime place. Though he trailed Francis in that day's stage, Henri held his first-place position in the general classification standings, twenty-three minutes ahead of Eugène in second. Francis sat almost four hours behind his older brother. The accident he had suffered in the first stage still dragged him down. For his efforts, Henri had already received nine hundred francs in prize money from *l'Auto* and individuals who'd organized their own prizes along the way.

Crammed into the small café, the cyclists spoke to each other and to the Brest residents who had come to see them, worn down but lifted temporarily on that Thursday evening. Henri stood apart, with the manager of La Sportive, Alphonse Baugé. Baugé's role was to ensure the La Sportive cyclists had as little work to do as possible once they arrived in a town at the end of the stage. He helped them find accommodations and he ensured they all had access to the mechanics from their respective bike companies, and to medics, when needed. In a year when accommodations were difficult to come by, when money was slim and when he represented more cyclists than before, his role had expanded, grown more difficult. Even the meals *l'Auto* had once guaranteed were now the responsibility of Baugé and the cyclists, apart from the warm cups of consommé Bouillon KUB handed out before and after each stage and snacks along the way. The broth had been enough to keep the men warm for a moment, when rain or cold drenched the area, but wasn't enough to replace their diets entirely. Baugé, a cyclist in his own right, offered his thoughts on a cyclist's performance in the preceding stage as much as they asked. He had watched Henri from the car that day, had seen his efforts to arrive near the front despite the roads working against him. Baugé offered Henri his congratulations; a comeback like that was no easy feat. Henri bluntly told Alphonse, "I'm a thoroughbred. My opponents are cart horses."

The cyclist didn't disguise the comment, didn't deliver it away from the others or in hushed tones in the corner of the café. The competitors stood around the manager and the skinny Parisian, wrapped up in their own conversations. Henri didn't resent his competitors, not acutely, at least. Many French cyclists took pride in the fact they maintained other jobs in the months they weren't racing, that they had lives away from their bikes—something Henri didn't share. His statement was in some ways a fact—he did little else but spend time on this bike—though it also reflected his self-regard. The cyclists who were talking in small circles, sharing their accounts of the day, overheard him. It confirmed their suspicions of the elder Pélissier.

Henri had turned professional in 1911, the year after his third-place finish in the Tour de France des Indépendants, after he'd been discharged from the military. His successes that year mostly occurred outside France. He won the Giro di Romagna–Toscana, Milano–Torino, and the Giro di Lombardia, one after another. Each was a one-day event, entirely unlike the Tour de France. The qualities they emphasized in a cyclist—their physical abilities and the necessary mindset and strategy—were distinct: a cyclist's decisions in a one-day event were simple compared to their calculations across fifteen dissimilar stages. The athleticism required was concentrated, either a cyclist's training and efforts would suit the particular route or they wouldn't, but his success wouldn't be defined by a preceding stage when he had strained himself beyond recovery.

Henri joined the Alcyon team in 1912 and rode in his first Tour de France that year, a competition that had taken a toll on him. He abandoned after the fourth leg with an ankle injury, his name relegated to Desgrange's "etc., etc." after the other, more prominent mishaps had been described. Despite his disappointing performance in his own country's Tour, he went on to finish second in the Tour de Belgique that year. He continued to improve. During the 1913 Tour, he finished first in the stage between Cherbourg and Brest, and came in second in the general classification in 1914.

Those who watched him—the journalists and the other cyclists—couldn't help but notice the lengths he went to treat his sport seriously. He didn't always win—too many variables existed on the course for that sort of consistency—but he always did everything in his power to tilt the stakes in his favor. Cycling was their sport, their social activity as well as their countries'. Cycling didn't encompass their lives, though, as it did for Henri. He padded his training with substances to improve his abilities, though he was hardly the only one. Strychnine stimulated muscle activity. Nitroglycerine improved his breathing, though it risked hallucinations and exhaustion. Ether deadened his pains, even while he rode, one hand removed from the handlebars, a handkerchief lifted to his face. It was tolerated by everyone—pharmaceutical companies advertised in *l'Auto*, and the drugs were freely given out by team trainers. Henri rubbed chloroform against his gums and dropped liquid cocaine into the corners of his eyes. He avoided alcohol due to its lingering effects the next day, but in that year's Tour, it was unclear what the state of drinking water would be in cities closer to the front.

He had never endeared himself to other cyclists, training well after others had settled for the evening, throwing his effort in their faces. His comment in Brest, however, rankled the others in a way his strict methods did not. His first-place standing was partly thanks to Jean Rossius's poor judgment and misfortune. Only three stages were complete, and two of those were considered warm-ups to the actual competition that would continue for another twenty-five days. The pack had not yet approached the alpine stages, where climbers like Eugène or the younger Honoré Barthélémy would find an advantage, where Henri's performance would lag, if his past races were any measure. Beyond those elevations lay the mottled ground between Strasbourg and Dunkerque, where the Circuit des Champs de Bataille had been fought earlier that year. Henri had failed to even place in the postwar circuit. The others could only smile ruefully for the moment. To the more hot-headed cyclists—those who were younger, in particular—as well as the competitors who didn't share Henri's success, and some of the other, more veteran racers, it was an affront to their self-images, a challenge that had been laid, to be disproved at the first opportunity.

The cyclists, those who rode for La Sportive as well as the two remaining B classification racers, were found housing in Brest. The city had few hotel rooms available due to temporary residents who entered and left from the city's port. They learned that an annex in a barracks had been set aside for them. The dimly lit room was sparse, not like other years of the Tour when a hotel would open its doors to them, but at least their efforts would force them to fall asleep quickly, no matter what they rested upon. In the annex the men found the same sunken bunks they had used as soldiers, at least those lucky enough to have been stationed away from the trenches. The soldiers there often didn't even have a thin band of cotton stretched above the dirt. "I feel like I've reenlisted," Jean Alavoine said as he lay down in one of the cots.

Cyclists continued arriving in Brest past midnight, the last one crossing the finish at 12:45 a.m., after twenty-two hours of riding. Despite the long hours, most of the men remained in good spirits.

They were visited by Desgrange and La Sportive's trainer, who ensured they were comfortable. When one of Desgrange's correspondents visited Eugène, he was humble to the point of frustration, admitting he'd lagged behind so far, despite his second place. He still believed he was perfectly capable of making up his time in later stages, particularly once the terrain became more difficult. The 1913 Tour was on his mind, when he'd suffered a catastrophic injury to his bike that would have forced other cyclists out of the race. Instead, he'd carried his broken frame down a mountain and repaired it before finishing the stage and the race. He wasn't one to give up like some of those who had already left.

A few cyclists who lay in the barracks were more strained by the preceding stages. Odile Defraye, Henri's rival in the 1912 Tour de Belgique and the first Belgian to win the Tour de France that same year, was ill in bed when the *l'Auto* journalists made their rounds. The thirty-one-year-old had been released from the military only a few weeks before the Tour started, giving him practically no time to train. Though he was near the bottom of the general classification standing, he hadn't abandoned the race.

The Pélissiers were absent from the barracks. They'd refused the free accommodations offered by their team. Instead, while the others were walking to the barracks, Francis had joined Henri in heading to one of the local hotels, where they looked for a single open room. Eventually, they found one and paid for it themselves. The other men didn't see much of the brothers until they were lined up for the next stage.

They had July 4th to themselves. From the hotel windows and barracks doors, the cyclists watched as the sky remained dark for hours on end, rain thrashing the ground around the buildings. Most chose to stay indoors, recovering together before the leg to Les Sables d'Olonne. There was little point in tempting the fates. Exiting the safety of their accommodations seemed as though it would only encourage the rain, convince the weather pattern they would happily walk and ride under a downpour for the rest of the race.

The Tour fans didn't share the cyclists' reticence. Late on the evening of July 4th, a crowd began to gather at Grand Café du Commerce once again, the townspeople braving the weather to mingle in the hours before the cyclists arrived. What did they make of the twenty-five men who showed up, just after night turned to morning? Their sunken faces in the spare, staggered streetlight didn't resemble those who had paraded from Parc des Princes just one week before, the ones described as something close to gods in Desgrange's editorials leading up to the Tour's first stage, "les géants de la route." They instead appeared one step from defeated. The two Pélissiers stood among the group that formed, Henri with his bristled mustache, Francis with his hulking frame. They were remote, though, and instead talked to one another in quiet tones that suited the hour. Henri's eyes contained an energy Francis's did not, a keenness in their glacial blue. In the younger brother's blue was melancholy, though his spirits had been lifted after the previous stage. Henri appeared confident among the remaining few. The ground grew faint and faded into nothing in front of them as a fog swept through the Brest streets, so thick Henri could scarcely see ten meters in front of his face.

More than four hundred kilometers stood in front of them that day. After that, the cyclists would confront the longest stage the Tour had seen. Then, the alpine climbs would begin. The Pyrenees would sprout in front of their tires: first unnoticeable, then unavoidable and unceasing. Both fans and journalists fixated on those challenging unpaved paths that ran between gullies; they predicted the cyclists who'd make the most of it, those who'd fail once confronted with the more demanding ground. The cyclists would spend the night in towns that existed less because of humans conquering nature and more because nature allowed humans a sliver of existence between the rocks and boulders.

The cyclists left Brest at 2:00 a.m. They doubled back on the path that had taken them to the end of Brittany. Then they headed south.

They neared the coast. The land shifted before them. It took its cues from ancient times, from humans pressing up against it, making only the smallest indentations. The scenes were almost designed to distract them from the kilometers ahead. They passed old walled cities, and green, incurable green between them—ferns and trees that ran in lines through farmlands.

They passed Quimper and Bannalec on the way to Lorient, the first checkpoint of the day's stage. In Quimper they rode along the Odet River and the Steïr, which came together to form the town's "Meeting of Two Rivers." Along pitch waters, walking bridges were filled with locals who stood and watched as the riders passed by. A slight haze rose from the rivers in the cold, early morning.

The pack was almost whole despite Desgrange predicting that this stage would shear them into smaller groups. They raced together through Le Faou. They passed the river mouth that split the town in two. At low tide, shorebirds picked through the silt for flatworms and exposed crustaceans. The cyclists smelled the salt and decay as they looked down from the bridge that passed over the river, the mud and sand expanding into Brest Harbor. Farther still, the Crozon Peninsula stretched blindly in the fog, a claw extending into the Atlantic Ocean, a ribbed and rocky coastline separating it from the water. There, stone fortifications stood: some still occupied by the military, others withered by a salty sea spray that browned iron and scraped sandstone into a smoothed pebble surface. At the tips of its trident, the landscape turned alien, with waxy marine fennel and ashy lichen. It looked more dead than alive, like a patch of scorched earth underneath a child's magnifying glass.

Henri led the others alongside Francis. They were part of the pack and separate from it. The mandate not to assist one another was hardly needed. Henri, in front of the general classification, distanced himself even further. Though every cyclist competed for himself, even those far from the front focused their attention on the Tour leader. They each hoped to unseat him. They could achieve their goal; all it would take was some consistency on their part and a slight failing—or even just bad luck—on the part of the leader. The challenges of that year's race only made that last condition likelier. Cyclists didn't necessarily need to come in first. The Tour's earlier points-based scoring ensured that an accident that caused a cyclist to ride into a town hours behind the others wouldn't necessarily ruin their place in the general classification standings if they had performed well enough otherwise. The system also meant racers weren't rewarded for pushing themselves when they otherwise might spend their last energetic bit. As long as they performed well enough to beat the others, they were doing all that was required of them. Desgrange switched to time-based scoring in 1913 and had continued it every year since. The winner would be the cyclist who consistently tested their limits through the end of the race. If no man was up to the challenge, there would be no winner at all. "If only ten make it back to Paris," that morning's *l'Auto* read, "they'll be the ones celebrated." The boyish cyclist Jean Alavoine had already benefited from timed scoring. He rested comfortably and consistently in third, a standing close enough to the leaders that he could push when he felt it necessary, while not drawing too much attention to himself in the process.

◆ ◆ ◆

Francis had arrived at the Twenty-fourth Infantry Regiment in December 1914, four months after war had been declared. He had turned twenty that June, the age when French conscription laws dictated every young man would start serving his three years of active duty, before he was transferred to the reserve.

In the unit, he acted as a cycling liaison, assisting in observation missions and in communications between the unit and higher-ups who were stationed behind the front. He fought with them in the Second Battle of Artois in May and June of that year, where Tour cyclist François Faber was killed on May 9th.

In 1917, around the same time that Henri transferred to the First Aviation Group, Francis received the Croix de Guerre. The year before, in the battle of Verdun, he had been on the receiving end of an artillery bombardment. The shells dropped around him; shrapnel pierced his left flank. On the ground, turned to craters, he saw his captain lying unconscious. Francis lifted up his officer and transported him to an ambulance waiting some distance away, only agreeing to be treated once he had seen that the officer was safe.

Both Henri and Francis had continued their service through the end of the war. Even during the Tour, they were only on leave, not yet demobilized from the military. It had been a costly war for the family, which was nothing special. Their home hadn't been destroyed, at least; the rest of their family remained safe, those who stayed away from the front, but plenty of people they knew and loved had been taken by the war and wouldn't be given back.

◆ ◆ ◆

After three stages, the racers were fatigued. While they had kept pace with each other through Quimper, their functions had slowed. Looking at them, fans saw deadened riders. The front-runners joked morbidly with the journalists in the car ahead of them and among themselves. Tire punctures were corrected with a quick stoicism, absent the frenetic energy of earlier stages or years. They were inevitable, if not predictable: not the fault of a careless cyclist but the treacherous roads and, it was increasingly clear to the cyclists, the administrator who had planned their path.

Twenty kilometers from the first checkpoint and 130 kilometers into the stage, they neared Quimperlé, a small town at the junction of the Ellé and Isole Valleys. The town flooded when the rains were bad, but fortunately it was dry enough for them to pass through that day. Of the 9,000 who made the town home, around 350 were missing or had died in the war.

Henri and Francis maintained a slight lead. Henri set the pace on the flat ground. He kept his body pliant to accommodate the small, constant imperfections in the road. However, soon his adjustments to the bull-horned handlebars stopped translating to changes in the bike's direction. A turn to either side only moved the front tire a hair. Over the kilometers, the bolt that connected the handlebars to the fork had become loose. At first, it hadn't made a difference to his steering, but in time it prevented him from maneuvering within the pack. He turned to the side of the road to tighten the bolt. It was a small repair, barely a repair at all, just an adjustment to keep the bike in its optimal form. It took him another moment to remove the water-resistant coat he was wearing, which had been stifling him in the clearing weather, though the fog remained.

As the others watched him slow, a quiver ran through them. They picked up their pace on the sodden ground, though much of the stage remained. They spurted forward. The change in their speed was almost inexplicable, that they would choose this moment to advance, that they would do so together instead of one determined racer leaving the others behind. It was as if they spotted a mirage of the finish line off in the distance.

With his handlebars tightened, Henri pulled back onto the road as quickly as he was able. He'd lost a few minutes behind the others' quickening tempo.

The cyclists in the pack set each other's speed. There was no rule barring them from doing so; Desgrange only wanted to prevent them from slowing down for another's advantage. Their movements were collective—even Francis had little choice but to keep up. Henri pedaled after them, drawing from the same spring of energy that had allowed him to advance in the previous stage. He still couldn't see through the fog that enveloped him and the others, but he had a rough idea of how far they'd advanced. The others hadn't been able to do much to prevent him from returning in the previous stage; how would it be any different now?

Along the peninsula, the cyclists passed the town of Vannes with its ramparts still protecting the city's old center, its wattle and daub exteriors appearing tall on the narrow, cobbled streets. At La Roche-Bernard, they were directed onto a newly built bridge that crossed the Vilaine River. Train tracks ran parallel to their section of the bridge. Henri continued behind the others.

As the afternoon progressed, the saturating fog gave way to a bright day, then turned yet again into bouts of rain punctuated by the occasional thunderclap. Lakes had formed on the dirt roads. Mud coated the cyclists who, between the uniform gray-and-blue wool jerseys and the brown gradient that extended up their frames, were barely distinguishable from one another. The journalists could only keep track of them with a close eye on each member of the pack. They determined their positions by a process of elimination—looking for markers like Henri's mustache, or Eugène's glowering face, the remnants of visible numbers on their bikes, anything that separated one cyclist from another.

Henri hadn't yet caught up to the others. Only a few riders, however, could keep their quickened pace over hundreds of kilometers. One by one he passed by those who'd been left in pursuit of the leaders. The spent cyclists dragged behind, without the advantage of having their headwinds blocked and another man setting their pace. They'd given everything they had in the wake of Henri's stop on the road's side; they could not beat him still. Henri then caught up to Francis. His younger brother was exhausted and teetering on his bicycle's frame. Henri stayed to race alongside him; they kept pace with one another.

The brothers reached the Nantes checkpoint, 321 kilometers in and 91 from the day's end. They continued. That far into the ride, their scant energy restored during their stop only lasted for a brief moment before they again reached the end of their reserves, straining against the smallest obstacles as if they were Sisyphus's stone.

Saint-Mathurin was the final town before Les Sables, their destination. The leading pack had continued to split apart as their lively pace over that distance proved unbearable. The limited supplies they had been offered in Nantes and Lorient had run out: the two water bottles, the small scraps of food held in their pockets. Henri had been riding for over sixteen hours at an average pace of nearly twenty-five kilometers per hour. He had lost Francis. The brothers now rode in different races. Francis knew he wouldn't win the stage. The general classification was more distant. It would be better for him to conserve his energy. Henri was slower than what would have been expected in any other year, but it was enough for him to pass by several of his competitors. He was five kilometers from the end. The leading pack still wasn't in sight. Unsure how far ahead they were, only that their numbers were diminished, he stayed atop his bike.

He passed a small cottage and found that he had nothing left. Collapsing against the home, he screamed to no one in particular. An old woman came out of the cottage, startled at the commotion. He asked her for water. The two bottles attached to the bike frame had long since been emptied. He reached into his pockets to find some form of compensation, as Desgrange's rules had mandated. He decided then. The race had taken everything from him; nothing was left. *It's Desgrange,* he told himself. *He created a test not a race.* If no one returned to Paris, perhaps then the editor would see. Henri slaked his thirst. He returned to the bike and pedaled toward Les Sables, more slowly now.

He entered the town near avenue de la Gare, where the finish line had been erected. The first cyclists to arrive had already gathered at café du Commerce, signing their names into the logbook. He looked around at the people who had waited for his arrival. They still cheered when they saw him. He could only imagine how they felt. Would they be disappointed? Should he explain himself? They'd understand it couldn't have been any other way. A lesser cyclist might have continued, convinced he could stick it out. It would be all he needed to possibly win. He had not arrived so far behind despite the other cyclists' efforts. If enough people gave up or fell victim to one of the road's hazards, he'd place admirably enough: it was just a matter of elimination. But in Henri's estimation, the cyclist who did so wouldn't be the best; he'd only be a survivor. There may have been some honor in it, but it wasn't any sort of glory Henri wanted for himself.

Jean Alavoine, who hadn't even finished Paris–Roubaix, signed into the book first, after fifteen hours and fifty-one minutes. Eugène signed in third. Henri sat thirty-five minutes behind them. No longer in first, instead thirteen minutes behind the leader, Eugène. Henri headed to the café to inform the officials of his decision. If he had anything more to give, he could make up the lost time on the next stages. If anything were to happen to Eugène or his bike, he may not have needed to. All he had to do was continue. But the race wasn't even one-third over and already he felt broken. At the desk where the officials sat, surrounded by the people who had come from nearby towns to watch him, he told them that he was abandoning the race.

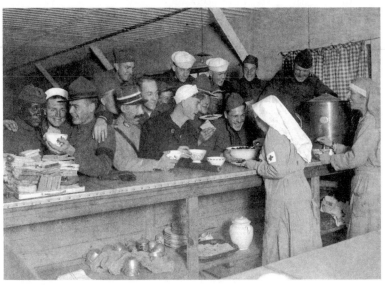

Allied soldiers get food, drink, and tobacco at the American Red Cross canteen in Bordeaux, France, October 1918.

6.

In 1518, Strasbourg was set upon by a dancing plague. The afflicted danced for days on end, their bloodied feet stamping the caked dirt underneath them. Their eyes spoke to a fear that their whirling motions didn't. Town officials claimed the source was hot blood; dancing was the means by which those who suffered from the ill humor could release themselves. By constructing a stage and providing music for the dancers—who had been swinging on their own without accompaniment—the afflicted would triumph over the condition more quickly. The officials' accommodations only persuaded others to join. In time, around four hundred citizens left their homes to dance on the erected stage. Of those, a number died from exhaustion, heart attacks, dehydration, and other afflictions that stemmed from their unceasing movements. They had neglected their necessary functions for survival. What had once seemed like a curiosity, a strange celebration, had become a macabre affair as the dancers continued for longer than anyone could have expected, and then some, before dropping in place.

As they left the country's main roads, the cyclists' bikes had tumbled over inhospitable paths. Henri wasn't the only victim in the stage to Les Sables. One cyclist saw both tires pop at the same time as he rode over the northwestern ground. Others fell from their bikes in accidents, became ill along the way, though none had given up as dramatically as Henri. Only Francis came close, dismounting his bike and lying down in a roadside ditch for a time before reaching the day's end. Though Desgrange was quick to compliment him—expressing that Francis could be a champion, if not this year, then a future one—Francis followed Henri, informing the officials he wouldn't take part in the race's next stage or any that followed.

Eighteen cyclists were to leave Les Sables for Bayonne on the night of July 6th. Eighteen of the sixty-seven who had registered for Desgrange's race, just one-quarter of the men who'd set out at Parc des Princes, still competed for the editor's prize. They had only finished one-third of his route. That night, they would leave the city and bike 482 kilometers. They would cover the distance in a single go, apart from stops in La Rochelle and Bordeaux. The distance they had ridden in one week would grow to 2,051 kilometers. The stage between the two cities, which would bring them to the southern tip of France's west coast, was longer than most every single-day race. Those one-days with longer distances, like Bordeaux–Paris, which Henri had won in May, were paced, each cyclist having the benefit of a car or motorcycle to draft behind. Those cyclists also didn't need to consider another, more strenuous distance just two days later. Most riders Desgrange had first predicted to win the Tour were gone, having abandoned in the preceding stage: Henri Pélissier, Philippe Thys, and Louis Heusghem were gone, only Eugène and Jean Alavoine remained. Francis Pélissier and two other promising rookies had abandoned. Honoré and Émile Masson alone carried the mantle of those untested cyclists. Some wondered if Henri had been right, that Desgrange in fact hoped no cyclist would arrive back in Paris, that Desgrange had somehow decided to take advantage of the Tour's publicity to turn it into an event ending with the editor telling his readers that no cyclists were worthy of that year's—his—title.

With Henri no longer competing for the prize, Eugène rose to the top of the general classification. He was just fifteen minutes ahead of the second-place, Émile Masson. Desgrange had considered Eugène too old to claim that year's title. He was four years older, to the day, than Henri. Eugène had not yet won any of the stages. He had, however, remained a constant member of the leading pack to rush through a finish line. His performance on individual stages had been consistent enough that no other competitor had a lower overall time than him, even if others had performed better in individual stages. His lead was hardly dominant, but no other cyclist had shown themselves as the one who might unseat him.

Though Desgrange may have thought otherwise, Eugène leading the others felt right, as they rode through the small towns in the countryside before reaching the northeast, and as others back in Paris read of the cyclists' progress in *l'Auto*. He bore those kilometers; he didn't triumph over them or fail, proclaiming what it meant for him or the race or the editor. The Tour had always reflected and was shaped by the towns those cyclists rode through each year. Whether the townspeople who watched the race saw themselves in the cyclists depended on the individual, the one who rode and the one who watched. Many of the cyclists still came from the nation's capital, and some from Belgium or Italy. Eugène was no different. In him, however, the people he passed saw something of themselves. He had experienced what they had experienced those last five years, even if he did come from Paris. He would leave his bike and return to his job at the end of the Tour. He didn't see himself as any better than the others. He was only surviving the race better than anyone else.

Firmin Lambot, the thirty-three-year-old Belgian who sat in third, didn't share Eugène's heritage, but he matched the cyclist in how he approached the path in front of him. In earlier races of his career, he had surpassed others as the kilometers ticked up and each one grew more difficult. In the 1914 Tour, during the first alpine stage between Bayonne and Luchon, Firmin had managed to beat the second-place cyclist and overall leader by more than seven minutes, an improbable gap on the beaten mountain paths. Instead of relying on outright speed across flat ground, Firmin had distinguished himself on those roads others struggled over.

The fifth stage's distance cut the cyclists' rest short. If Desgrange's predictions in *l'Auto* were correct, they would arrive in the Basque city after seventeen hours of racing. So far, however, Desgrange's guesses had overestimated their speed. The Tour fans who had closely followed *l'Auto*'s coverage knew the journey would likely extend beyond the 4:00 p.m. arrival time and into that Monday evening. After they had crossed those 482 kilometers, the cyclists would rest just one more day before starting the alpine climbs, stages Desgrange once thought would be impossible for anyone to complete.

What rested between Les Sables and Bayonne might offer the ground Firmin or Eugène needed to separate themselves from the other cyclists. The landscape was flat and would have otherwise been suited for cyclists more reliant on sprints. The distance between the two cities was great enough, however, that the stage was transformed into a different challenge altogether. A shorter length after already grueling days of cycling would have still been a test of its own, but the vast distance between Les Sables and Bayonne meant any result was conceivable.

Firmin first rode over Desgrange's route in 1911. He placed eleventh that year in the general classification, beating roughly half of the twenty-eight cyclists who'd finished. In 1912 he almost mirrored the previous race, finishing eighteenth of forty-one. He performed better in the 1913 Tour; only three others beat him. He was as close to winning as he had ever been, though it was too soon to say whether that year's alpine stages would help or hurt him. If something happened to Eugène or the second-place Émile, all he would have to do was persist on the difficult stretches, finish each stage from the fifth to the final one delivering them back to Paris. For the time, his third-place position was a safe one; few looked to beat anyone but the first-place competitor.

Firmin escaped others' notice even when he'd won individual stages. It was a skill he had, even if it meant fewer supporters and annoyed fans when he won against their favorites. Though he was strong in climbs, he was otherwise understated while cycling. On that year's Tour, he only tagged behind those nearest to the front; he hadn't led any sprints. It had helped him avoid conflicts others had been inextricably drawn into in earlier years while they jockeyed for positions up alpine climbs. As cyclists continued to drop from this year's race, he hoped it would be enough to remain near the top and spend as little of his energy as he could manage.

Born to Louis and Alphonsine Sibille in the small, French-speaking Belgian town of Florennes, Firmin had turned professional in 1908, at the age of twenty-two. That same year he won the Belgian National Championship and a handful of smaller, regional races. Like the other cyclists who maintained regular jobs, Firmin could be found working on horse saddles those days when he wasn't racing, commuting from his home to the leatherworking shop on a bike purchased when he was seventeen.

In Florennes was another young man, his neighbor, who shared an interest in cycling. Léon Scieur was born just down the road from Firmin's family house. The two became friends in time. When Firmin bought a bike with money earned from work, Léon borrowed it so that Firmin might teach him to ride. The younger of the pair by two years, Léon had turned professional after Firmin, in 1911, following behind his friend. At times he had passed Firmin: he finished the 1913 Tour de Belgique in fourth and won the stage between Antwerp and Brussels after Firmin had abandoned after the third stage. That day in 1919, Léon was in ninth place in the general classification, more than two hours behind his onetime neighbor. Though the pair had competed against one another as professionals riding for two different teams, they rode together under the same banner now. In the years before the war, Firmin had raced for Griffon-Continental and Peugeot-Wolber while

Léon rode for Thomann-Soly. They might as well have been twins when fans saw only their gray-and-blue jersey backs, cycling together toward that stage's starting line.

◆ ◆ ◆

A quarter moon illuminated the cyclists as they left Les Sables at 10:00 p.m. that Sunday. The riders headed east in the darkness, away from the coast, to Luçon. Residents of the city stayed awake to see them off, turning in after the pack had left the city, sleeping in the next morning. Shortly after the stage began, another cyclist left the race; he saw little point in straining himself that day. Seventeen others remained.

Firmin rode alongside the pack, near the back, behind Eugène, Honoré, Jean, and ten others. Unlike some of the younger cyclists, who had only competed in regional races against those who lived near them, Firmin knew many of the men he raced against. He understood when each competitor would be strongest in a given stage, which terrains slowed them down, whether they were likely to push aggressively to the front or lag behind until the end, waiting for an opportune moment while the other cyclists were tired. His ability to measure the others was necessary for any cyclist who hoped to do well on the fifteen stages, but particularly for Firmin, who hoped to conserve himself and calmly seek out those advantages when they arrived. He responded to the others' movements and made gains when they cost him the least. Those who watched from the roads hoped for something more striking and heroic, a cyclist who took another's bait and threw himself against the rushing air, beating back its drag in an effort to pass through the finish line a second or a length quicker. Directing the crowd's eyes, even those of the officials, only helped Firmin's quiet insistence.

He rode into the Marais Poitevin. The wetland stretched one hundred thousand hectares across France's western midsection. Canals ran along small farming towns built on the Marais's rich soil. For hours in the darkness he passed waterways, thick tree trunks sprouting from the banks. In front, the Brasier's headlamps illuminated the stretch of ground immediately before him, but little else. The poplars and ash trees lining the road stood between the cyclists and the sliver of the moon, darkening their path even more. Above the creaking of the bikes and the words that passed between them and the journalists in the car, the sounds of the wetland were an uproar. Stretches went by without any spectators in sight. The crowd's absence left only nature's disorder to intrude on their paths, though the Marais creatures stayed off the roads and kept their assault verbal. The overall effect was still something close to peace.

Their distance from civilization created its own problems. The night and the roads strained the cyclists, even in their first hours. Much of the land remained unpaved. Punctures continued to plague them through the final hours of July 6th and the first hours of the 7th. When one struck, the unlucky racer found himself alone in the Marais, only the faint moonlight illuminating his task. The sounds crescendoed without the Brasier's rumble. The cyclist's sleep-deprived mind concentrated, attempted to ignore the woods' shadows that sprung his neck hairs. He finished replacing his tire and mounted his bike a little quicker, pedaling harder to catch up to the light and the sounds of the pack.

The group rode together out of the Marais and reached La Rochelle on its southern edge at 1:55 a.m., after almost four hours. The port, still dark, was crowded with freight ships. Fuel and wood that had been continuously off-loaded in wartime years were still needed for new infrastructure and for rebuilding old, battered buildings away from the coast. Not all wartime retrofits made to the boats had been removed from the vessels. Some weather-beaten, rust-stained fishing trawlers still carried heavy guns mounted to their bows, as if concerned they'd encounter a lost U-boat unaware of the war's end.

◆ ◆ ◆

Firmin had been living in Marcinelle when he received news a war had broken out. Before some of his fellow cyclists even considered whether the conflict might need them, his country had been occupied by German forces. The life he had started to create for himself ended. He avoided the front, at least; his hours were still his own, not ordered by another, even if the troops stationed in his town prevented him from living his life fully. He married Maria Anwera in 1914 and moved to her hometown of Antwerp the following year. He opened his own saddlery there and waited for the war to end. Few races were hosted in those years. He avoided the races that his teammate, Philippe Thys, didn't. Peugeot-Wolber, his sponsor, didn't pay him for events he didn't compete in. Instead, he cycled when he could, without a sponsor supporting him, and continued working at his day job. The four years under occupation afforded him more than what the soldiers at the front received; he lived more than they were allowed to live.

His life had not been entirely free. In the first months of the German occupation, thousands of Belgian civilians were massacred. He arrived in Antwerp after the eleven-day siege of the city had ended and the country was firmly within the grasp of German troops. Belgians were asked, then told, to work in Germany. By 1916 a forced deportation policy had been put into place; hundreds of thousands of Belgians were sent to Germany under the law. Firmin managed to avoid that fate. Patriotic Belgian displays were suppressed, and those that did take place were performed by men and women willing to take part in underground resistance movements. "La Brabançonne," the Belgian national anthem, was rarely heard above a whisper. Most newspapers were described as "rubbish," though a few chose to go into exile instead and continue to report without the constant eye of German censors.

◆ ◆ ◆

By the time Firmin and the others passed the *l'Auto* correspondent stationed in Saintes, they had ridden 171 kilometers. Eugène pedaled toward the rear of the leading pack, in front of only Firmin, who was eight minutes behind after suffering from one puncture then another. Even Jules Nempon, one of two remaining B classification cyclists, passed the correspondent before the Belgian. Three hundred eleven kilometers remained in front of the men; plenty of time for the distance between them to grow or for those fortunes to change. The day was so long it was almost pointless to note those early distances, only the longest gaps between one and another. In Blaye, a complete peloton of seventeen re-formed. They rode into the city, where the correspondents checked over their bikes, then they rode out again, a flock of birds resting briefly at a pond.

They passed south. Farmlands extended in all directions. The fields didn't end, just gave way to a clear sky, a painted film backdrop more than a tangible, three-dimensional space. The farmland was sparer than the land to the north. Khaki dirt was visible through scrub. The earth tones were broken by neat crop lines ascending the hills around them. Weathered trunks, cracked and broken, ended in lush, wide leaves. Between the leaves, grape clusters grew. The vineyards extended for kilometers. The oldest vines had turned into crone's toothpicks, splintered offshoots and twisting trunks. Where vines were young, they stood like gnarled saplings. Workers picked the grapes year after year; some had been harvested for more than a century.

Eugène stopped in Bordeaux around 9:43 a.m. with the others. According to Desgrange, they were behind schedule by thirty-six minutes. The crowd's impatience was palpable. He watched them shift, bend over to look down the road, watching him near café de la Avenue. Those who had woken up early were seated along a terrace that wound around the restaurant, while others crowded underneath and around, on avenue Thiers, wherever room remained. They jammed onto the landscaped median out front. Their eyes looked to the street leading out of the town.

A cry started from down the avenue and neared the café. The shouts reached Eugène after the others. "Les voilà!" They're here! Men and women and children shouted to others in the rows behind them who couldn't yet see the cyclists over the mass that was pushing one another on either side of the road. The fans were nearly in Eugène's path as he entered the city, but each person moved just before he crashed into them. Hats waved, hands reached out to touch Paul Duboc, then Jean, then Félix Goethals, and Eugène. Firmin rode in behind them. By then, some of the crowd had given up containing themselves and took to the street, following behind Eugène, not noticing the cyclists who remained on the road. Firmin arrived in eighth, ahead of Léon and a few others.

The first three cyclists to enter the city received prizes from the Bordelaises before mounting their bikes again and exiting the city. Eugène left after those first competitors. Outside the town, the ground was no longer endless. It instead extended upward in small hills around him. The hills intruded on layers of clouds and the blue between them. Their inclines were small, not more than a short walk or ride to ascend, and they barely slowed the cyclists. Eugène rode in second behind Émile, Firmin in front of Léon. There was little the two Belgians from Florennes could do for one another, any small show of physical assistance would be enough to trigger a penalty from the officials who watched them. It was something, though, to have a friend they had known for years to ride with after hundreds of kilometers, with over one hundred more to go that day. At any point, a seed of doubt could have sprung up in one of their minds. It might have left after just a few moments, but if it arrived at the right time, the seed could have been enough to force Firmin or Léon off his bike, to persuade him to sit on the side of the road, or in a ditch as Francis had done, as others passed him by, others who weren't troubled with such images. Each second the seed remained with him would have been another second he would have to make up to return to the pack. The seed would grow in response. Having someone else to set his pace and offer a sense of teamwork or goodwill could be enough to wash the feeling away.

A little before 5:00 p.m., the people packed into the stands in Bayonne heard cheers from beyond the hairpin turn along route nationale 10. An earlier rain had cleared the sky, and the evaporating water thickened the air in the southern sun. A bugle call sounded as the people around the finish line spotted Jean, coated in dried mud, as he picked up his pace, sprinting along the final hundred meters of the course, away from cyclist René Chassot, who responded with a sprint of his own. The crowd cheered for them both as Jean cleared the finish line less than a length ahead of René, who was followed by Léon, Joseph Van Daele, Jacques Coomans, Aloïs Verstraeten, and Luigi, all within ten seconds of one another.

One hundred men from the Forty-ninth Infantry Regiment stood around the edge of the finish. The unit's thirteen hundred soldiers had been garrisoned in the town for decades, left to fight in the northeast, in Verdun and Somme up through the last days of the war, and had only just returned to their homes. Plenty of men in the unit were still up there, in the north, and had not yet been demobilized back to the garrison town. The men who had been demobilized, who had left the front and who were now back in the Bayonne, didn't know the fate of all the soldiers who hadn't returned. The Great War, for them, was over; their unit occupied a liminal place until it returned to Bayonne and was finally accounted for. Their initial return had been a celebratory time, when they rejoined their families and their neighbors, but it was allayed until the other soldiers joined them.

The dull blue of the Forty-ninth's uniforms was darker than day. It was a blue closer to the sky of an industrial town, or one washed out by the milky yellow of latent chlorine, with the light gray white of shell explosions. Official documentation called it horizon blue, the color of the ground meeting the sky. In more regular terms, it was gray-blue lead, a blend of the cyclists' La Sportive jerseys.

The Forty-ninth's uniforms had replaced those worn in the first years of the war, vibrant ones that had distinguished the French army since 1870. Red kepis and trousers with a deep, rich blue had adorned those old soldiers, announcing their presence from hundreds of meters away. Cuirassiers on horseback kept polished and plumed helmets. The uniforms had come from a different time with different convictions, convictions broken as the war ground to a halt in the trenches.

The Forty-ninth's pressed steel helmets, the same horizon blue as their uniforms, were imprinted with a grenade, a flame, and the initials R.F.—République Française. They had been temporarily replaced with soft side caps as the soldiers waited at the finish line. No incoming fire endangered them. The crowd remained respectful and yielded to the soldiers as the first cyclists arrived at the finish line, though there was little fear of anything happening, and one after another the people who watched the cyclists slipped beyond the soldiers' grasps and walked among the riders as they slowed and stepped off their pedals.

◆ ◆ ◆

The cyclists traveled to Brasserie Schmitt, where the local cycling club helped the *l'Auto* journalists staff the signature table. The celebrations continued as they had in the other towns. In each city, a hesitancy hung over the cyclists as one after another dropped from the race. Their diminishing numbers increased the chance that those who were left would find prize money somewhere along the road or acclaim at the Tour's end, but it also gave each cyclist reason to doubt their attachment to the ground in front of them. The roads ahead had never been the most well maintained, not traveled too frequently. With the accompanying climbs, few knew what to expect from here to the Mediterranean Sea on the far side of the ninth stage.

For their effort, the town threw the cyclists a champagne lunch the next day. They were joined by Desgrange and the *l'Auto* correspondents, as well as officials from Bayonne. The politicians didn't focus much on the race, though they couldn't help but ask their preferred cyclists how they'd found the journey so far and congratulated them on their performance, but with only one night's rest separating the cyclists from 482 kilometers, their responses were subdued. Instead they talked about the poet and playwright Edmund Rostand, who'd died one year before, and really anything else that would keep the race at a distance, to the chagrin of their hosts.

The cyclists weren't the only members of the Tour to have mixed feelings about how the race had gone. A nagging tugged at Desgrange. Over the past day, the Pélissiers' abandonment had curdled into a more noxious feeling than any superiority he'd felt as soon as they had left the race. It congealed into something ugly as he sat down to write his column for the following day's newspaper. "I want to go back to the Pélissiers' defection," he started writing in his room. He laid out his case against the brothers. He focused on minor complaints Henri had made at the time about his health, aches and pains the cyclist had found at the end of stages. "His kidneys couldn't have been too bad," he wrote. He described how Henri had stopped at a bistro on the fourth stage, while racing to Les Sables. "He drank too much," Desgrange claimed, "and by Nantes, he was zigzagging across the road as the others looked on in disgust. Only then he told me about his pains.

"If there are so few racers capable of racing on his level," Desgrange continued, referencing Henri's remarks to Alphonse Baugé on the evening of the third leg, after he had placed just behind Francis, "why couldn't he stay?" Desgrange addressed his critiques to Henri directly, confident the cyclist would see them, or at least hear of them. "No champion of the Tour de France has had the nerve of Pélissier," he wrote.

Desgrange continued to write about the cyclists who remained in the race, but his words were few and tempered in comparison to those directed at Henri. The brothers had already arrived back home in Paris by the time Desgrange sat down to draft the column. Henri was a perfectly good cyclist, Desgrange would freely admit, but it was not as though the Tour hadn't seen others like him, others even better. If he didn't have what it took to complete the stages and instead thought it better to give up, so be it. The roads ahead of them now would only become more difficult, both Henri and Desgrange knew that. It would be better, safer, and more tolerable to give up if he couldn't cut it rather than to suffer through the Pyrenees. "Compared to Pottier and Petit-Breton, he ran with muscles like a sensitive woman," the editor wrote.

Alice Milliat

July 6, 1919—rue de Varenne, Paris

If Henri Pélissier or any of the other cyclists in that year's race weren't willing or able to finish the 1919 Tour, Alice Milliat knew plenty of other athletes who would be more than happy to take their place, if only Desgrange allowed it. She had other, more pressing concerns, but if the *l'Auto* editor sent her a telegraph with a request for competitors, she would have found the time to answer. If the editor changed his ponderous rules and let her know, she'd set down her efforts with the International Olympic Committee for a moment and happily put out a call to the women of Fédération des sociétés féminines sportives de France, or FSFSF, if the Tour couldn't find men who would last until Paris. She was sure her members would be ready at a moment's notice to fill their places.

"Let me tell you what I think of bicycling," Susan B. Anthony had said to Nellie Bly as the journalist interviewed the suffragette for an article published in the February 2nd, 1896, Sunday edition of the *New York World*. "It has done more to emancipate women than anything else in the world." The *Tribune* described the bicycle as "a great equalizer of the sexes . . . In no other sport can they hold their own so well with men. Mounted on these machines, if equally proficient in the use of them, the average man and woman are nearly equal as they perhaps ever can be in any undertaking requiring muscular energy and skill."

On Ocean Parkway, in New York City, administrators had built the first path dedicated to bicycle use. The dirt track between Coney Island and Prospect Park carried women and men alike as they rode safety bikes, which had recently replaced old high-wheel designs. It was so popular, the path had to be expanded shortly after its creation to keep up with the flow of cyclists who, for the most part, dutifully maintained the twelve miles per hour speed limit. Before setting out on the parkway, women exchanged their heavy, layered gowns for shorter skirts and bloomers. Ambitious clothing designers even sewed pulley systems into their skirts' linings so the garments, which first appeared like any other piece of clothing, could be bunched up when women mounted their bikes, ensuring their hems stayed far from the bikes' drive chains. Countless cautionary tales of injury or death began with a woman failing to secure her garments while atop a bike. Sitting side-saddle, as one might have done on horseback, simply wasn't an option.

Alice thought recreational cycling perfectly fine but was more interested in competition. She had recently ascended to her role as the president of FSFSF from her position as general secretary of the organization. She was tasked with overseeing the hub of women's sporting clubs in the country that were making headway finding are-nas and sponsors to support tournaments that could now be more readily held at the war's end. Alice helped FSFSF organize women athletes who competed in the same sports in different regions of the country and acted as their spokeswoman, helping the athletes reach new audiences and drive competition in additional sports. Under her leadership, FSFSF had just held a women's football championship that March at Paris's stade Brancion. She oversaw the organization's opera-tions from its Paris headquarters at 17 rue du Faubourg Montmartre, just down the street from Desgrange's offices.

FSFSF had been founded in April 1917. The war's direction hadn't been clear then, but by that time, Alice knew women's involvement in sports would grow over the coming years. It was only a matter of how quickly and in what particular sports. FSFSF grew for two years. Alice, however, was the first woman to hold the organization's top position. She knew she could better represent the administrators and athletes who made up FSFSF's membership—who competed in football, soccer, and rugby, among others—than the men who had come before her.

As an active rower, Alice was at least more familiar with sports than her predecessors, whose involvement came from a clinical distance. Rowing may not have been as practically liberating as cycling, perhaps, but it still relied on its athletes' independence. In FSFSF's members' minds, at least, it made sense that a woman like Alice was at its helm, instead of the men who had filtered the athletes' needs and professional desires through their own sense of what women were able to accomplish.

Despite settling into the president's office at FSFSF, Alice was still accompanied by two men who sat on either side of her as vice presidents. She was seen as the outward face of the organization and its internal organizer, even if men outside the organization would have sooner gone to them than to her. Sports dailies like *l'Auto* mentioned her by name when she attended events around Paris. She'd taken to writing in the newspaper's pages at times, using her role to detail advancements in the field of women's sports: that FSFSF wouldn't join the Fédération française de football, the national men's organization formed in April 1919, and congratulating her athletes on their performances throughout the city and the country.

Her most immediate task was negotiating with Baron Pierre de Coubertin, president of the International Olympic Committee. In his role, the slight man, a Parisian aristocrat, oversaw the body that helped organize the Olympic Games. Privately, from her office, Alice had written to him with the hope he would include women's track and field events in the next edition of the Olympics, set to take place in Antwerp in 1920.

Women had competed in the games since its second modern iteration in 1900. During the months of events that coincided with the World's Fair hosted in Paris, twenty-two women sailed and played croquet, rode horses, and competed in golf and tennis events. Women's archery had been added to the 1904 St. Louis, Missouri, games. They had skated in the 1908 London games, and swum in the 1912 Stockholm Games. Every organizer of the Olympic Games had added women's events to their international celebrations.

Each new addition displeased Pierre de Coubertin as much as it pleased Alice. Of the sports traditionalists in France, who thought women shouldn't be permitted to compete, few stood taller than him. "Impractical, uninteresting, unaesthetic, and improper," read a section of the IOC's report following the Stockholm Games on women's competitions. Even recreational sledding had been too much for him, he'd decided on a 1908 trip to England. "Painfully ugly," he had said of the encounter. It wasn't that he opposed women exercising, it was that he thought they shouldn't compete with one another or do so in public.

That women had been included in past instances of the Olympics was a product of the limits of Pierre's power. In earlier games, the organizing committees of each year's event—appointed by the host cities—decided on a schedule and the particular competitions that made up the games. Representation from the IOC had not been mandatory on these boards. It was the cities, not Pierre, who decided to include women's events in one Olympics after another.

As the 1920 games neared, the IOC's rules changed. Pierre had never liked giving up so much control to his hosts. He thought the games, or at least their organizers, should have similar ideals about what athletics were good for and their place within a society. He held a common patrician sentiment that athletes should be amateurs—not unlike the Tour cyclists who kept their day-to-day jobs, even if they were otherwise professionals. He disliked money being exchanged for athletic performance and thought it muddied the waters and corrupted athletes' incentives. Pierre believed sports should be competitions among men and exist for no other aim than honor or glory or achievement. He believed athletics had the power to achieve something close to peace, taking his inspiration from the Olympic Truce of the ancient Greek games and an agreement that prevented the host country from being attacked while the Olympics were ongoing. It wasn't an entirely accurate view of the ancient games, but it was part of the new games' founding myth. It was idealistic if not naive. If Pierre had his way, countless athletes—many of whom were the most accomplished among their peers—would never have competed in the games because they had received sponsorship money and compensation for their performances. To allow women in the games would have been a tacit recognition of their athletic equality, or, if not a sign of their outright ability, then at least of their place within society.

It mattered little to the IOC president that women had played an integral role in the Great War. When men left small towns and large cities, abandoning their jobs and businesses, women had filled their absences. Women came closer to the front, too, taking on roles at Red Cross stations and in hospitals run by armies and navies. In most countries, women had only approached the front directly when their homes were caught near it, but, in Russia, some military battalions were composed entirely of women, both as officers and enlisted soldiers. Without women, the war could not have continued; without them, their countries would have ground to a halt as economies flagged and supply lines dried up.

Once the war ended, the men began returning home. It had been a slow process. Even as the Tour went on in the summer of 1919, seven months after the armistice's signing, units still watched over the occupied German territories and worked near the front, constructing buildings and helping displaced people return home.

In time, however, the men would leave, resume the lives they had before the war. When they did, most would no longer be employed by the military. Others wouldn't return at all—over one million, it was predicted, had died. The wives they had left behind, the ones who had taken up their jobs and their roles in the community, had seen the horizon of their solitude extend in a way they never asked for, as much as the accompanying freedoms and opportunities might have been desired. Many of their husbands had simply stopped returning letters one day and were buried in one or another unmarked grave in an otherwise common stretch of ground, far from home. Women were kicked out of their factory jobs as some, but not all, men returned. The unemployed widows weren't sure how they could continue to provide for themselves and their families.

Before the war started, some women had already been seeking the right to vote. Each time the issue arrived on a ballot, or gained some traction in public, it had been shot down. L'Union française pour le suffrage des femmes, or the UFSF, an organization founded in 1909, was one group leading the continued effort. It was a coalition of republicans and Catholics who advocated for a more moderate approach to suffrage, who were willing to work with the existing government. Others, like the Conseil National des Femmes Françaises, and the Ligues Française pour le Droit des Femmes, didn't advocate for the UFSF's limited approach. The UFSF was led by Jane Misme, the editor of the feminist journal *La Française*. During the war, she had suspended the UFSF's suffrage campaign in order to support the government. With women's roles in those years, the right to vote appeared like a reasonable expectation once the war was through.

Earlier that summer, in May, it looked as though UFSF's support of the government would pay off. The Chamber of Deputies, the lower house of parliament directly elected by the people, voted on a measure to grant women suffrage. The bill passed with 329 votes. It dictated in even clearer terms the role of women as citizens and in politics, more than what UFSF had asked for. Instead of being able to stand only in local elections, the bill described full equality on the basis of sex in matters of voting and citizenship. Misme was cautious. The senate, the body of government elected indirectly by other elected officials, still stood in the way of the bill's passage. The right-leaning Democratic Republican Alliance controlled the senate. Jane had every reason to believe the bill's voyage through the higher body would be more difficult than the clear victory they had achieved in the lower house. She had few connections there; all she and her members could do was wait for the senate to take up the bill.

◆ ◆ ◆

With voting on the table and women's place in society clearly changed, Pierre's desired ban on women's sports in the Olympics was particularly out of touch. Alice felt distant from Jane's battle with parliament and was consumed by the shakier ground she and her members stood on. Women's proposed role in sports didn't hinge on any sense of duty but on competition and entertainment—undoubtedly less serious matters than citizenship. She believed women's increased participation in sports could bring them closer to suffrage, for what it was worth, and vice versa, but it was her association's goals that consumed her.

Since the International Olympic Committee was a private organization, it had no legal necessity to allow women to compete on equal terms, but outside pressures had caused individual countries to accept women competitors in the past. Pierre didn't see any way to backtrack on those women's events the games had already included.

Around Alice and Pierre's country, men now competed on bikes, the machines that had liberated women elsewhere. If Desgrange had included her athletes in that race, one that bound its competitors and their country, perhaps she, Jane, and all women who didn't yet know what their role in France would be in the coming years, could have found themselves on steadier ground.

Port de Vénasque, as seen from l'Hospice de France, just south of Luchon.

7.

The path the cyclists would follow up col d'Aubisque was a narrow trail that connected one spa town to the next. The dirt path was invisible at almost any distance. It had originally been beaten flat for Empress Eugénie, the wife of Napoleon III, during his reign in the mid-1800s. She'd used it to travel by carriage across the remote terrain. There, small hamlets dotted the valleys and gulches of the Pyrenees, the seam between France and Spain. The empress sought out those towns fed by a warm spring, where water burbled up from the dash of tectonic plates underneath their foundations.

Aubisque's summit lies at 1,709 meters, at the intersection of the Ossan and Arrens Valleys. The mountain pass rests on a slope of Pic de Ger. The path is barely more than a hiking trail once it leaves the towns below since there has never been enough traffic between them to justify a more permanent path than that. In the winter months, the path closes. Regional and national governments allowed it to erode while other, more regularly used roads were maintained. The towns it connects—Eaux-Bonnes and Argelès—are mostly self-sufficient. Those who do use the path do not do so often. It's wide enough for a car to drive comfortably along, but too narrow should two approach in opposite directions: one would have the unenviable position of veering out toward the road's edge, which falls away to hundreds of feet below.

Desgrange's first Tours avoided this difficult region. Most of the first Tour cyclists had arrived after training and competing on flat, regular tracks. Their longest competitions were one-day events, a single Tour stage. When Desgrange announced the race, it was the first of its kind. The cyclists never had to consider how they'd sustain their efforts day after day, week after week across those distances. To add climbs thousands of meters in height would only diminish the cyclists' numbers further. Desgrange was fine with the thought that only a few cyclists would remain by the time they arrived again in Paris, but he doubted whether anyone could finish an alpine stage after toiling on the Tour's more regular distances. He wanted to push racers beyond any other race, but he didn't want the men to die on the narrow mountain paths or have a race that ended with no cyclists remaining: it would be bad for business, if nothing else.

The Tour began its annual procession; the number of willing competitors grew. Desgrange grew confident in the Tour's model, just maybe the cyclists could be pushed further. The editor was persuaded to include the first climb by his employee, Alphonse Steinès. Steinès, a bookish reporter, thirty-two years old at the time, who wore pince-nez and had a gradually receding hairline and neatly trimmed beard, managed the newspaper's section on the sporting industry. He had a higher opinion of the cyclists' abilities than Desgrange. If the mountain roads were of a good enough quality, he told the editor, the Tour riders should have little trouble climbing them from basin to peak. *L'Auto* would simply have to find a route that included the proper traversable paths—not too difficult, in decent maintenance—and ensure that at the end of the day, after not too long a distance, the cyclists could arrive in a town that would be able to accommodate their numbers. Desgrange agreed to a trial in the 1905 edition of the race, with an ascent of Ballon d'Alsace, just above Switzerland's knuckle into France. Cyclist René Pottier ascended first. He climbed the mountain's 1,178 meters without lifting himself from his bike's seat, single-handedly convincing the *l'Auto* journalists that ascents were possible. It was the proof Desgrange had asked for, but the editor still held doubts that any more alpine stages on the Tour could happen, or a more strenuous climb than the mild Ballon d'Alsace.

Four and a half years later, in the winter of 1910, Steinès left Paris to head to the Pyrenees. There, he would survey mountain passes for possible inclusion in that upcoming year's Tour de France. Steinès arrived at the Spanish border. Gradually he ascended from the flat ground of the Aquitaine. The roads that were not shut down entirely thinned as the elevation increased, unattended and untrod in the winter months. Snow packed the untrammeled ground. A fresh storm powdered the dense white with a soft crust as Steinès neared the mountain pass of col d'Aubisque. Eventually, his car slowed to a halt. He was unable to drive over the snow in front of him. If he sent word back to Desgrange of his halted progress, before he reached the peak, Steinès knew Desgrange would be scared away from adding alpine climbs to the Tour. The editor was more comfortable in his role than four and a half years back, and had a clearer vision for his Tour champion, but was still a cautious manager at his center. If a car couldn't drive across these roads, how could cyclists? Determined, Steinès left his car behind and climbed up the mountain pass on foot, surveying its state where the snow was not too heavy. The climb nearly killed him, but eventually he managed to find his way back to his car and eased its wheels out from the accumulating snow, driving back into town where he sent a telegraph to Desgrange. The path was traversable, he said. Tour cyclists would be able to make the crossing. The unqualified declaration convinced Desgrange that the Tour route could be moved south, closer to the Spanish border, and into the Pyrenees.

Later that year, when the cyclists approached Steinès's route on the ninth stage of the clockwise Tour, Desgrange claimed he was ill. Instead of watching their progress from a car, he received reports from his correspondents on the road, eventually meeting back up with the group after the stage was through. The editor was relieved to hear the cyclists had all climbed col d'Aubisque. Octave Lapize, the first to make his way to the summit, spoke to the cyclists' feelings about the climb. Turning to the administrators who had been tracking their times, he called out, "Assassins." The Tour maintained its alpine stages every year since.

◆ ◆ ◆

The early kilometers of the sixth stage weren't so different for Eugène than the previous ones. He left Bayonne at 2:00 a.m. and began riding. The roads he crossed weren't well maintained, but they were still traversable. The ground gently sloped, but still only hills surrounded them; the mountains were far in the distance. He quietly rode through and along small valleys that mirrored one another, crossing a bridge above the Nive River, whose dark rushing waters were swollen with rain.

Eugène wasn't the oldest cyclist in that year's race. His competitor Louis Heusghem had a little more than two years on him. And Paul Duboc had been born nine months before Eugène. But Paul was riding in sixteenth, behind Eugène by eleven hours and fourteen minutes, and Louis had given up as he rode into Les Sables on the fourth stage. Firmin, just over a year younger than Eugène, was in third, behind by forty-eight minutes. After Eugène's ninth place showing in Paris–Roubaix that year, and after being put on leave from the army on March 17th, just a few months before the start of the race, he had little to complain about.

He'd been born to working-class parents in Paris. A taciturn but obedient child, he didn't take well to school. He instead started working as soon as he was able. He left the classroom behind at the early age of thirteen to begin an apprenticeship as an iron worker down on 13 rue Chapon in the Marais. It had been a twenty-five-minute walk to the shop from his parents' house on Île Saint-Louis, a small island in the middle of the Seine. On a bicycle, however, he could arrive at the shop in less than ten. On Sundays, Eugène spent some of the money he'd earned in the shop to rent a bike from the Sainte-Catherine Market. He'd take the bike outside the city and into the surrounding areas: Vincennes, Villiers. He didn't naturally take to the machine. Instead, a man who worked as a bicycle dealer noticed his determination and gave the young Eugène free lessons. As he improved, Eugène spent as much time as he could on bikes, cycling in and around Paris.

◆ ◆ ◆

The racers passed through Basque towns. Over the centuries, the local people had been subject to the whims of countless rulers. To each of those who governed them, the Basque region, their towns occupied different places within their lands—the distended Roman Empire, years of the relatively independent Duchy of Gascony, which gave way to the incorporation of the territory into France itself. They had only recently lost home rule with their distinct government institutions, including a separate parliament and a separate legal system, with the abolition of local governments in the French Revolution. Despite the legal shift, the people who lived there maintained their cultural and societal systems through the upheaval: matrilineal inheritances, the bird-like sounds of chiroula players who took to the streets during the bonfires of Saint John and the maskarada. They could just as easily be identified as Spanish as they could French, though they were neither. They had enough pride for their country, but their world was distinct, not only separated by their distance from the capital, but in their way of life that didn't entirely accord with the rest of the country.

The Tour that rode through these towns was smaller than a pinprick in the wild landscape. The cyclists were nothing to it. The ground around them was fragmented, pitted with roots of old sycamore trees on either side of their path. By the time Eugène left the check-in at Saint-Jean-Pied-de-Port, after riding fifty-one kilometers, the Pyrenees were within sight. Their crowns peered through broken green foliage; they stood steadily against the gray morning sky. The cyclist continued, underneath storm clouds again. The trees broke the rain droplets, softened their sounds. The weather refused to let go.

Desgrange and the other correspondents were quick to mention Eugène's age whenever they wrote about his prospects for the coming stages. If he held his place through the end of the race, he'd be the oldest Tour winner in history, but the journalists were still reserved when discussing his progress. They had concerns he would be able to sustain his position through multiple alpine stages.

They expressed their doubts that he, like the other older cyclists, could compete against the younger ones on the climbs, even if Eugène had once distinguished himself on that difficult terrain. His energy didn't fade as it did for others. He held his frame tight with effort, but he continued on, holding steady on the dangerous descents where others slowed their pace out of caution.

◆ ◆ ◆

Eugène's first military job as courier for the 119th Infantry Regiment left him without the camaraderie of the other soldiers, but it at least kept him on his bike and gave him an independence that was more important to the twenty-one-year-old. He entered the reserves and continued to race before he was called up again and sent to the First Cycling Group in the first general mobilization order of 1914. They were part of the infantry foot hunter battalions, distinguished from line infantry units in marksmanship and in their ability to maneuver independently, without the support of engineers, artillery, or logistics, though the western front cared little for their status. Eugène rode alongside the infantry soldiers and maintained the bikes they used to traverse the ground. They wore silver hunting horn insignias that marked their lineage. The job felt less foreign to Eugène than his first years in the military, though his time in the cycling group was more grueling and devastating than what he could have imagined. He rode alongside the soldiers at the Battle of the Marne in September of 1914, when the northeastern ground was still flat and soldiers built small dirt berms to hide behind. There, bicyclists could ride to and from the front to flank enemy movements and dip away before a counterattack could be planned. Eventually the bikes were useless as permanent, deeper trenches encased the soldiers, but on the flatter terrain between France and Belgium they provided a mobility and speed marching on foot could not. In time, he'd been transferred farther away from the battles, to serve as a mechanic in the Second Aviation Group, but his time with the bicycle infantry unit helped him realize the nature of the war he was fighting in and the ground they would all ride over soon enough.

◆ ◆ ◆

Eugène neared Aubisque's ascent in Eaux-Bonnes. He and a few others slipped from their bikes before they began the climb in earnest. On the side of the road, in the tiny spa town whose bright white buildings stood out against the dark green that jutted up from behind, the cyclists pulled off their bikes' muck-coated chains and flipped their back wheels, aligning the larger rear gear with the front one. Each subsequent push against their pedals would be done more easily, at the cost of power transmitted to their wheels. Once they had reattached the chains, the riders began riding up the steeper mountain road. A few chose not to stop. Luigi, Jean, Léon, and Louis Mottiat rode past them under the power of the smaller back gear, straining against its resistance.

Already the roads were an unnatural part of the landscape. Their flat lateral planes stuck out from sharp upward slopes. On one side then another, the path dropped down into rushing spring waters. The cyclists pressed against their bike's pedals. Seventeen kilometers separated them from Aubisque's peak, though there would be little relief for them there.

Once they reached the summit, they would still have 147 kilometers until the stage's end. Eugène turned left in front of Eaux-Bonnes's hydro facilities. A church was on the opposite side of the road, and black-robed nuns had come out to watch the cyclists pedal past, quiet but attentive. Luigi and Léon accelerated, as close to a sprint as they could muster, given the steep grade. If they distanced themselves enough while they still had excess energy, they could risk slowing down later in the climb and regain what had left them once the descent began. They reached a pounding waterfall. Small cafés lined the hairpin turns, and patrons watched the race from their respective terraces. The spectators were few in number, but their eyes fixed to the racers and they cheered for them all the same.

A few kilometers into the ascent, Eugène passed shacks scattered on a bluff overlooking the city. Local zinc-mine workers watched as each figure passed by. The miners had dutifully taken part in national strikes earlier in the summer. Railroad workers, seamen, metal and transportation workers joined them in solidarity. They continued negotiating with the government after an eight-hour workday had been secured earlier that year. Others hoped the French government would halt its intervention against Russian Bolsheviks, who had first established some of the labor reforms they now saw in their own country. The road no longer existed by the time they passed through the mining village. Only a path led up the peak. The miners who carried ore back and forth from the mine's shafts maintained it on occasion, but the snow and rains wore it down faster than it could be kept. Deep gutters ran along its edge, and the racers' slow speeds emphasized every pothole and rock their eyes may have missed. They teetered back and forth, climbing between eight and sixteen degrees up toward the peak. When they slowed down enough, or left the bike's seat to walk up a section of the pass, their wheels skittered before catching the ground again.

Those cyclists who hadn't changed their gear for the mountain worked more wearily. They had to push harder than the others to advance; sweat ran in streaks down their dirty faces. Their tense bodies flexed. Jean slipped off his bike for a few meters and began to push it up the path. He reached a section with a less severe incline and returned to his seat, accepting those first slow revolutions to regain his speed.

Eugène rode behind the boyish Parisian cyclist. He kept his pace steady and didn't exert himself too much on the final stretch to the summit.

The approach to the top was biblical. Looking back down the path, it seemed impossible he had come so far. The grassy slopes he had encountered in the first hours of the day still surrounded him, but clouds now lined them as if on the banks of a gauzy pond. Only rocky peaks broke through the small islands.

When Eugène reached the top, two hours and twenty minutes after passing through Eaux-Bonnes and starting his climb, a small group of journalists stood to the side of the path, waiting for him. Behind those on the right stood Pic de Ger, in front of the still rising sun.

The other cyclists were only minutes ahead of him, but he could not make them out on the winding path. He began his descent. Only a small supporting wall kept the road from washing away in a storm. The riders all trained their eyes to the ground in front of them, trying their best not to veer from the path's center or ride over a wayward rock that would throw them from their bikes.

He sped toward Argelès. Once in the town, he'd cut south toward col du Tourmalet, his next climb only thirty-six kilometers away. He took advantage of each new stretch of road. Even descents were ground that could be won and lost. He sliced toward the green forest. The pack had broken up on Aubisque's climb, but the route was narrow and traffic had not been cleared. Men and women who watched from the side of the road were joined by cattle and horses that roamed near the valley floor. Between the cyclists and the animals—who sometimes strayed onto the path—were blind turns around boulders and trees that humans had not been able to cut into. Descending cyclists were in danger of tumbling off an unprotected stretch of ground. If they did, all they could hope was that they would come to rest on a small ledge, utterly by chance. Those who took their descents with little consideration for their own safety, however, could sweep past more cautious cyclists at their own and others' peril. Eventually, the ground flattened out in front of Eugène.

The cyclists sped along the valley base that led into the last town before Tourmalet, Luz-Saint-Sauveur. The sun beat down on them. As they turned west out of the town, the destination stood in front of them, less specter than unmoving golem. The clouds were part of the landscape, no longer distant and inaccessible but as real and mutable as a patch of hail or a yellowed field of grass.

The cyclists' scattered procession rode along a gentle bank at Tourmalet's base. Luigi, first to sprint up Aubisque, led Eugène by thirteen minutes. Minutes separated each cyclist from another. At the back, Eugène found himself not far from Léon, Émile, and Jules Nempon, the B classification cyclist. At the distance that remained between them, he had no one to pace himself against nor anyone to push him along. The drafting, the collective effort of a pack didn't exist on those mountain roads. The flat stretches between climbs weren't long enough for a group to rejoin. Each cyclist had to compete against themselves and their own strategy; sprinting on these flat sections seemed pointless, but at least it would mean the tired cyclist would drop as little behind the others as possible while they rode along the mountain's gradient, if they could continue at all. All Eugène could do was decide on his speed and keep to it as best as he was able.

They continued their march, eventually reaching a small plateau that gave way to another lush mountain path. They were still not through with Tourmalet. The distance between them grew as the mountain exacted its toll. Only the young cyclists—Luigi and Honoré, in particular—seemed to have energy for the climbs. For them, a sprint up the mountain could make their leads decisive. The ground shifted between ten and sixteen degrees along the seventeen kilometers to the summit. Their limits, those months crouching, sitting still in shallow dugouts, wore on them.

All around, peaks looked down on the racers. Luigi climbed first until Honoré and Firmin struggled by him before the maximum. The Italian eventually passed the journalists at the summit sixteen minutes after Honoré and six minutes after Firmin. Eugène would do the same after another ten. The older cyclists tested the young ones but could not definitively push past them despite the strain of higher gears.

It's impossible to know what memories were jogged in Eugène's mind when he took one last hairpin turn and began his descent into the valley, heading toward Sainte-Marie-de-Campan. Perhaps the descent alone was enough to occupy him: the pitched ground in front of his tires whipping past as he tried to make up the distance between him and Jean. He knew other cyclists had a lower tolerance for risk on this terrain. They weren't willing to injure themselves or destroy their bikes, particularly in a year when those inconveniences troubled them even on the safest paths. His speed changed the sounds around him: drowning out most, heightening the pitch of others. At one point or another, however, he almost certainly recognized the same path he rode down in the 1913 Tour.

That year, along that same descent, he had been just a few hundred meters behind Philippe Thys, sprinting behind the Belgian. His general classification position was safe. He led Philippe by thirty minutes, but it wasn't in his nature to let Philippe keep his temporary lead so easily. There was still plenty of time for Eugène's fortunes to change. To relax then, when he was most confident, wasn't the behavior of a soon-to-be Tour winner. Eugène had been a favorite to win that year, and he was on track to do so. The thought carried him through one stage after another.

They had been flying down the mountainous descent, crouched low against the frames of their bikes, waiting for the path to bottom out. The promise of gaining seconds and meters drove them against their pedals. The cranks turned quick to overcome the wheels' speed. Eugène's absorbed the shocks from the dirt and rocks underneath as he violently glided into each turn.

He then felt his bike's frame crumble underneath him. He must have not seen a rock, a small dip in the road before he trampled over it. His wheel locked and his front fork sagged. He managed to stop his bike just before falling. Inspecting the frame, he saw the front fork had fractured in two. Philippe continued his descent, becoming smaller and then disappearing as Eugène considered his options. After a moment, he placed the ruined bike frame on his back and began to run down the mountain, but the soles of his cycling shoes slipped dangerously on the road's surface. Tears flooded his eyes; he considered whether he should simply give up—seventeen kilometers separated him from the next checkpoint, and the town may or may not have had the tools he needed to repair the bike. When a car full of fans passed by and offered their assistance, he briefly hopped onto the car's running board but then felt ashamed and resumed walking as the other racers passed, one after another.

As he neared Sainte-Marie-de-Campan, a young girl greeted him. She led him to a shop on the other side of the town. Eugène asked the blacksmith there whether he could use his tools to repair the bike. The man agreed, standing aside after Eugène's brief explanation that he couldn't receive any assistance from the shop owner. Then Eugène began, using those skills he had learned in Paris, those he would use time and again in 1914 and in the four years after, in far different conditions, to weld his fork back together. He shaped a new sleeve for the fork's top as the blacksmith and race officials watched his progress. Eugène still had to redrill holes in the fork to secure it to the bike: a two-person job. While Eugène held on to the fork, the blacksmith turned the drill. The official noted the assistance, adding another ten minutes to Eugène's time. Officials later reduced the penalty to three out of pity. He returned the fork to the bike's frame. Before leaving with his repaired bike, now sporting half as many bearings around its front fork as before, Eugène asked the blacksmith where he might buy some bread and butter. After having witnessed Eugène's effort in the shop, the local that the blacksmith directed him to refused to accept payment. Eugène knew if the official saw the transaction, he would add more time to his performance that day. The local insisted. It annoyed Eugène, but ultimately meant little. With Desgrange's time-based scoring that year, he knew he had already lost to Philippe.

◆ ◆ ◆

Six years later there was little stopping the same accident from happening on that downhill stretch. He could slow to watch the terrain more carefully, but Eugène hoped to extend his lead. Even that year, it didn't feel proper to slow on the stretch of road where he held his greatest advantage. He instead continued; his bike torqued against the ground and into turns. He let himself almost disappear with the speed of the descent. No, a slower descent wouldn't happen. He kept his pace, though all he could do was hold on to his ground.

Eugène neared Luchon around 4:15 p.m. He rode through the town's length, toward the thermal facilities that abutted the mountains on its western edge. An elegant white building with Doric columns and a two-story entrance housed the spa facilities. The stage ended in front of the spa's entryway. Management had opened its doors to the cyclists for their stay. Back behind Eugène on the street, in Café Central, the Tour administrators sat with their open logbook for the racers to sign.

Once he had inked his name, Eugène confirmed that he had held on to his first-place position. Just over thirty minutes separated him from Firmin in second. He still had to watch the Belgian and check his own performance at the end of each day. Every stage to Strasbourg featured similar terrain and equal opportunity for disastrous mistakes.

Each had descents capable of tearing a cyclist from his bike and rending his machine from its precise geometry.

In Luchon, the cyclists spent much of their time in bed, recovering from the first alpine stage. The casino and theater opened their doors to them, too, should any of them wish to take the businesses up on the offer. La Sportive's trainer took care of Honoré more than the others. The cyclist's thin leather shoes had given him blisters as he'd pushed his bike frame uphill over hours. When a *l'Auto* journalist visited him, Honoré asked him to put out a call for any photographers who had taken photos of him as he rode up Aubisque or Tourmalet. He hoped to have a souvenir of the occasion. He had finished his first Tour de France climbs and arrived in first, at some cost to his own body.

Desgrange received a letter after he arrived in Luchon. "Monseiur le Directeur," it began. "Each year the valiant cyclists have passed through my small town and I've never failed to give them a bit of assistance." The letter continued, "For four years the Tour didn't take place. Like all of us, I became a soldier and I regret it this year because I'll be deprived of applauding the kings of the road when they pass through my country.

"But I do want to do something for them. I would therefore be grateful if you would give the final cyclist to pass through Narbonne the modest sum of five francs, which I'm pleased to offer to the Tour. Please accept it from a petit poilu who would like to do more, but who can't right now."

The letter had a return address to Parc Aero no. 8, in the Marne, and was signed by Alphonse Rouvier. The letter spoke to Desgrange, though plenty of larger sums had been donated by groups along the way. He sent the letter to the newspaper's offices to be included in the following day's paper. Rouvier represented what Desgrange had hoped for when he first announced that year's Tour. The editor then knew there were people in the country who didn't view the race as froth, something that would just pass them by, but an event to be remembered.

◆ ◆ ◆

As the cyclists rested in Luchon, the temperatures started to warm and the rains left the area. The town was peaceful despite the tourists who arrived for the thermal baths and to watch the cyclists pass. The mountains dampened the movements of those who lived there; they cast shadows and a humility on the visitors. In his room, Eugène considered the ground left in front of him, and the nine chances that remained for him to fall from his position.

A French orphans delegation in Marseille gathers to welcome young Serbian refugees from the war in 1915.

8.

Firmin had arrived in Luchon behind Honoré after sixteen hours of cycling, thirty-three minutes ahead of Émile. With his time, he had caught and overtaken Émile, replacing the cyclist who had been sitting in second place. Only Eugène remained in front of him. If Firmin could hold his position, it would mean another five hundred francs at the end of the race in Paris; if he could somehow pass Eugène, it would be one thousand more. More than that, it would mean winning the race and the glory that arrived with it, even if the immediate celebration in the capital would be muted in comparison to what would have been had a Frenchman won their race. Firmin didn't even have a toehold yet, with just fifty seconds separating him from Émile now in third, a meaningless time given the hours they had ridden to get there, but as each stage passed, the cyclists considered what their place would mean for their future years.

If the cyclists still fought for their positions in the general classification, their strengths and the molds they occupied as characters in that year's Tour were clear to Desgrange. He began to refer to the cyclists in shorthand on *l'Auto*'s pages. What had once been speculation before the race began, when untested cyclists were evaluated on early results and predictions based on veterans' past performances, had been adjusted, upended, or confirmed over thousands of kilometers. Luigi, the young climber. Honoré, quicker than the rest of them, even if he didn't yet know what to do with that speed. Firmin, Jean, and Eugène were still the Tour's leaders, the race's veterans, who had not yet turned over the mantle even if they couldn't beat the best of the young cyclists when the roads were rough.

Desgrange argued with himself as to why the young cyclists sat so firmly behind the veterans, who were undoubtedly weathered from the race stages that had taken place. The editor always considered the Tour one long race, not the accumulation of fifteen shorter ones. When he shifted the Tour's scoring from points to overall times, it was in response to his vision for who the race winner should be, which had become clearer each year. He didn't think the shift would make the race any less athletic; in fact, it should push the cyclists harder, and those who couldn't keep up would fall behind. His Tour would be less tolerant of mistakes after the change, even those that were just a matter of bad luck. Any cyclist who finished poorly one day—due to accident or personal negligence—not only finished last in that stage, but also saw their overall time grow to a degree that couldn't be regained. In a race that used scores instead of times, a seventh-place cyclist who finished one minute behind the sixth was scored the same as if they had been one hour behind. That would no longer be the case. A cyclist who led the race but arrived two hours behind the others on one stage—not an unlikely spread when considering accidents that took place at least once per year—would have to make up those two hours, not just six points. Racers received similar benefits for an anomalous success on a stage, though such a success usually only came about through someone's misfortune. The cyclists who were most advantaged by the time-based scoring were those who were consistent: not necessarily those who placed first in individual stages but those who weathered the distances and the road conditions without significant failures. That consistency was enough to beat out others who performed remarkably in portions of the race but who lagged elsewhere, in both a confirmation and refutation of Desgrange's desires for the Tour. It rewarded a strategy of conservation, of knowing one's own strengths and weaknesses and those of one's opponents. The Tour was then definitively a race of endurance, or a test more than a race, in the eyes of those who distrusted Desgrange's shift.

The pages of *l'Auto* reflected the change in its race. Instead of a series of scores, readers of the paper now saw their preferred cyclists, the position they occupied in the general classification, as well as a list that delineated the cyclist's time on each stage: 16 33 24, 15 51 45, 18 54 7, 16 11 28. No longer did the numbers march evenly from first place to the lanterne rouge, the last-place cyclist. Instead, tens of minutes if not hours separated each competitor. The simplification extended the real and imagined distances between the competitors. With their cumulative times the only thing that mattered, the cyclists raced against their own abilities as much as they raced against the cyclist in front of them. Whether they spent their last bit of energy sprinting alongside the stage leader to pass through the finish line first that day, or whether they held that energy for another time, the general classification standings would be more or less the same—seconds rarely mattered. The only motivation that drove them forward in those small moments was the glory that came from winning an individual stage, and the money that arrived with it. Neither were insignificant, but they were a distraction from where they would wind up in the general classification.

The veteran cyclists and their conduct reflected a familiarity with this way of racing. Desgrange still held doubts, however, that the veterans would be able to keep up with the younger cyclists who had joined the race for the first time, as the alpine stages continued then gave way to the northeastern landscape. Cracks in his predictions, however, were already clear.

The younger cyclists had been called up for training with the first groups of able-bodied men before they were sent to the front. Honoré had served in infantry units throughout the war, traveling back and forth on foot from the trenches to towns behind the front to rest with the other soldiers of the Sixth Dragoon Regiment. Luigi had been subject to Italian conscription at the end of 1911, when he turned eighteen. He left the service after his term was through but was brought back into uniform once his country issued a general mobilization order in 1915; he'd managed to continue cycling in Italy, at least. Léon had been a wartime mechanic, like Eugène, while his older friend, Firmin, avoided the front entirely.

The cost of Honoré, Luigi, and Alfred Steux's push on the alpine stage became clear as they rested in Luchon on July 10th. They couldn't recover entirely before the next stage began. It was true for all the cyclists, but particularly the young trio who had exerted themselves beyond the others on those first climbs. They had decided to hold fast with their bikes' higher gears, and the decision would follow them as they set off for Perpignan the following day. The trio had recognized their advantage on the course—the bursts of speed they could muster on the uphill climbs when Eugène, Firmin, and Jean lagged behind. In one way, they acted in accordance with Desgrange's desires: for cyclists to expend their energy when it was most advantageous. In another way, they had not thought any further than the stage they were riding on; he hadn't considered what the next stage, and the one following that, would bring.

"Here we are, after one million three hundred and sixty-five thousand deaths," Desgrange wrote in the July 11th edition of *l'Auto*. It was as if he believed that year's Tour winner would be crowned on a kingdom of dust; the only one whose bike teetered back to Parc des Princes. As if winning had become only a matter of surviving after the others had fallen.

◆ ◆ ◆

The racers left for Perpignan on the morning of July 11th and raced until evening. Jean arrived at the finish after thirteen hours and twelve minutes. Eugène came in just one length behind him, with Firmin trailing the first-place cyclist by another length. Despite the climbs along the stage, the three veterans remained close to one another throughout. They passed by the younger cyclists as their performance cooled following the first alpine stage. As the veterans neared the finish line along allée des Platanes, the crowd cheered, and they sprinted in response. The band of the Sixty-third Infantry Division played as they passed along the promenade. Sweat streamed down their faces, and they grunted with exertion. The attention granted them an energy that had been absent in the uninhabited climbs. Each man convinced himself of the essential nature of the remaining one hundred meters. He pushed past whatever signals his brain sent. He passed the finish line in a rush and coasted for a moment, spent, as the crowd surrounded him.

Jean and Firmin were again unable to unseat Eugène from his first-place position. He maintained twenty-eight minutes between himself and Firmin in second, while Jean remained nineteen minutes behind the Belgian with Émile now in fourth.

After another day's rest, they headed to Marseille, the port of the empire. The flat 370 kilometers to the fortified city was a respite from the two alpine stages on either side. The cyclists left the mountains and turned back toward the sea. Before they reached the light-blue Mediterranean waters along Marseille's beaches, they turned left toward parc Borély. Long rows of trees and grass marked the way to a château. It was a Sunday, and crowds, unable to be maintained by the police, flocked around the racers as they rode down the avenue toward the park. Troupes coloniales supported the police. In other years they would have been abroad in one of France's African or Asian colonies, but some of the men from the colonies had returned to France so that they might fight in the war. Colonial subjects fought alongside French soldiers for the country who claimed dominion over them.

Five other cyclists rode behind Jean, each competing for whatever ground they could find. Luigi, Léon, Firmin, Eugène, and Paul arrived one after another, seconds separating them. For his effort, Jean won Desgrange's praise as "The Sprinter," in the following morning's *l'Auto*. Despite the flat route between Perpignan and Marseille, the Tour continued to shed competitors. Aloïs Verstraeten, a Belgian B classification cyclist who had been in last place, had been found holding on to the back of a motorcycle on the road between two towns. He was disqualified from the race by the end of the day. Jules Nempon was the only remaining amateur who hoped to finish that year's Tour. Another cyclist had been fined thirty minutes for not paying for his food at an Arles café, which bumped him into last place in the general classification. Émile, whom Desgrange had once predicted would be in contention for the general classification prize, abandoned after entering Marseille. His knees had begun to trouble him on the alpine climbs, and with more coming up, he saw no way forward.

Whatever respite the cyclists hoped to be granted in Marseille was quickly shaken. The city's population had grown in the war, with those who'd left their hometowns from the north and those who'd entered the country from another—by choice or by necessity. The city had not been able to build housing to keep up with their numbers. Few hotels had vacancies, and those that did were closer to flop houses than any accommodations the cyclists would have found in other years. The cyclists shared rooms; Eugène and Honoré bunked together. Privacy was slim, and they found little rest in the beds their managers secured for them, but any bed was better than nothing. A few made a point of complaining to Desgrange about the bed bugs they found in their rooms, but there was little for the editor to do except sympathize with their complaints.

Outside their rooms, la fête nationale erupted. The soldiers who had watched over the finish line paraded down the Marseille streets, celebrating the storming of the Bastille 130 years earlier. Along the esplanade, locals lit off fireworks. In Paris, victorious generals joined the troops who marched beneath the Arc de Triomphe, Foch, Joffree, and

Pétain riding on their horses through the Parisian streets. A thousand French soldiers, mutilated by the war, marched in front.

◆ ◆ ◆

The cyclists headed south, past parc Borély and into the city's suburbs on the morning of July 15th. The homes were smaller there, made from large, scarcely shaped stones that blended into the cliffs behind them. The pack made their way into the nearby hills. It was still dark in the early morning, but they could make out the gentle slope of col de la Gineste overlooking Marseille. Behind them, they could see the expanse of the city. The Mediterranean Sea stirred underneath a nearly full moon. Desgrange had earlier described the ninth stage as the most beautiful they would encounter, and for once, his editorial did not need or want to overpromise. The pack rode along. To their right, just beyond their sight, steep cliffs led into the hidden coves of the calanques. The azure water at the cliffs' base was bone black that night, flecked with growing and decaying white shapes in the moonlight. The road dropped the cyclists into a small town along a rocky cove before they continued along the coast.

The first group—Eugène, Jean, Firmin, Luigi, Honoré, and five others—arrived at Hyères after five hours and forty minutes. Ten of the twelve remaining cyclists rode alongside one another through the town and its thousands of palms—vegetation that had been introduced in the middle of the last century. The morning sun was beginning to warm the roads underneath their tires, the heat reflecting up onto their bent-over bodies. Only Jacques Coomans, whose bike had failed between Saint-Cyr-sur-Mer and Bandol, trailed behind the other A classification cyclists.

Outside Fréjus, 173 kilometers into the stage, the wind picked up and buffeted the back of the cyclists' jerseys. The warm breeze felt pleasant as they rode along the unprotected coastal cliffs. Before it had reached them, the mistral had blown through the Rhône Valley to the north where it accelerated. After brushing past them, it would reach out over the waters of the Mediterranean. Off the racers' right shoulders, white peaks dipped in and out of existence, as if drowning in the sea. The wind shaped the land around them: trees took on the bent frames of old men, houses were built with low outside walls to protect the fragile fires within. Over thousands of years the constant wind had claimed mastery of the region.

After passing through Cannes and Antibes, the cyclists raced toward Nice. The route took them through the coastal city. Along promenade des Anglais, a crowd greeted them, but the cyclists raced past without acknowledgment, keeping a quick and constant pace. On the edge of the town, they began a loop that would take them away from the coast and into the two climbs of the stage. They veered toward col de Braus, the first climb, more gradual than what they had encountered in the Pyrenees. Stone houses lined the road almost up to its summit, where the structures finally dropped away and the length of the valley became clear. The pack had thinned from the earlier, flatter portions of the stage. The riders were visible to one another on the straight sections of roads, but persistent tire punctures had stretched their procession out hundreds of meters.

Back toward the water, the coast was not quite visible through a scraggle of trees occupying the hills. There were high peaks on either side of the path, covered in green. The road was made from compacted dirt. In more occupied sections, where it gave way to cobbled stones, their ride felt as though a hammer was striking up through them, reverberating in every bone of their bodies. If the untended sections of the road didn't destroy the bikes, the tended sections just might.

In time, the green valley led to the town of Menton. Luigi raced alongside Honoré in front of the others. The French cyclist had just managed to pass by the Italian, less winded from his climbs. They turned back toward Nice after passing through Menton and again rode along the water. They biked through more stone towns built on the side of winding hills. Children poked their heads out from wooden doors, and old women lined the street. Young men raced alongside them—some on bikes, others on foot—for those final kilometers.

Horns sounded as the cyclists entered Nice again after thirteen hours and thirty-seven minutes of racing. As he and Honoré neared the finish line, Luigi saw the usual crop of journalists tracking their times. Interspersed among them was a crowd who cheered for the Italian more than any of the others, even though he still trailed Honoré. His supporters were almost indistinguishable except for the flags they waved, green, white, and red. He rode through the finish line in front of the ice cream store, café Riviera Palace. The Italian contingent rushed up and offered a bouquet. They patted him on the back and gave him their congratulations, expressing how proud they were of his accomplishment. They didn't seem to care that he hadn't won the stage. They'd traveled to the finish from their hometown, Monaco, northeast of the racers. The cyclists had passed by the town when they had looped back to Nice from the climb. The Treaty of Versailles had put the city-state under the protection of France in exchange for Monaco sharing the political priorities of the country. It had retained its independent government, led by the Prince of Monaco, Albert I, just as it had kept its history and the culture running throughout the town since its days as a part of the Republic of Genoa.

Luigi was the last Italian cyclist remaining in the Tour. None had won the general classification in the race's history. It was his first international competition and, though funding for an Italian team had dropped in the weeks before the race's start, Luigi still made the trip to Paris to represent the rest of them.

The city of Nice turned out to celebrate the riders. The question of Nice's allegiance—to France or to Italy—had not yet been resolved, but it had at least been temporarily stalled with the war. The town was annexed fifty-nine years before; generations of residents had lived through its last changing of hands. Of the 140,000 Niçois who lived in the city, 3,655 had been killed in the war, fighting on behalf of the Allies. About one-quarter of those who died were Italians who had immigrated to France.

Nice's proximity to the Mediterranean meant goods and people had continued to flow as the war closed other port towns. Nice was far from the front but close enough that companies could make the journey north from the port, if needed. It didn't have the mass forma-tion of troops, hospitals, and industrial factories like some cities along France's western border, but that didn't mean it had been untouched by the war, either. Serbians who left their country fled to French colonies and to Nice. The Saint Sava Blessing Serbian Children's Orphanage had been set up in town to care for the refugees. The local economy, whose tourism industry had grown in the years prior, had dipped and unemployment increased. With the announcement of armistice, there was cautious optimism that the town's routines might return to normal, but it was still unclear how long that recovery might take.

Eugène arrived thirty minutes after Honoré. He again held on to his general classification position. By the time he rode into the city, the crowd around the finish line had spread out as some of the people left to watch the racers sign the logbook while others, no longer under the watchful eyes of the police officers, crowded the area just beyond the finish line. As Eugène crossed it, a police officer stepped back from his place tending to the crowd and crashed into the cyclist. It was enough to knock Eugène from his bike and the officer onto the ground. Eugène lay on the cobbled path for a moment, shocked by the accident. He lifted himself. Blood trickled down his leg. When he placed weight on the leg to get up, he felt a pang up through it. It didn't hurt so much that he needed assistance to walk, but that night, he made sure La Sportive's trainer came by to check on him and ensure he could keep racing in the following stages.

Most of the racers left their rooms that night to have dinner at a res-taurant across the avenue from their hotel. They had traded their racing jerseys for dressing gowns that the hotel provided. When Desgrange spotted them from down the street, he almost mistook them for a procession of ghosts. Even without the flowing gowns, some of them might as well have been transient spirits after the nine stages they had just barely completed.

Later that evening, when Desmarets, a *l'Auto* correspondent, checked in on the cyclists, he found Luigi sharing a bottle of champagne with a few members of the Italian crowd; Félix, a French cyclist from Rinxent, enjoyed a glass full of cognac alone. The alcohol at the end of the stage had become a constant presence since the strict Pélissiers left. It provided some relief, a way for them to get by between the stages, to escape from the festivities that surrounded them, to celebrate the race, to deaden their limbs and bring on a deep sleep after hours of cycling. Even with their aches, the cyclists found it difficult to sleep, to drive away the phantom motions of their limbs after days of cycling.

The land in front of them would take them away from the coast and up the country's eastern border. The climbs would continue for another few stages, past Geneva, toward Strasbourg. After that, they would approach the western front. What they would find there was a mystery to some degree. The land's newness meant that shifts to its structure were quickly growing and decaying. Not much had taken root, and even the cyclists who had experienced it during Paris–Roubaix, the Circuit cycliste des Champs de Bataille, or the war itself didn't know how much each town had rearranged itself in the months since they last saw it.

Eugène's fall wore on his hip that night, enough for him to visit a medic again the next day. Honoré's toenails had become ingrown from his tight leather shoes. An injury not dissimilar to those wartime ones that plagued all infantrymen: feet stuck in damp boots, undried for days while they waited at the bottom of trenches, pests feasting on them in the dark, dirty ground. Félix had been suffering from hemorrhoids, the reason for his lonely cognac glass. Unlike the others' injuries, the pain was too much for him to bear. That night, he notified Desgrange and the eleven others that the stage to Nice would be his last.

Marguerite Alibert

July 16, 1919—avenue Henri-Martin, Paris

Marguerite Alibert had seen the parts of France that the Tour cyclists rode through the day before, and Italy just on the other side of the border. She preferred Italy to Nice. In summers, she would sooner visit Lake Como than the south of her own country, like so many others did. When she couldn't make the trip, however, Brittany would do, particularly the past few years when travel had been difficult, less accommodating to a woman traveling alone. She didn't care much for a strict sense of national identity, or the requisite politics that came with it—she cared more for culture and held an interest in those outside her own borders. She only turned to politics when it was a matter of joining a dinner party conversation, or when it interacted with her own place in society, a standing she cared about deeply. She understood for all her personal disinterest, the letters and time she had spent alone with one of Europe's postwar leaders could shape what came in the years ahead.

Not that she had much need for Prince Edward as of late. From her honeymoon view last month, looking out at Venetian palaces across from her window—those ones merchant families had built hundreds of years ago with views of Venice's Grand Canal—she saw something for her future the prince was unlikely to provide. Her husband, Charles Laurent, had leased an entire home for the month-long celebration after their wedding ceremony in May. They were living like princes, so what need was there for one? Still, she couldn't imagine what it would have been like to come from a family like those of the merchants. They had histories that couldn't be bought or created whole cloth—the Barbaros, say, who could bring out a map of their family's roots and point to generals, admirals, diplomats, and governors whose names still meant something even though the family's money was long gone.

Marguerite's job in Paris had allowed her entrance to a life otherwise impossible for her to achieve, even if society was only willing to look at the job obliquely. Her father, Firmin, a taxi driver, and her mother, Marie Aurand, a cleaning lady, were never able to provide the wealth and status that she had achieved on her own.

Marguerite's hazel eyes and long auburn hair stood out to men when they arrived at the maison de rendezvous where she'd worked as a courtesan—first Madame Denart's and then Madame Sonia de Théval's, on 20 rue Bizet, whose wrought-iron balustrades looked down onto the sixteenth arrondissement's streets. Its exterior might as well have housed a private bank or a society club. The men who frequented the maison reflected its outer appearance. They came from noble families or those that had come upon newer industrial fortunes. Once the war began, men from England who owned large parcels of land back home, who took part in wartime strategy and political bargaining, began to enter the lobby doors, too. They paid her for the sex, yes, but also the experiences she shared with them—the pressed duck at la Tour d'Argent, the glowing ballrooms and the smoky parlors where she led them gracefully through the crowds. She might as well have been showing them her own stratum, that of the other partygoers in the room, for all the time she spent around Paris's cultural and political elite, but she was as distant from them as her parents were, even with those fleeting invitations.

She had only been able to gather the outward symbols of status— her apartment on avenue Henri-Martin in the sixteenth, with servants and a stable that could house ten horses. She had been able to secure two hundred thousand francs from a settlement with her first long-term relation, Andre Meller, who had also given her the name she'd gone by in recent years, Maggie Meller. It took her some years to come upon that most difficult symbol, a history or a family who would naturally attend such events, be in the permanent company of politicians and artists and thinkers. After her recent marriage, Charles had started to pay rent on the apartment and its upkeep, in addition to giving her an annual allowance of thirty-six thousand francs. Her marriage, more formal than her relationship with Andre, gave her that legitimacy she could not otherwise obtain. She could walk more or less freely through society circles as the wife of an upstanding Frenchman, who had not only served admirably in the war but also came from a well-to-do family. She had already cultivated the connections, a few knew her name, but she could finally participate fully in the society she had always wanted for herself. What Charles offered was better than the prince did—there was no crown to attend to above her personal needs, after all.

It was for the best that Prince Edward had broken it off. The letters he had once sent to her were safely stored away. When her marriage with Charles ran its course—a divorce, she imagined, or a drawn-out separation for one reason or another—she could at least turn back to the prince's letters.

It was not that Edward's gifts hadn't been nice—the bottle of Coty Chypre perfume, the turquoise bracelet. But the lack of money hadn't been. "The Prince of Wales never pays," she had been told. The experience of being with him had been her enticement: she would be seen with him, she would receive his letters, addressed to "Mon Bébé."

Marguerite could use those letters to receive the money she needed to continue moving on in the world once Charles was gone.

There had been nothing personal about the note she'd sent to the prince in November 1918, reminding him of his letters' existence. He never should have been so careless. He knew he'd never marry her. His family wouldn't have allowed it, even if he'd wanted to, which seemed equally unlikely. He shouldn't have taken advantage of his relationship with her to bemoan the war as a hopeless endeavor. Nor should he have insulted his father, the king. He may have had a private courier, but she had no such privileges. She enjoyed reading them; it fascinated her to hear from someone like him, closer to the battle and with a stake in its outcome, but he shouldn't have trusted her with them.

With her marriage, however, Marguerite could give her twelve-year-old daughter, Raymonde, a sense of legitimacy so that she wouldn't have to live the same life Marguerite had. She would never know her real father. He was a man Marguerite had had an affair with while she worked in the home of the Langois family. The Langoises became embroiled in a financial scandal in 1902 but had survived it. They lived in a mansion on 65 avenue de la Grande Armee. At times Marguerite told people that Raymonde's father was a twenty-eight-year-old whom she had grown up with and become engaged to, but whose family hadn't accepted her insufficient dowry. At other times, she said it was the son of an English colonial administrator who needed his father's approval to marry, which he didn't receive. In any case, once it became clear she was pregnant, she was cast out from the household. If Marguerite and Charles could provide Raymonde with enough support, at least for a time, she wouldn't ever have to consider working at a place like 3 rue Galilee. If Raymonde could bypass that hardship, if Marguerite could ensure that she'd skip those years entirely and grow up with the respectability that Marguerite had achieved, that was all her mother could ask.

◆ ◆ ◆

Marguerite had been hired by a few members of the prince's crowd before she met him in the ballroom restaurant of hôtel de Crillon, along place de la Concorde on April 23, 1917. The prince had been on leave from his post at the British army's XIV Corps headquarters to the east. Francis de Breteuil, the son of Marquis Henri de Breteuil and a friend of the prince's grandfather, had made the introduction. From the restaurant, the trio could look out onto the northwest corner of the plaza, where the statues representing Brest and Rouen stood, the latter the site of the beheading of Louis XVI, a distant relative of the prince. They'd spoken French; Prince Edward had learned it from his earlier years in the country, and Marguerite spoke none of his English. Their conversation had continued later into the day, into the afternoon and evening.

She couldn't show him what Paris had been like in the years before the war, before the city had shut down early. She couldn't take him to Abbaye de Thélème, in Montmartre, where they could have danced until three or four in the morning and then found their way back to her apartment or to his hotel room just before the sun began to rise up over the city. Paris had still been lively enough despite its trials. Recent coal and grain shortages meant that bakeries sold limited offerings. Restricted hours on clubs and cabarets necessitated that those seeking nighttime entertainment leave the city for its outskirts, for locations that were less likely to be targets of German zeppelins and artillery guns. The distractions had instead moved to palatial mansions or run-down farmhouses, popping up and shuttering depending on the night. Paris couldn't be subdued entirely.

Then, after only a few days, the prince had been off again, back to the war that first brought him there. For his upbringing and station, the prince spoke and wrote as if he wanted nothing more than to be a common soldier, or at least an officer along the front, a posting that he'd been denied by the secretary of state, Lord Kitchener, and his family. Germans would almost certainly have tried to capture him if they knew he had been out there with only his men protecting him. Instead his war had been dull and disappointing: he spent it holed up in old châteaus like a royal hostage to prevent that same thing happening to him. He had served his country as a staff officer to Major General Lord Cavan. He'd neared the front when he could, but for the most part he'd stayed away from any work resembling fighting.

He'd taken up writing to Marguerite in the times between visiting the front. His letters arrived via royal courier; no one else would see what he had written. She'd responded, but without access to the same channels he had, she'd sent them by regular post. He became restless, even more than before, less tolerant of the war and those who had been leading it. He took up running great distances by himself to relieve the anxious energy that grew the longer he was away from her and the front.

She'd spent that summer in Deauville, just south of Le Havre. When he visited her there, the war seemed distant apart from the few almost invisible military hospitals that had been set up in converted hotels. He visited the hospitals often, more than anyone had expected of him, though he never took her with him. Stories claimed he'd once kissed the face of a soldier who needed facial reconstruction surgery; no one had seen a king, or a king to be, do that before, not that older wars had left men like that alive. He left his mother in Rouen while she'd been visiting and drove ninety kilometers to the coast in his Rolls-Royce coupe to visit Marguerite and spend the night with her, getting back early the next morning for his royal duties.

Marguerite's job hadn't changed with the war. The doting prince wasn't enough for her to leave her position, nor did he expect it of her. When the prince was not in Paris, she continued working under the eye of Sonia de Théval, greeting the men who asked for her by name in the saloons. The men liked her wit and the artlessness with which she greeted everyday matters. They saw little of the tempestuousness that ran underneath; she cared about her work and didn't allow her feelings to threaten it.

With her recent marriage, all that she wanted was hers, everything she wanted for herself and Raymonde. In October, one month before the end of the war, Edward ended their relationship. Since February of that year he had been seeing Winifred Dudley Ward, a married British woman he met at a London party. She wasn't a viable candidate for marriage, but at least she came from a status closer to his own, and without the stain of Marguerite's work as a courtesan. When air raid sirens had sounded, Winifred, or Fredie, as he called her, had been forced to take refuge in the party host's home. There, she'd met the prince. The charm of Paris and Marguerite melted away for him quickly after that, though he continued to see her in the months leading up to sending the October letter that broke things off. He had mentioned off-handedly to Fredie there was someone in Paris, someone he now only referred to as "IT" in his letters to close friends, but that was all that he let on.

Their correspondence cooled for a bit after the letter she sent him in November, reminding him of those she had kept. In August 1918, while convalescing from an oophorectomy in a nursing home, she'd met Charles Laurent. Charles had been recovering after a stint fighting the Bolsheviks in Russia. His father was a director of the Société du Louvre, which owned the department store the Grand Magasins du Louvre and hôtel de Crillon, where she first met Edward. Charles quickly fell for her. Marguerite stashed the letters from Edward away: they would only threaten her budding relationship, which was moving quickly. Less than a year later, they had married.

It mattered little that Charles was too serious for her. He was different from the men she had spent time with before—which was at least refreshing, if not sufficient for long-term love. Marguerite took what she could from him: the society connections and money that would establish her and Raymonde further. Then, she'd leave him. She might craft a story for why the marriage failed, a reason why she had to move on, for those who would ask. Hopefully it would be enough of an explanation. Then she could return to those letters the prince had sent, which she held on to like a deed for her and Raymonde's future. She could reach him. She knew he'd read her letters, no matter from where she sent them: Deauville, her honeymoon home in Italy, from Paris, or whatever unnamed stretch of ground she could find along the French border.

Mont Blanc.

9.

Eleven men left Nice on July 17th. Until the moment they exited the city at 2:00 a.m., Desgrange hadn't been convinced even those few would continue. For every cyclist who remained, more than four had left. La Sportive's trainer could only do so much for Honoré's toenails before the cyclist had to race again; he could only give the young cyclist treatment to reduce the pain, so that he might ride for another stretch before it again became too much to bear. At the end of each stage, his feet were raw. The trainer could help the cyclist soak them, give him drugs, and rub ointment on them in the hours before another stage, but he couldn't fully treat him until he was off his bike for longer than a single day. Each time Honoré pushed himself, on a climb or on a sprint, he realized he did so at the cost of pain and immobilization at the day's end. On July 16th, while the locals fêted the cyclists, serving them a traditional Niçoise lunch and placing a gold medal around Honoré's neck, the cyclist considered whether he shouldn't just leave the race now, when he was as triumphant as he would be in that year's race. Three hours separated him from third and its associated prize; he had already won two stages, perhaps it would be best for him to leave before any permanent damage was done. The thought had retreated by the morning of the seventeenth, however, and he lined up alongside the others outside Riviera-Glacier, on the edge of the city's wide public square.

They followed the roads away from the southern coast, from the idyllic route Desgrange had described, for the country's eastern border. They had reached another corner of France, turned onto one more side of the French hexagon, the rightful and natural shape of the country according to *Encyclopédie du dix-neuvième siècle*. France was situated an equal distance between the equator and the North Pole, between both the Atlantic and the Mediterranean. Three borders of the country were formed by water, three by land. Just as the tripartite motto of the Third Republic, "Liberté, égalité, fraternité," wrote its author. It was now as it should be.

The lands they would soon pass through were those won in the war even if the country's political leaders had considered them part of France long before that.

French claims on the Alsace-Lorraine had traditionally been slightly stronger than Germany's, but they were still only claims. After taking the territories at the end of the Franco-Prussian War, Germany had placed the inhabitants of the Alsace-Lorraine under direct imperial control. The Alsatians didn't receive the same freedoms the typical German citizen did. The citizens resented imperial rule and the lack of representation it offered. The French Alsatians who remained in the territory and German Alsatians were pushed closer under the conditions of a shared struggle, exacerbated when local political leaders were forced into exile at the war's outset for fear of German reprisal. If the French won the war and took the territory back, at least the citizens would have more freedoms than what they had found as part of the German Empire. Many men and women instead hoped for a bolder solution— for the region to be independent, free from either country. The question had again been decided for them when the Treaty of Versailles was signed and the Alsace-Lorraine was returned to France.

The cyclists traveled north and neared the edge of the Alps. The remaining stages would have them ride through the border with Switzerland and into the neutral territory before they reentered France, tracing a path along the country's new border with Germany, beating its bounds. On July 23rd, the fresh division would give way to the country's firmer border with Belgium. On July 25th, two days after that, they would reach the English Channel again.

They climbed Colle Saint-Michel first, just over 1,500 meters, though fortunately for Honoré and the others, the path was only one-half the grade of the earlier mountain climbs. They raced through Barcelonnette, a forested town lofted 1,100 meters above the sea and 170 kilometers from their start. The land didn't feel so different from the Pyrenean ground that had once been underneath them. It was colder now, however, and though no trees existed at the peaks of the Alps, a lushness still ran through the surrounding earth. Snow instead of rubble coated the mountain peaks, and the cyclists found themselves along steep cliffs and the deep green of spruce and pines.

Outside Lauzet-Ubaye, around 180 kilometers into the stage, the landscape dominated their path. To the journalists who watched the cyclists from the Brasier, it was difficult to focus on the race. The scenes dwarfed the competitors. They saw the waters of the Durance cut through the land. The journalists could see Eugène ride alongside Firmin. On their right, the valley swung low behind them. They were two minutes behind Jean, himself behind Honoré, the young cyclist setting pace for the veterans despite his injuries.

The road continued to wind downward, canopied by networks of mountain ash trees. To those who rode below them, their fernlike stalks appeared almost yellow, filtering the midday sun. The tree cover broke at the edge of the Ubaye River. Bushes leaned over the river's edge where rocks were ready to tumble into its blue-green water. A curve in the river revealed a towering mountain, Le Mourre Froid, on its opposite side, some way off in the distance. Behind and around it, the lesser peaks extended to the north and west for thousands of miles and across eight countries, splitting them like a saw blade.

The Alps hadn't seen war like other stretches of the French border. Italy hadn't joined the other members of the prewar Triple Alliance—Germany and Austria-Hungary—in forming the Central powers at the war's outbreak. Their interest had been purely defensive. Their two allies had compromised Italy's security by acting as aggressors. In response, Italy remained unaligned and consulted with diplomats from both sides for a year after the war began. Each promised Italy territory—the Central powers offered land if the country stayed neutral; the Allied powers offered them the same, though they told Italy they would receive land from Austria-Hungary if the country joined their fight. On May 3, 1915, the Triple Alliance had fractured. On the twenty-third of the month, Italy declared war against Austria-Hungary.

At altitudes higher than Mourre Froid and at temperatures as low as minus twenty-two degrees Fahrenheit, Austro-Hungarian and Italian soldiers dug trenches down into the frozen ground, whose icy crust hadn't been broken through for as long as anyone could remember. Soldiers from both sides died in the snow, on machine-flattened peaks and along roads made of ice. When they did, they often just lay there like so many other stretches of the front, eventually coated by a dusting of snow—an immaterial shroud—until it became impossible for others to find them and carry their bodies to a proper resting place. The armies continued fighting in the Alps until the end of the war. Though the battles started there one year after the war began and the ground they'd fought on was small in area, five hundred thousand Italians died on the peaks in 1916 alone, a number that failed to include the civilians who were displaced by fighting, who died in refugee camps from malnutrition and illness. The men who were killed in the battles on the Alps became part of those peaks as they re-formed, in time.

◆ ◆ ◆

Jean had been born to the north of where they rode, in Roubaix, even if he thought of himself as Parisian more than anything else. By the time his brother, Henri, was born two years after Jean, his family had moved to Paris. He took advantage of the independence the city and his family allowed him, the freedom to walk down the streets of his neighborhood and farther afield in the city. He took in the sights of the Belle Époque, the theaters and the showy mansions described by so many writers of the time who spoke of Parisian high and low society. The city had a name for young boys like him: titi Parisien. Quick, troublemakers, able to dart off around the corner of a seemingly dead-end street only to disappear by the time the police officers chasing them had arrived.

Jean's boyish looks had held fast despite the fact he was no longer one of the young cyclists and lagged behind Honoré and Luigi on the mountain climbs. He could at least hold his own on the flat sprints. His dark, middle-parted hair was streaked with sweat that day. It still looked as if his mother had combed it before he set off. He had a heavy brow and attentive eyes, his nose cockeyed from an earlier break, with two deep wrinkles on either side of his mouth, signs of age his other features hid. Despite those two creases, his face was not rough like most of the others but was instead round and clean-shaven.

Jean's brother, Henri, had died in a plane crash on July 19, 1916, just north of the cyclists' path on July 9th, between Bayonne and Luchon. He had been attending an aviation school in Pau, where he was receiving flight training along with his unit, the First Aviation Group. Planes were by then a reliable part of both sides' war effort. Single- and two-seated planes were sent back and forth on bombing and reconnaissance flights over European cities and trench networks. After surveying troops, pilots returned to their side and dropped messages via streamers, small packages that ensured the intelligence could be used by friendly soldiers before it became useless. Eventually, photographs and radios allowed for short, more complex and timely messages to be transmitted. The planes themselves were still a recent technology. The Nieuport and SPAD planes flew at altitudes that were within bullets' arcs. Pilots still needed luck to arrive back to their base safely, or, short of that, a measure of skill to crash land without injury. The military pushed airmen through classes to ensure that a steady supply of planes remained flying. The insufficient training only added to those strains. Mortality rates among flyers grew as the war progressed.

Jean and Henri both became professional cyclists in 1909. Jean, however, showed an aptitude for the sport that Henri didn't. In the first Tour they rode together, Jean took third in the general classification, winning the eighth and the fourteenth legs, while Henri came in thirtieth overall. Subsequent races reinforced the pattern: in the 1913 Tour, Henri received the lanterne rouge, the dubious prize for the last-place finisher. Jean was sponsored by well-regarded Alcyon-Dunlop while Henri rode under the smaller Femina Cycles' banner. But Henri had been gone for three years by the time the 1919 Tour took place; Jean rode in the race alone.

◆ ◆ ◆

Past the town of Gap, the cyclists rode up col Bayard, a smaller mountain pass with an elevation gain of roughly five hundred meters. The pass connects Gap with La Mure. The road was still well traveled and had been kept in relatively good condition compared to the Pyrenean roads the cyclists had traversed. The leaders held their positions through the morning, Firmin and Eugène riding just next to one another, both strained yet too far from the finish to speed up and challenge each other. Eugène's skill on climbs and descents slowly reaped its rewards over the gradient. Firmin had fallen slightly behind him by the time Eugène reached the Bayard's summit.

Just past Chauffayer, Eugène cut from the main road, a detour mentioned by Desgrange in the itinerary that had circulated earlier in the week. The Drac River had recently overflowed, flooding the mountain road Eugène had just departed. It had formed shallow rapids across the ground. Stones and gravel littered the cyclists' usual path. Riding or walking across the road would be difficult, or at least unpleasant, the cold mountain water soaking their shoes, the tumbling rocks potentially damaging their wheels. Eugène instead took—as instructed—a wartime communication path, with blind turns and an unpaved surface. As Eugène's bike lurched over the path, the cyclist absorbed the shocks of the ground. He followed the detour for a few kilometers until it met the main road again, where he could safely descend the nearby slope, running parallel with the river as it flowed away from Grenoble.

Eugène was close to the finish, he knew, just another thirty-five kilometers or so remained. He wasn't in first; he'd miss the twenty francs the local bank had put up as a prize. He'd not won much yet at all, in fact, only seven hundred francs, less than the third-place prize at the end, while others who had won more stages outright, like Jean, had gathered up nineteen hundred francs. As they rode past locals on the street, the people continued to hand the cyclists sums of money, holding out their hands as if in offering to a passing clergyman. Some gave the money to the first cyclist to ride through their town while others supported their favorite, no matter when he arrived. Desgrange had encouraged them to send their money to the paper's offices. He said he'd distribute it to the cyclists once they arrived back in Paris, but many didn't listen or didn't care: they wanted to meet the cyclists, for their heroes to know which face had given them the money, that they were supporting them no matter when they arrived. The money was a nice boost to the La Sportive salaries. In other years, when there was competition between teams, cyclists had more leverage over managers to negotiate their salaries—the bonuses they would receive for races, the amount they would receive monthly—but with few alternatives to La

Sportive, their salaries were under a tight grip. No one knew how long they would have to rely on the conglomerate—months or perhaps years.

Eugène and Firmin's old sponsor, Peugeot, was part of the collective, as was Jean's, Alcyon. In the war, Alcyon had produced military motorcycles. The town where the Alcyon factory had been, Courbevoie, was also where the headquarters of Eugène's 119th Infantry Regiment, his first unit, had been. Eugène knew firsthand the site had been the target of regular bombing runs; it was going to take time for the company and their employees to rebuild what they had lost, much less a cycling team.

Eugène and Firmin reached the outskirts of Grenoble. Eugène's injury from his Nice finish had worn on him, and with the relatively flat ground that unfolded ahead, Firmin pushed himself harder, catching up with Eugène and beginning to overtake him. They passed the Château de Vizille. A bell tower sat atop the imposing black-tiled mansion; it marked his time: just after 3:21 in the afternoon.

Vizille, a vestigial limb on the edge of Grenoble, was itself barely recognizable from the last time the Tour had passed through in 1914. The nearby Drac gave the town an abundance of free energy, and the town used it to grow its heavy industry, even before the war began. Once the war started, however, the city's location and its structural investments made it even more appealing to those who hoped to profit by manufacturing materials needed on the front. The war required some of the city's power, as well as artillery shells and the explosives that formed the core of those shells, not to mention fertilizer and foodstuff for the soldiers who fought to the city's north. The war had been a hungry beast, and the Grenoble industrialists had responded to its call. Those with large factories and with capital to spare considered what the conflict might ask for, what contracts they might be in a position to secure, and shifted their production schedules to match. Even smaller family-run businesses adjusted their catalogs and where their products were shipped. Each producer was paid handsomely for their efforts, to the point that industry nearly underwrote the city's whole existence. Grenoble, which had been a tourism hub in its earlier years, saw the number of visitors drop. It instead became reliant on the goods its companies sent to the front. Despite the mobilization of fighting-age men, the city continued to produce fifty thousand shells per day after local women took the place of men in the grime-soaked factories.

Firmin rode up pont de Claix, just south of Grenoble. The Drac curved below the neighborhood, holding it in a cupped palm. The blocky industrial hulls that made up the neighborhood sat as close as they were able along the river's edge. Large vats of brine were placed in some of the factories. During the war, rods were lowered into the salty water. Electrical currents shot through the metal poles. Small bubbles formed, then drifted off the metal; a noxious smell—pepper, pineapple, bleach—rose from the vats. Tubes above the tanks transported the gas that had formed to metal canisters, which were sealed once full. These factories cropped up later in the war, between 1916 and 1917 when the French demand for poison gas grew.

Soldiers eventually released the gas from the canisters. It drifted over battlefields on an unwitting wind. The first symptom was respiratory: a hardened breath, a persistent cough. A burning sensation filled the eyes and throats of any men who had not donned their gas masks. Above one thousand parts per million, fluid filled the lungs and drowned the victim within a few minutes.

Germans first used chlorine gas on April 22, 1915. They used chlorine, in particular, because factories already manufactured it for industrial purposes; it stayed low, hugging the curvature of trenches and craters, and dispersed in not so long a time, allowing the assaulting army to march over the ground they had just cleared of life. They released 170 tons that first evening. French and Algerian soldiers watched as the sage-green fog drifted toward them. Around a thousand were killed in the attack, and seven times that were wounded. The French public's response was visceral and outraged; they couldn't believe the enemy would use a weapon so pitiless and cowardly on their soldiers. They held on to their outrage but qualified it: if anyone was using poison gas— chlorine, phosphene, mustard—those on the receiving end shouldn't cripple themselves with principles; there would be time to think about that after the end of the war.

Soon, the factories in Grenoble began to produce gas according to the instructions of Victor Grignard and other reluctant chemists who had been enlisted into the wartime effort. The gas didn't hasten the end of the war. Its efficacy on the battlefield was limited. Instead, it deformed those who came into contact with the gas and stirred people's emotions who saw its effect on their soldiers.

◆ ◆ ◆

Firmin rode through an opening in the wall surrounding Grenoble. It had been a garrison town before the war, housing soldiers from the 140th Infantry Regiment, the 105th Territorial Infantry Regiment, the Second Artillery Regiment, and the Fourteenth Alpine Battalion, among others. Over twenty thousand men had been stationed there, men who had been called away once the war began. Their population had been replaced by others who came as the town's industry grew. More workers were needed: immigrants and war widows and those men who had not been called up, who had been too old or otherwise unable to fight. The men who had left and then returned were able to find places to stay in the town, but Grenoble's accommodations were stretched thin. Many slept in one of the military barracks or at the hospital set up at the boys' high school. Others took rooms at the annex of the hôtel Suisse, or at the wealthy Raymond family's home on cours Berriat. The Raymond family business had been built on the production of snap fasteners for clothing, but during the war they'd expanded to manufacture bullet primer and shells.

Riding along cours Saint-André, a straight artery through the city, Firmin neared the finish line. The afternoon sun doubled the shadows of the trees lining the promenade. People bordered the promenade, too, held back by garrisoned soldiers who had joined gendarmes on horseback. Scarlet oriflammes flapped lazily in the breeze behind them.

Firmin rode through the finish line outside brasserie des Marronniers and greeted the crowd who waited there. As the cyclists finished each stage, and as Paris marched closer day by day, the racers had started to pay more attention to their times, aware of the distance between them and the cyclist just in front. No other competitor was more watchful than Firmin, who looked at the timekeeper's mark after each stage to see whether he had cut away at Eugène's lead. The "Old Gaul," as Desgrange called Eugène, though he no longer wore the distinctive mustache, rode through the finish just three minutes after the Belgian cyclist. Firmin's gains were too small to quickly upset Eugène's position, but Firmin saw a clear path ahead. If Eugène's injury became worse, perhaps those three, four, or five minutes stage after stage would be enough to change their roles by the race's end. He would only need a few more leads like that one to change his fortunes.

Desgrange and the *l'Auto* journalists continued to watch Eugène, but his consistency began to be taken for granted—if he lost ground, or if he switched his strategy and became more aggressive on one of the stages, they might make note of it. As it was, the editor was more interested that day in Honoré, who arrived first for the second stage in a row, an entire twelve minutes in front of Jean, who crossed in second. Honoré hadn't moved from his position in the general classification, those three hours were still insurmountable, but his athleticism excited the crowds as they watched him ride past. The journalists were thrilled, too, to see someone push themselves as hard as he did despite only a few months of training and an injury that grew worse with each passing day.

The cyclists gathered at café de l'Ascenseur on cours Berriat. Eugène had known his time had been good enough to hold his position before he rode through the finish. Maybe, he started to believe, this was the year he'd do it. He'd been cautious, strategic, but that strategy had been enough for him so far. One after another, the other cyclists had been struck down by faults of their own, or the unreliable roads. Perhaps, if he remained cautious, consistent until the end of the race, that would be enough.

The next day, Desgrange walked up to Eugène. He held a bundle of woolen fabric in his hands. It was yellow, the same shade as *l'Auto*'s pages. Desgrange gave Eugène a stack of new jerseys. The editor instructed the cyclist to start wearing them, on the next stage to Geneva and as long as he led the general classification. Up until that point, the racer in front had not been distinguished from the pack, with the exception of a green armband that Maurice Garin wore during the first Tour in 1903. The mud on the earlier stages had made it difficult to identify the racers as they'd passed through towns. With this yellow jersey standing out against the muddy gray and blue of La Sportive, Desgrange believed that the spectators could more easily pick out Eugène as he jockeyed with the others toward the finish line.

Eugène had little of Henri Pélissier's pride; he respected the other cyclists. Paris was ten days away, however, and he knew his competitors would look for whatever chance they could to change their fortunes. A yellow jersey would separate him from the others, just as Desgrange wished, would draw attention to his position as they rode. Eugène didn't need that type of visibility, a constant reminder that might cause the others to act differently toward him. With his jersey signaling his position, the others might notice an opportunity they'd otherwise have missed, sprinting away as soon as they saw him repairing his bike, pushing harder than they otherwise would when he was just behind them. Those who were nearest to him had seen him clearly, but now the entire field could. With a strategy that hinged on managing his strength and stamina, using as little of both as was needed, he'd have to push himself to keep up with their attacks, expending energy that otherwise would have been left for a final sprint. With those remaining days, that scrutiny, the pressure of losing his standing, would mean a more difficult race for Eugène than for the rest of them. The cyclist realized how the jersey changed the nature of the competition. Eugène protested. Perhaps his good-natured relationship with the editor would be enough to change Desgrange's mind. The editor, however, held firm.

The next morning Eugène arrived back at café de l'Ascenseur and signed into the logbook. The stage before him was only 325 kilometers long but included col du Galibier. The climb pulled cyclists in with a comparatively easy early ascent. The final 8 kilometers, however, became more difficult. The ground ascended to 2,558 meters before falling into the Maurienne Valley. As Tourmalet had been for the Pyrenees, Galibier was for the Alps.

Even before Eugène left the café, the calls began. "Cri-cri!" the crowd cried as he walked past. The familiar name took on an unusually high pitch. Amid the expected cheering, a new phrase peppered the crowd's chants. They saw the yellow jersey uncreased on his back. "Canari!" they jeered. He was no longer another cyclist but the leader of the Tour, a marked rival for the others to beat.

The 1939 Tour peloton ascending col du Galibier in the sixteenth stage of the race, between Briançon and Annecy.

10.

Desgrange watched from the Brasier as the cyclists neared Galibier. He saw Honoré ascending the unkempt mountain trail. Behind him, out of sight, Eugène struggled up the terrain. They were remote, in a place few Frenchmen had seen, near towns of only a few hundred, but on that day the population had grown as crowds drove out to witness the cyclists race across the 2,558-meter summit of the mountain pass.

The Brasier stopped; Desgrange noted the time on the timekeeper's watch. One minute and thirty seconds passed before the springy Luigi caught up to their position. It was a substantial gap between the first- and second-place cyclists. The car followed the Italian as he continued riding up the mountain. The last town they'd passed through, La Grave, was invisible behind the khaki bluffs on either side of them. Small grasses broke through the ground, and the crowd grew the farther they drove along, but the mountain otherwise appeared lifeless.

They sped up to catch Honoré. As the Brasier neared him, the journalists consulted the watch again. They followed behind him, then slowed to watch the others' progress. His climbing was unlike the others—Firmin, Jean, Luigi—it was artless, not graceful or efficient, but it was as if that energy that would otherwise go elsewhere instead allowed him to power ahead. They checked the time; Luigi was now two minutes and fifty-eight seconds behind Honoré.

Rocks flicked from the path as the Brasier drove over them. The journalists neared the tunnel marking the end of the climb, the passage that would take the cyclists to the rest of the stage. Hundreds of kilometers remained in front of them. One last time they noted Honoré's time and waited for Luigi. The car sputtered among the crowd that had gathered on the thin mountain road. The people and the cars they had used to arrive at the summit encroached on either side of the cyclists' path, barely enough for two to ride next to one another, not that the space was needed with so few cyclists remaining. Four minutes and fifty-five seconds later, the Italian picked up his pace as he reached the flat ground. Wasted from his effort, only to have Honoré extend his lead as if Galibier was just another flat sprint to the finish line.

"That's it for a year," Léon told the editor as he passed by another three minutes after Luigi.

Firmin had watched as Honoré first sped up the mountain. He looked around at the frost that surrounded them: tan brown, a translucent crust covering the dirt underneath, a permanent feature of the landscape. Firmin rode alongside Eugène and Jean in a small pack as they followed the younger cyclists up the incline. The climb was steep, and they hopped off their bikes when it overcame them, the exhaustion reaching the ends of their toes and fingers. When they rested, the cyclists had a moment to look behind them and observe the rocky path that had guided them so far, that would continue to test them. It seemed at once impossible and insignificant from where they stood. By any measure Honoré should have been exhausted, barely able to pedal up the mountain.

If Firmin had Honoré's younger legs and heart, if he could have siphoned that youth from him, rewound his own body's aging, the competition would have looked different. Of course, the same could be said for Eugène or Jean, all the cyclists whose prime years had passed, wasted during a war that couldn't use them fully but had halted their chances to compete against one another. The 1919 Tour could have been postponed instead of forcing them to compete so soon. They could have trained, spent time understanding how they would fare in a race like this one before they had to go through with it. Perhaps a few of the older cyclists would have decided they had enough, particularly after they saw Desgrange's proposed route—180 kilometers longer than the 1914 Tour—and the poorly tended roads, which would not be finished for some time, that strained their muscles and broke down their bikes. Instead, they only had enough time to register for the race and arrive for its start. Instead of a competition, the cyclists' physical tolerance and mental stamina mattered most; those who recognized that kept count of both as they exerted themselves and could survive each successive stage. The younger cyclists could defy the strategies of the older ones who paced themselves. They could gain minutes on the worst stretches of road, but the older men held on to their limited reserves and waited for those long, flat stretches where they might be most effective. Honoré continued ahead and didn't stop, even if Desgrange's praise and that day's prize were the only things he could hope for.

Honoré hadn't even turned professional by the time the war had started; he had only competed in a few races around Paris and had won the championship de France des indépendants in 1912. He had been a promising cyclist, no doubt, but the war had come before he'd had a chance to prove himself.

His name was on the military register of the thirteenth arrondissement, where he'd lived with his parents, Léon and Noel, on rue de Patay. When he turned twenty, he became eligible for conscription. He was mobilized one year later, in October of 1913. After training, Honoré expected to be sent to the unit where he would spend his remaining active duty years before joining reserve units. Two weeks before his arrival to the Twentieth Battalion of Foot Hunters, however, parliament instituted a change to the length of mandatory service, extending it by one year. Despite popular demonstrations against the law, it passed. He saw his future, those years when he'd potentially be away from the bike and still in uniform, extended in the same law from twenty-five to twenty-eight years.

Once the war broke out, the laws mattered little. Those who could serve did. Honoré's Twentieth Battalion had been one of the first units to cross into the Alsace once the fighting began.

He fought at the Battle of the Frontiers at Donon and at the First Battle of the Marne, just one month after fighting started, when the Germans had come crashing through Belgium, and the Allied armies—including units like Eugène's First Cycling Group and Honoré's Twentieth Battalion of Foot Hunters—stopped them. In that first success came the seed of the war that would continue, when the battle maneuvers ground to a halt and the armies dug themselves in, advancing and retreating incrementally as the deaths carried on for years without much hope of a decisive victory.

In the summer of 1917, Honoré had been transferred to the Sixth Regiment of Dragoons and fought with the unit at the Second Battle of the Marne. The battle represented what the war had become, how it had changed since the same armies had last fought on that land. The Allied victory in the battle cost one hundred thousand casualties, men who had been shot in the German attacks and the Allied counterattacks over twenty-three days. Honoré had been released from the unit on January 18th that year, and began training on his bike, returning to his life. He finished third in Paris–Roubaix just two months later.

◆ ◆ ◆

Firmin continued toward the peak, alongside sparse grasses. He rode through a flat stretch of ground. It tilted up again, and he rose from the seat of his bike to bear down on his pedals. He was five hours into the stage. Reaching another plateau, he cycled past the waiting journalists, who recorded his time. He rode through the tunnel at the top of Galibier. As he descended the steep path into the valley below, grasses again peeked through the frozen dirt, the sound of water rose above the dirt crunching underneath his wheels. Murmurs carried from hikers—spectators—who'd made their way up the path. It was loud up there, as if the mountain was asserting itself over him. The volcanic rocks leered as he swept past them.

At least Firmin had something to show for his times. As he left the Alpine section of the stage, he rested for a moment, taking a more relaxed pace as trees whipped past him on the hairpin turns leading down from Galibier.

Firmin watched as the other cyclists sped up to attack Honoré's position at the front. Luigi and Léon pushed most aggressively from their positions behind the young cyclist. Their efforts yielded no results. Each time one approached his tail, Honoré picked up his pace, keeping it steady and elevated until they fell behind again, spent from the energy of sprinting toward him. His energy never appeared to falter. It was as though a battery inside him was replaced before each day of racing began.

The scenery around them stunned. They found themselves in the midst of the Alps, riding from one valley floor to another, punctuated by moments when they veered up a mountain pass. They exited one minimum and entered another. They passed through a tunnel that man had gashed into the Alps. Inside was dark except for the spot of light that grew steadily larger before releasing them again into the day. They continued. Craggy walls jutted up on either side of them, skittering streams poured over rocks arranged just so. The beauty was a shock to their senses. They rode toward peaks in the distance—not so large when the cyclists first regarded them, but which towered over them as they pedaled on a low path just barely in the mountain's shadow. They had known all along, of course, that these places were here. But they had not seen them in years.

Not even war could destroy these features. The cyclists stationed near the front saw the flat land to the north changed into something unrecognizable, made even lower with each passing day, pitted with innumerable craters and hills. What had once seemed impossible, to change a landscape so completely, had been realized. It was more striking and sweeping than any tunnel cut through a mountain to connect spa towns. Firmin and the others cycled through that undamaged region. Few men had many uses for these mountains and cliffs, apart from the occasional coal mine. The ground was difficult to traverse, not worth whatever could be found there except for the sights.

If the French people could have seen this enduring place, maybe they would have had fewer doubts about what came next. The cyclists passed through Flumet. To their right, behind a row of nearer peaks, stood Mont Blanc, the tallest in Western Europe—a monument to those things humans can crawl their way up but not alter. The cyclists pressed on. They cut south after passing Thônes, then looped back to ride along the waters of Lac d'Annecy. On the other side of the ultramarine lake, mountainous bluffs were layered, one over another. A few buildings stood on its shore: a château on a small finger reaching into a crook of the lake, some scattered homes and lodges. Firmin stayed along the water until he reached l'Abbaye de Talloires, an old monastery that had been converted into a hotel during the revolution. Its stuccoed walls remained along the lake's edge, white sided and brown roofed, with the spires of Pointe Centrale standing guard. The town of Annecy signaled to Firmin he was just forty-five kilometers from the end of the stage. He could only see Luigi nearby. They rode together through the town, past canals filled with alpine water that gave this place its nickname, the Venice of the Alps.

Firmin rode through the crenelated gate of pont Charles-Albert, a suspension bridge 147 meters above the Usses River. The gorge's white walls were covered in dark-green trees barely holding on to its sheer walls. The gorge seemed determined to shake from it anything affixed to its rippling, eroded face. At the bottom was an old Roman thermal bath, fed by deep springs. Civilizations had taken advantage of the springs at times over the centuries. Histories were layered one after another onto the land as different groups inhabited the area, then allowed it to fall back to nature before the baths were discovered again. They had been rebuilt seventy years before. The baths didn't have the accommodations that facilities farther south did—the high-thread-count towels, the waiting attendants—but their proximity to Geneva made them a popular local respite. Nearby, a specially designed car ran to the foot of the gorge and unloaded passengers at regular intervals.

At the bridge's far end, Firmin passed French border guards who looked at the cyclists without comment. Desgrange had already provided the cyclists' passport information to both sets of border guards, so the riders were allowed to cross through without stopping.

◆ ◆ ◆

Switzerland had done what France could not in the preceding five years. It was not to say that France had been responsible for Germany or Austria-Hungary's decisions at the beginning of the Great War, but a combination of luck and strategy had allowed Switzerland to maintain its neutrality while France was bound up in the fighting. The country had taken pains to defend itself while not siding with either of the warring factions. The two mandates—that of neutrality and that of defense—were in opposition to each other. This strain led the country to fortify itself while the war continued outside. It mobilized its military with the strict order to defend only its borders and would remain peaceful, not antagonizing the countries that destroyed each other over the western front's wasteland. Switzerland would fight, however, anyone who attempted to route the war through its borders.

The Swiss neutrality created its own set of confrontations with those on either side. The task of the Swiss government was to keep both sides partly satisfied, or at least not so angry that they attacked the neutral country. Within Switzerland, French- and German-speaking areas tended to ally themselves with the countries that shared their language. In the opening salvo of the war, those sentiments created a climate of mistrust and rumor. Those on one side thought the others were working to force their country's hand to enter the war on behalf of their allies. The Swiss government and social leaders managed to tamp down these rumors and ensure they didn't bubble up into violence.

Untouched by the physical destruction that surrounded it, Switzerland had been able to expand its humanitarian programs. The Red Cross, headquartered in Geneva, supported prisoners of war and their families, providing them with food and supplies, and helped prop up medical professionals when influenza broke out. Though its borders were closed, the country assisted displaced civilians in repatriating once it became possible to return to their towns. More or less, with great care and strict policy, the Swiss managed to keep the two sides satisfied and equal.

◆ ◆ ◆

Past the Swiss border, Firmin picked up his pace along the flat road through Plan-les-Ouates, the final sprint to the finish line in Geneva. He rode alongside Jean, Léon, and Eugène, all within a length of one another. They gave the sprint all they could muster. Honoré had already breezed through the finish ten minutes before second-place Luigi.

Firmin set his eyes on their destination, café de la Couronne on the south side of Lake Geneva, at the mouth of the Rhône. The rest of the city was on the river's opposite bank. Just across from the finish on the other side of the Rhône sat one of the more prominent structures in the city, the five-story hôtel National.

As a result of its neutrality in the war, Geneva had been named the future site of the Society of Nations. The Paris Peace Conference, where the victorious Allied countries continued to determine the nature of the peace, included provisions for an international body tasked with maintaining that tranquility once it had been found. It was an ambitious aim. With so many lives lost, it was only understandable that the winning nations thought the cost imposed on the losing ones should be great. It wasn't clear that a small group of men could remain focused on an optimal peace and not be distracted by others' calls for revenge. If peace didn't make itself known after such a difficult war, perhaps it never would. It seemed inconceivable, given the technology at the front, that weapons with such destructive potential could be used time and again in the same way.

◆ ◆ ◆

The city held a reception for the cyclists at café de la Couronne the next morning. Desgrange and Victor Dusseiller, a member of parliament, toasted them on making it so far. The men otherwise kept to themselves, except for short appearances at Jardin anglais and pont du Mont Blanc, the bridge connecting the two halves of the town. They managed their exhaustion as best as they were able. Eugène tried to recover, but his crash at the Nice finish line still caused pain to shoot up his legs. "It doesn't surprise me, running into a cop without suffering is difficult," he joked with the *l'Auto* correspondent. Still, the first-place cyclist praised Honoré's abilities. He knew the younger Parisian had worse troubles than him.

Desgrange wrote that the imminent journey to Strasbourg was the Tour's crux. The stage was long, at more than 371 kilometers. There was one more major climb, col de la Faucille, which would test the cyclists before the flat ground of the north. In other years, the stage would have ended in Belfort, 234 kilometers into that year's stage. But the racers would have found few accommodations in the town. It was the state of countless towns across this stretch of France—some familiar to the cyclists, others they would never see. Some were broken, others gone, all had been marked. The temporary loss of Belfort would extend their ride and force them through the Alsace that same day. They would bring the region into the Tour's fold—the towns that had been German for nearly a half century until postwar concessions repatriated them. The people who lived in them would see how Desgrange and the others considered them part of their own country, a country that countless people in the region regarded with some caution, before the race once again left them on their way home to Paris.

◆ ◆ ◆

The cyclists departed from place Montbrillant at 1:44 a.m. The eleven left Geneva's center, riding along the tramway northward, toward the city's outer suburbs. It was still dark when they exited the neutral country.

A crater lake created by a mine that exploded during the Battle of the Somme in 1916.

11.

In the week leading up to the Battle of the Somme, British forces fired 1.5 million artillery shells toward German lines. Those steel shells that flew over Allied heads and into no man's land varied in size from just a few pounds to thousands. Many were just filled with explosives, designed to approach the ground but not quite touch it. Instead, they detonated in the air just above. Then, the force of the explosion sent out a shockwave that carried scraps of the shell in all directions. The blast and the metal shards crashed like a wave against trench walls. Other shells contained hundreds of lead-antimony bearings, which melted in the first heat of the explosion and cut through soldiers' woolen coats like a biting wind.

Each shell left an impression in the ground, shrapnel dusting it with metal pellets that quickly hardened, while large, high-explosive shells cratered the ground with depressions the size of small lakes. In an instant—and then over time—the explosions shifted the topography underneath the soldiers' feet. The armies used shells as though they would never run out, and they launched far more than what was needed to secure their objectives. Their lives then were not ones of regimented order, as much as training had promised otherwise, but were in fact random and chaotic. At some point, all the soldiers could do was resign themselves to whatever might come. Around them, shells stamped and scuffled across the muddy terrain, with scarcely a moment's notice before impact. Soldiers claimed the blast that would kill a man was the one he never heard, though no one was around to confirm that theory and it did nothing to diminish the terror that came with the low whistle that bore down upon them, directionless, it seemed, to humans' imperfect ears.

When rains came, the newly created pits filled with water. Small tributaries quickly formed and hurried it down the pits' sloped sides, along with any remnants of chlorine gas that still hugged the ground and blood-soaked scraps of wool, horse flesh, trench waste, browned metal flakes, anything left in the immediate area. It all collected in the pit. Unlucky soldiers and horses who had been running across the dark ground sometimes fell into the rising waters, their woolen uniforms and heavy packs weighing them down. Over time, the water evaporated and exposed mud-coated remains like artifacts of fallen civilizations until they were covered once again by the next storm's rains. And yet, despite the noxious collection, when the sun was out and the pit was now behind a new line—out of the territory between the two enemies—one could still see the occasional butterfly landing on its lip or a wildflower sprouting on its edge. Life had not been extinguished from the land, despite the war's best efforts.

◆ ◆ ◆

It hadn't been clear if the race would survive its own weight in the Tour's first years. During its initial edition in 1903, only Géo Lefèvre, the *l'Auto* correspondent who had proposed the idea of the Tour to Desgrange, followed the cyclists. Along 2,428 kilometers, Lefèvre served as the race's sole timekeeper and finish-line judge. He was also responsible for overseeing the Tour's day-to-day administration: looking after the racers' accommodations and corresponding with the leaders of towns along its six stages. While the cyclists rode at night, he had hopped on his own bike to follow alongside the otherwise unaccompanied competitors—having no domestiques or coaches—and make sure they were adhering to the Tour's strict rules. He'd then board the next train to the stage's end and greet them as they arrived. On top of that, he filed stories for *l'Auto* along the way. The newspaper's circulation grew with each passing day of the race as French people heard about the Tour that was approaching their towns.

Cheating was as common as it was creative in the next year of the race, assisted by supporters along the roads. An early favorite, Hippolyte Aucouturier, held between his teeth a cork tied to a length of string that was in turn attached to the bumper of a car. The cork gave him the appearance of grimacing as he was pulled along by the car. In another incident, masked men swung at Maurice Garin and Lucien Pothier, attempting to knock the two cyclists off their bikes, but the bikes were nimbler than the car the men rode in, and the racers dodged the attacks.

In the second stage between Lyon and Marseille, a mob of fans attempted to stop all the cyclists except Antoine Fauré, a hometown hero. They were only broken up after *l'Auto* organizers fired rounds from the starting pistol.

Rocks were thrown and nails were placed on the ground, shortcuts had been discovered, lemonade once thought to be a gift to a cyclist was poisoned. Cheating and outright violence was so common that Lefèvre wasn't sure that year's results could be guaranteed at all. The corruption was enough that Desgrange considered shutting down the entire operation after that second year, still not convinced the race was worth its risks.

And yet, in 1919 the cyclists would follow a route through a stretch of their country that had been destroyed, on the longest Tour de France attempted to that point. Though their numbers had winnowed, it looked as though at least a few of them would finish the race. As it had been in those first years, the competition wasn't a matter of determining the most proficient or athletic cyclist. It had become a different sort of race, between those who remained, who had simply managed to continue riding.

Just after leaving Geneva, Firmin and the others ascended col de la Faucille. Firmin rode past a crowd of young boys who looked on. It was the first time they had seen the race; they'd been too young to watch it before the war began. The hill was small enough that Firmin arrived alongside the others, their pack unbroken. Behind them, Lake Geneva extended into the distance, its color deepening toward the center of the lake, dark and undisturbed. The Alsace lay just next to it. It was peaceful at the moment, in those first hours of the day.

◆ ◆ ◆

The first people who visited the region saw its value. How the animals they hunted had gathered on its plains between the Vosges Mountains and the Black Forest. In time, grapes were planted in the rich soil; they fed the viticulture of ancient Rome. The Holy Roman Empire eventually took control of the land in its entirety. It was violently traded between France and Germany for centuries after that. Both knew the value of the crops that flourished there. The people who lived in the region reflected the nature of the conflict. Many spoke a language close to Swiss German, but others spoke only German or French. More German than French in their culture, small towns were dotted with half-timbered gothic buildings, and their food was more like what one would find in Berlin or Frankfurt than in Paris.

The French took control of the Alsace in 1674, when Louis XIV led his army in the Franco-Dutch War and gathered up the remaining parts of the country his father had failed to secure in the Thirty Years' War. In 1871, France ceded the Alsace to the Germans after the Franco-Prussian War. Under German control, at least one hundred thousand Alsatians decided to keep their French citizenship and leave the territory; those who stayed felt the burden of the kaiser's power after he declared the

Alsace-Lorraine a reichsland, a region directly controlled by him, and denied its inhabitants self-government for thirty years.

The Great War hadn't started because of France's desire to regain the Alsace. Nor did it occupy the most strategic ground of the war: German troops had been concentrated to the north after their army stormed through Belgium. The region wasn't just a symbol, though. Its hops and tobacco were riches for the country that controlled it. The French towns along its border had been fortified; they would be costly to capture. One was the former Tour stop of Belfort. Rather than fight to challenge these positions, Germany first stayed away.

In the last days of the war, the territory's future had been uncertain. Few knew how the Alsace would be governed at war's end. Those who lived there had their own opinions on whether France would retake the land and exert control, or whether they would finally give Alsatians a choice in the matter.

France's decision came down after a self-proclaimed government was declared in November 1918 in Strasbourg. French troops were sent in to quash the fledgling state and reassert control. The French government also began a cultural campaign, ensuring that Alsatian ways of life bent toward French norms. As French citizens had once left the land, a similar number of German citizens did the same, of their own accord and by the demands of the government.

◆ ◆ ◆

Firmin rode through these Alsatian towns. Seven of the cyclists stayed together as a pack, in front of the four others. None of the seven were riding aggressively, for there was no reason for them to attack yet. Those who remained were the riders who had survived the race, who had found themselves on a level playing field even if they had lagged in earlier stages, as if their diminished numbers were a weight now shed from them. Jacques and Paul both suffered tire punctures and fell away. Joseph and Alfred slowed, injured from earlier falls. After the bright alpine days, the temperature dropped, and the riders again felt the effects of the cold on their energy and limbs. The sky was gray; the clouds were so common they receded into the flat sky. It was an atmosphere the cyclists had become used to over the years, one that seemed to hold steady toward the front, planed further by the haze that had once drifted over the lines.

Firmin had not seen how the weather seemed to change near the front. The changes to his atmosphere had been subtler, though the war still socked his city. Both his hometown and his current city, Antwerp, had fallen under control of the German Central Government, a governing body set up by the Germans for the Belgian occupation. Those in Antwerp and Florennes at least had it better than the towns nearer to the front that had been placed under direct military rule. The small conveniences Firmin had been allowed—a job, religious observance—were even more difficult under military rule. The civilians there had been treated as prisoners lest they use their proximity to the front to transmit intelligence to Allied soldiers or lend physical support to the German enemies.

He had still faced daily grievances. The occupying forces had been a parasite drawing on Belgium's economy, demanding regular monetary contributions the Belgian government could not have paid even under normal conditions. People from Firmin's town had been deported to work on roads and on railways, then to man German factories, farms, and mines, when the country could not meet growth aims with its existing workforce.

Firmin had spent the war in that miasma. He had avoided its worst sufferings—the deportations, the forced labor—but his life had existed in a country entirely constricted by another. The saddle shop he opened in Antwerp before the war began at least kept him busy. He had been able to cycle, but he took on few professional racing opportunities. Still, his had been a better existence, he knew, than those who were fighting to the west.

The landscape had changed. Fresh dirt, exposed worms and muck of underground strata, had been brought up, then pounded flat. A railway connecting France to Switzerland had been commissioned in 1915—in the midst of war—but construction lagged. The cyclists followed the twin line of assembly. It was a Monday, and the railroad workers stopped to watch and cheer as the cyclists passed by the unfinished, crosshatched tracks.

The new railroad was one of many in the area. Construction and reconstruction of local utilities and transportation gave the cyclists the feeling that they were traversing an industrial wasteland. In that construction was evidence, too, that there was movement along these roads, even if they were in disrepair. Few knew how long the boom would continue, whether the funds would dry up before the tracks were completed, whether the lines would eventually wither back into the ground, or whether the region would join as neatly with its country as those in the government hoped it would.

For all the construction, for the gray day around them, the war was as obvious as it had been since they first left Paris. Firmin crossed through the checkpoint in Pontarlier and then reached rue de Vannoles, where men in uniform milled about and watched them with interest. Their garrison, the fortified Fort de Joux, looked down on the town. The soldiers' mission wasn't clear to the cyclists; whatever it was, there was little tension in their movements. They simply existed in the town, made up part of its population, showed the people that the French government was taking care of the region. Between towns, simple white signs placed by the military directed the cyclists. They marked the way to locations on the front and to towns where units could rest before joining others in the trenches.

Firmin entered Belfort just before noon. By then, Jacques and Paul had caught up after their punctures and rode alongside the others, nine in total, who formed the leading pack. On rue Vauban, they passed another crowd of blue-uniformed poilus. An officer by the name of Berger approached Desgrange as the Brasier idled in the town. He handed Desgrange a stack of bills that he and his men had gathered, and instructed the editor to give part of the money to the first cyclist to pass through the town and part of it to Jules, the last remaining B classification cyclist.

The streaks of war were still visible in the town as Firmin rode through it, but Belfort was at least inhabitable. Many of the buildings still served their more recent wartime purposes: schools had become hospitals, warehouses stored logistical supplies. The town, stretched beyond its capacity, couldn't accommodate the racers for anything more than a pit stop, to the dismay of its citizens.

After they checked in with the race administrators, the cyclists rode east. Just before leaving Belfort, they passed the town's citadel. The fortified building had first been a castle in the 1200s and was strengthened through the 1700s as the Alsace became contested territory. At the foot of the citadel, carved into rose Perugia sandstone, a twenty-two-meter-long lion sat, its front right paw crushing an arrow beneath its weight. The arrow faced east, toward the German border. It had been built to represent the resistance of the city for 103 days against the Prussian army during the Franco-Prussian War. Belfort's fifteen thousand garrisoned men had fought against forty thousand Prussian soldiers. The town surrendered at the end of the war, but its fight went on longer than any of the French strategists and politicians had imagined. At the end of the war, the Germans occupied the town for two years, until 1873. Instead of claiming the town for its own, it exchanged Belfort with the French for cities farther north. After the Germans left, the city's fortifications expanded again; the wall between their city and the surrounding countryside grew. Alsatians from other towns made their way to Belfort after the region was ceded to Germany, the nearest place where their way of life could continue. Once the Great War broke out, the most vulnerable civilians left Belfort on the orders of General Frederic Thevenet. The city supplied French soldiers to the front, only fifteen kilometers away. The Germans responded by shelling the town with long-range guns and bombers, though its fortifications held.

Two hundred and fifty kilometers into the stage, Firmin hit a fork in the road near La Chapelle. Another plain white sign pointed him toward Soppe-le-Bas. The small town held no more than five hundred inhabitants in a typical year, but with the war, the population had dropped. People had sought out safer terrain and hadn't returned once the war ended. The town itself had only two intersecting streets. Firmin rode through it, continuing eastward. He looked at Eugène, whose yellow jersey stood out against the landscape. Neither had been able to break away from the other along the stage's length. The flat terrain didn't suit their strengths. They rode through Soppe-le-Bas, their tires kicking up dust and shifting unsteadily along the pockmarked ground. The day grew darker.

There were people along the route, but they were few and far between. Dressed in simple clothing stained with earth and hand sewn, the townspeople stood out from the soldiers. Every now and then they passed by a station on the road—small huts, only large enough to keep a few people out of the sun and rain. The soldiers didn't stop the racers like they would for others crossing the land—checking their passports even though they were part of the same country. Instead, the poilus only looked on and occasionally cheered.

Imperceptibly, the cyclists crossed the outdated border. There was nothing notable left to pass over; the land between Germany and France had moved kilometers away. Instead, they continued riding. They headed to Mulhouse. In the distance, the cyclists made out pont d'Aspach. The bridge slumped into the water. Stones and wooden planks were strewn underneath it. It had once connected Mulhouse with Belfort but had been destroyed by artillery to delay troops and material from crossing.

To the right, the cyclists began seeing deep gashes in the ground. A little more than two meters deep, the trenches had covered the heads of the soldiers who fought within them but had still allowed the men to scramble out from their protection. Some were more complex, following a quick zig-zag pattern to prevent shrapnel from crossing too large a distance. The occasional trench perpendicular to the others allowed soldiers to move between lines, communicate plans. The German trenches were more elaborate than the Allied ones, deeper and with concrete constructions, stairs and spherical pillboxes. Some German soldiers didn't see the sky until they had left the trench entirely. Around the trenches the ground was pitted. Bird nests of barbed wire sat in irregular bundles, like rusted tumbleweeds. The land was empty.

The battles that took place in the Alsace were unlike those farther north. They were smaller and moved more quickly across the land. Immediately to the cyclists' north, where the ground ascended into the Vosges Mountains, there had been alpine fighting. French and German men had fired at one another on slopes between sixteen and twenty degrees, land so steep it would have been difficult for the cyclists to ascend. They lived and fought in trenches like those on the northern battlefields, but above the cloud line the ground froze in winter. Sometimes only a few meters separated the soldiers on the Vosges from enemy machine guns and men who had trudged up the mountains just like them, dragging their artillery guns behind them on makeshift lifts. The landscape had separated those soldiers from the rest of the war— thick with trees when the war began and inaccessible to trains. They were self-sufficient and expected little relief if they found themselves fighting against a superior force. By now, most of the land had been sheared. Its trees were cut to make way for excavations, and the wood was used to make the duckboards that supported the soldiers on the sodden ground. Those plants not felled were destroyed in the beat of artillery shells and bullets.

The pillaged ground surrounded the cyclists. Firmin hadn't seen that sort of war, nor had Eugène. The machines Eugène had fixed while it went on couldn't operate on those Vosges Mountains; they were suited to the flat ground where the largest battles had been fought, where the decimated earth waited for them on the other side of that day's ride. The front hadn't disappeared with the end of the war, the cyclists knew as much. Eugène, Firmin, and Jean continued, setting pace against one another as the gray deepened.

The former town of Hartmannsweilerkopf, in the southern Vosges, after the Alsace-Lorraine evacuation.

12.

When exactly a war begins is a matter of debate. After it is over, after the thing is said and done and the consequences are clear—though they are bound to change as the years go on—historians and other interested folk mark a time or day when the first soldier was killed in an opening gunfire trade, or when foreign troops crossed the border and marched into the countryside. The particular day may vary from source to source. In a book that reconstructs the war's history, a frustrated historian will make clear the time they chose leaves even them wanting, that it has sheared from the history an important set of events preceding the moment, which that historian then summarizes after some bemoaning its incompleteness.

Franz Ferdinand's assassination is often selected as the moment the Great War's gears began creaking, its pistons sliding, the war's trajectory inexorably fed by its own mass. The archduke's assassination is an easy event to turn to: public and brutal and in near enough proximity to the first exchange of fire between Belgian and German soldiers that not much string is needed for historians to connect the two violent facts. In marking the event, historians give the reader an absolute point, a backstop to the infinite causal regression that is part of life but is unsuited to bound copies. Questions go unanswered. Why did the death of a royal at the hand of a quasimilitary group led by Serbian nationalists lead to so many other countries becoming embroiled in a war? What conditions led to the decision to assassinate Franz Ferdinand, presumably made by a small subset of Black Hand members, or possibly only one person? For readers who seek those answers, the limitations of a single moment are clear, even if starting at a particular instant is still practical. Historians, to some degree, must leave out the other important moments that had taken place before, which indicated what would soon happen. There just isn't enough room for them all. It's rare that at the end of this backslide, a historian can simply say "a leader decided he wished for it to happen" without describing the motivations that existed before or the world that surrounded him, which prove just as important as his own thoughts on the matter. The historian has to be satisfied with a crumpled start.

◆ ◆ ◆

As the cyclists rode toward Strasbourg on July 21st, they passed north of the small town of Joncherey. There, on the morning of August 2, 1914, the Sixth Company of the Forty-fourth Infantry Regiment was stationed, observing a ten-kilometer neutral zone, a buffer along the French and German border. The neutral zone had been declared at the same time as the French general mobilization orders, one day before, at 4:00 p.m. The unoccupied strip of land had been one last attempt to stave off war.

That morning, a young girl in the town was heard shouting that she could see Prussians. Corporal Jules-André Peugeot went to meet the German patrol of the Fifth Mounted Chasseurs, usually stationed at the nearby Mulhouse, who were approaching the road that ran through Joncherey. Peugeot walked toward the patrol. He expected to arrest the lieutenant who led the small unit, since no war had been declared. Before Peugeot could approach the officer, however, the lieutenant, mounted on horseback, pulled the revolver from his hip and fired three shots toward the French soldier. "The first and third shots went wild, but the second entered Peugeot's right shoulder," an article in *Le Temps* read. Peugeot shot the lieutenant with his rifle before collapsing without another word. The next day, war was declared.

Eugène had received notice of his activation that first day in August, the day before Corporal Peugeot was killed. He left to join the First Cyclist Group just fifteen days later. When the war broke out, Honoré had already been with his unit, nearing the end of his three mandatory years of service. By the time he turned twenty-three in 1914, the war was one month old; his three-year anniversary in uniform came and went without him hanging up the purple-brown tricolor cloth of the early French outfits. He would serve until the end of the war, though he was at least able to leave the front in February of 1916.

Jean, Luigi, and Eugène rode alongside one another through a suburb of Mulhouse, the city of nearly one hundred thousand, where Alfred Dreyfus had been born before Germany annexed the region and forced inhabitants to declare their allegiance to Germany or leave. The roads the racers cycled over had been pitted from neglect in the early stages, but they were now worn with use. On August 8, 1914, just one week after the war began, forty-five thousand Frenchmen advanced into the area. The soldiers arrived on foot and horseback. Trucks full of bullets, rations, whatever else might be needed for a fight followed the young men who would use the materials—enough for a few days or weeks, an umbilical cord that would have to remain continuous if it was to be of any use to them. Two days later, French troops were forced back in a German counterattack. The town changed hands from country to country, back and forth until August 24th, when the Germans finally secured Mulhouse, a position they would hold until the war's end. In November 1915, the city's chemical factory was destroyed in a strike; the gas stored within leached from its broken confines into the area, killing forty-two workers. When the fighting was dormant or farther away, the roads were used to resupply the soldiers. Militaries consumed even in the absence of exchanged bullets. The routes were worn down further as soldiers moved between locations, on leave or as they were needed elsewhere. Little upkeep could be completed in those few moments when the roads were not in use.

The cyclists rode down chaussée de Dornach, then turned left at the fork toward rue Franklin. The fighting in Mulhouse had been close to constant, but it had not been so threatening that civilians ever left the town. Most battles between soldiers occurred outside Mulhouse, in the surrounding area. Besides, where did the townspeople have to go? If they stayed in their homes, they would be safer than if they moved on roads through the night to some undetermined location. In the city, lines existed between the French and German people. The troops who occupied Mulhouse used both populations for their wartime ends. Hostages from the opposing population were taken, and prisoners were forced to work. They rebuilt trenches outside the city and tended to crops that would be used to feed the soldiers. Less fortunate prisoners were sent to Germany to live in camps, coined "industrial laborers' lodging" to distance the sites from concentration camps, in name if not in conditions. They had been removed from their communities. They didn't know the fate of those who stayed behind. They had little idea what their own fate might be, apart from the scant food they were provided and the disease that was a constant presence in the camps.

When the end of the war was in sight those first days of November 1918, German soldiers established a town council in Mulhouse like the one that had formed in Strasbourg to the north. They attempted to form a Soviet-style republic in the wake of their country's defeat. They were secure in their position—why should their country's loss undermine that? In response, Mulhouse's mayor established a militia to enforce its sovereignty over the German soldiers. Only the entrance of French soldiers on November 17th put an end to the microcosmic war forming.

When French soldiers first arrived in the city after the signing of armistice, the lines that had existed between citizens appeared to collapse. People greeted the poilus in their traditional outfits and in uniforms from the Franco-Prussian War, as if in recognition that these two conflicts weren't so distant from one another, that they had fought for the same things. Surely the French would be better than the Germans, who didn't even allow the Alsatians to govern themselves. To those who lived in the towns, it again seemed like independence might be possible. But soon those thoughts were done away with. Individuals most likely to remain allegiant to Germany were expelled. Others were investigated, surveilled, or arrested. Those who remained received identification cards that displayed their origin. Germans denounced other Germans in an attempt to give themselves a better future; Frenchmen denounced Germans for perceived wrongs. Those who weren't sent away or arrested faced danger from those who sought to take the law into their own hands.

Some on either side of the conflict lined the streets the racers rode down. They stood along the canal that connected the Rhône with the Rhine, past the Riviera Express railway tracks that had, in the years before the war began, connected Berlin with Nice. The people who watched had left their jobs early that Monday afternoon. They sat in cafés past lunch, shared another glass of Gewürztraminer. There was a peaceful camaraderie in the race that blanketed Mulhouse for at least a brief moment.

Jean, Luigi, and Eugène sprinted through the unfinished city. They beat against one another. The cheers and the wind battered their ears, pursed their vision down to the competitors next to them. *L'Expresse de Mulhouse*, a local newspaper, had offered 20 francs to the first racer to sprint through Mulhouse, as well as half that for the second racer and the first B classification cyclist, of which only Jules remained. Jean had received 2,400 francs in prize money so far. Eugène had won 1,000 while Luigi had received 925. They were energized from the recent pit stop in Belfort, and as they sprinted through Mulhouse, their tires kicked up dirt that wafted behind them on the constricted streets.

Overhead, the sky was an endless quicksilver: mute, unabating. Jean managed to hold his position through the town. They slowed almost imperceptibly once they left the confines of the city, no longer in competition for an immediate prize. They conserved some energy for the ninety-six kilometers remaining between them and Strasbourg.

The sky then opened up. The rain filled the grooves and the craters in the road. Poilus had once waded to the front. Off the road were pits like the ones soldiers and horses had once drowned in. It was as if those unlucky men had been called into the ground, as if they were never there, except for those who had known them. The men who were injured in no man's land could be heard in the distance calling for someone before they went quiet, but the soldiers who'd drowned in the pools went quickly, were swallowed whole.

Between towns, the racers approached single buildings: a lone café, two or three small houses with a shared barn. The buildings were spare, not so different from the ones on the outer reaches of Brittany. Stretches went by with no towns at all. In those places, there was little evidence of the war. Neither the Central powers nor the Allies had ever wanted to destroy the land entirely: their trucks and columns of soldiers had marched through, taking what they needed, but avoided the lands where fighting wouldn't result in any gains. The more populous areas of the Alsace, where factories had supported wartime efforts, had borne the brunt of the attacks.

◆ ◆ ◆

Jules and Jacques both dropped away from the pack when their tires were punctured, one after another. Flats had become so common that they were little more than an inconvenience. They pulled the unfortunate cyclist from the pack by a minute or more, but unless the damage happened at the end of a stage when the cyclists were advancing on the finish line, the time was surmountable. Two others dragged behind from lingering injuries after earlier crashes.

The group of seven neared Colmar with sixty kilometers left until Strasbourg. The military commissioners stationed in the town, responsible for overseeing the return of the Alsace-Lorraine region, had put down a prize for the first racer, so the cyclists began their sprint as they entered the more or less undamaged city, past the brightly painted old town on the banks of a canal. Jules and Jacques made repairs on the side of the road as the others picked up their pace. After they had sewn their tires and taped them into their wheels, they mounted their bikes again and followed the pack into town.

The cyclists rushed past another set of barracks on the tree-lined rue de Strasbourg. Each of the towns near the front had these military structures. The war had grown over even those undamaged places, leaving a mark without entirely suffocating the country beneath it. There were still people walking in the street, Saturday markets still had produce, the town continued to function. A few banners here and there welcomed the riders into the city. Soldiers presided over most of the towns, but stretches went by in Alsace when the only dusty blue the riders saw was from an occasional break in the clouds. Jean and Luigi led the pack toward Strasbourg, racing next to one another. Paul Duboc followed them, then Firmin, Eugène, Honoré, and Léon.

They continued on the road. A little after 5:00 p.m. they reached Strasbourg itself. It looked as though the rain had given up; the clouds had withdrawn and left a deep-blue sky. The pack rode together, separated by only a few centimeters as they sprinted along a straightaway toward the finish line at Grand Café de la République.

The crowd was ecstatic. The racers were reduced to their most essential and immediate needs: the road ahead of them, those riders who were nearest. They tried to avoid any more accidents as they drove forward. Members of the Alsace Military Commission, the local police, and sporting and cycling clubs from the nearby area, correspondents from the German-language local newspaper, *Straßburger Neueste Nachrichten*, and *l'Auto*, and local fans watched. The cyclists charged for them. The twilit sky behind the cyclists silhouetted their swinging frames. Behind them was the land their country had fought over for centuries and the 4,437 kilometers they had crossed to arrive at this moment. The men were wet and panting as they slipped into those final moments. Some were injured, but they stayed atop their bikes until they crossed the line and were at once relieved. It could have been the first stage they had ever attempted. If not, it looked as though it could have been their last.

The Tour had pushed its way as far east as it was able. It cut along the country's humpback. Desgrange had shoved the cyclists through a region where the conflict was old, even if the weapons used this last time had changed. War became something to be endured. Before, the land had been granted a modicum of safety; battlefields had been kept to less populous areas where soldiers could move unimpeded.

The Great War had instead broken over the region like a wave. With each acre it traveled, each minute it moved across the land, it picked up more in its froth: businesses, remote pastures, small, insignificant towns. The people who cheered the cyclists on had seen the wave first hit, had been caught in its wash, not in control of their fates, only able to gasp for air as it carried them along. It still wasn't done with them. France had welcomed them, as had the Tour, but neither asked the Alsatians for their thoughts on the matter.

As it had in preceding years, even with the paper quotas, *l'Auto*'s circulation had grown in the preceding weeks as the Tour circled the country. Copies of the newspaper sold out at stands. Those who had read recent editions knew the cyclists who barreled toward them. Honoré, the climber, among the best the race had seen. He had still not broken into the general classification's top three places, even after his effort on the recent climbs. The two hours and ten minutes between him and

Jean in third mattered little when the people on the side of the road saw him sprint out in front of the others. There were three stages left to go, plenty of time for him to take advantage of someone else's misfortune and continue winning individual stages. Luigi, the youngest of the bunch, had pulled out in front and broken Honoré's streak of first-place finishes with his sprints, following the model of the older Jean. And Eugène, still wearing his yellow jersey, though he had not yet won a single stage, still pushed himself just enough to beat the others, without once failing. Had Desgrange not changed the Tour's model, Eugène would have fallen behind the others. Firmin had been mostly absent from Desgrange's editorials, despite sitting solidly in second place, just twenty-three minutes behind the first-place cyclist. With even less style than Eugène, he had been able to tail him through the race and escape notice.

Following their finish, the *l'Auto* editor penned an editorial about the day's events. "Our Lambot doesn't usually shine," he wrote of Firmin. "He's the poet of the course," he added dismissively.

Despite Desgrange's snub, Firmin had done exactly what the editor had asked of him. His strategy had been to respond to his competitors, first Henri and then Eugène. He had beaten Eugène in four of the eleven stages, but he had avoided the attention Eugène drew with his first-place standing, with his new yellow jersey. For Desgrange, however, he only saw that Firmin was not the best at any one part of the race: not in sprints, nor in climbs—younger cyclists had him beat in both. He didn't share Eugène's amicable attitude on the course, and he wasn't French.

The cyclists felt little in response to Desgrange's editorials; plenty avoided them altogether. Their exhaustion worsened, and they picked up one injury or another across the distances. The quality of the roads slipped with each passing stage. The cyclists were broken, but those who remained were determined, beyond the reach of the editor's pen. Desgrange estimated they were averaging between twenty and twenty-two kilometers per hour, down almost ten from the Tour average. The climbs were behind them, but that relief did little for them now. They still hadn't entered the worst stretches of land. A few of them had seen the conditions ahead when they raced in the Paris–Roubaix earlier that year. They knew they'd have to contend with long distances on the remaining stages, on roads that had been damaged beyond what any man or country could repair in so short a time.

The site of a former battle in the forests of the Vosges Mountains.

13.

When Eugène was first called into service, in October of 1906, the French military was still recovering from their loss in the Franco-Prussian War. Across the French army, reforms were being instituted—modeled on those of the Prussians. Even in peacetime, the French were considering what the next war would require of them. Conscription was expanded, more soldiers would be called into the military for shorter lengths of time, a ballot system was reintroduced, two years of service was eventually expanded to three. The kaiser responded that the last change was a prelude to a French-led war. Engineers from both France and Germany strengthened their eastern border for the next fight that may or may not come, and Germans built a line of fortifications between Metz and Thionville. Their engineers expanded other walls the French had built in the Franco-Prussian War years that the Germans now controlled, and French engineers did the same for those territories that remained French, strengthening concrete batteries and steel turrets to protect them from artillery fire.

The 119th Infantry Regiment, Eugène's first unit, had defended Paris during the Franco-Prussian War. Before Eugène joined the 119th, they had taken part in the bloody week of the Paris Commune, when the national government reasserted control over the forces that had declared autonomy in the capital. Eugène had been a child in Paris at the time, living with his parents at the edge of the ninth arrondissement, in a modest house dwarfed by the mansions on rue de Caumartin.

Six years after his active duty service ended, on August 1, 1914, Eugène was called up as a reservist. He had only recently left active duty, but more time out of uniform would not have mattered much; those older than Eugène had been recalled into line infantry units, too, as the war began. Then there were the veterans like Desgrange—well past his reserve duty requirements but who still volunteered to join the younger Frenchmen as a poilu in the trenches. There were stories that men as old as their late sixties—nearly old enough to have fought in the Crimean War—received special dispensations from the government to join the fight on the western front. By any measure, these reservists fought as well as the others; most of the time on the front they were in the trenches, waiting for the moment when the officers' whistles trilled and the soldiers would run up the walls and onto no man's land, through the pocked terrain under cover of darkness, until flares broke overhead. During those dashes, the punctuated shots of snipers joined the drumbeat chorus of machine guns and the irregular refrain of rifles. One's fitness might make a difference then between death and survival, but in those first moments of blindness, when a soldier lifted his head above the trench rim to begin the sprint, it was only luck that spared anyone, and older soldiers had just as much of it as the rest of them.

Three months of training had been enough time for Eugène, at least when most everyone found themselves under the same constraints. His yellow jersey was visible from a distance as he entered Wissembourg ahead of the others at 6:17 on the morning of July 23rd. Nine of the eleven remaining cyclists formed the leading pack. The new border of the country was to his right as he rode through the town. A firing range and barracks, still in use, sat alongside it. In the early morning, soldiers were beginning to leave their squat shacks. Some watched the cyclists pass while others began their morning physical fitness. Just beyond the town, a small finger of the Vosges Mountains reached down to cut across their path.

The forest's remnants were visible on some of the battlefields. Trunks were splintered into jagged stakes, limbs were tossed outward, a crater exposed whatever stubborn roots remained. In the east, German soldiers killed almost all the remaining European bison in the Białowieża Forest, dam locks were unleashed to flood plains, exploding shells excavated soil built up over centuries down to the bedrock at times, leaving a desert where plants once blossomed. The forests immediately around the fighting were gone for the most part. Henri Barbusse, a poilu who wrote about his experience, called them "fields of sterility." They had reminded him of French industrialization, but on a scale and a depth he had not witnessed.

The forests, once full of deciduous trees—oak, hornbeam, beech— had suffered the most. A blight had run through them with the war, and the Vosges had been one of the worst-hit areas. Now the soil contained that noxious mix of chlorine and mustard gas, hydraulic oil and gasoline, an assortment that suffocated pliant new trees that might have replaced the ones now gone. Those trees that remained in the forest had splinters of metal in them that would have to be divined before they could be cut down for lumber. Buried or uncovered between their roots were unexploded shells, making the ground underfoot dangerous for any creature.

Eugène rode through the vestiges of forest until he reached Sarreguemines around 9:30 a.m. He had biked 143 kilometers, and by then he had lost his place at the front of the pack. Firmin had taken the lead. Alfred and Jules both slumped from injuries and dragged behind the pack by about thirty minutes. Firmin was close behind Eugène's overall time, but not so much that the Belgian would pass him under his own power.

Unfailingly consistent, Eugène had taken to heart Desgrange's words that the Tour was much more than fifteen sprints. The editor had defended the race and its scoring over the past few days in *l'Auto* from the readers who would sooner see Jean, the sprinter, or Honoré, the climber, lead the race. "Alavoine has speed, but a cart horse should win the prize," he'd said, sticking a needle in the eye of Henri Pélissier's critiques. Despite Firmin's proximity to him, it seemed continually likelier that Eugène would be that year's champion. The race had been his to lose since the Pélissiers left at the end of the fourth stage. The yellow jersey rested more comfortably on his back now. For Firmin and the others, the bright symbol drove them toward Eugène like a beacon. Those watching from the side of the road took notice of his standing, too, and marked the man who would be their hero.

Before Boulay, Eugène's tire began wobbling. It was an easy fix, a matter of tightening the bolt that held the wheel to his fork. He pulled off and began to fasten the bolt. The eight others he had been riding with saw him get off the bike. They sprung forward, bringing their pace closer to a sprint. The movement was coordinated, not so different from that moment on the fourth stage when Henri Pélissier's handlebars had come loose. The cyclists pressed on quickly. The riders at the front of the pack alternated to sustain their collective strength against the gusts of wind; as one cyclist tired from the effort of setting their pace, another took his place. The roads' state made their quick and close movements more difficult; the potholes and irregularities were dangerous for a sprinting group. If one of the leaders were to fall, the rest of the pack would go with him. Still, they continued.

With the adjustment to his machine complete, Eugène hopped back on his bike and sprinted ahead, hoping to catch up with the pack. He could see Firmin in front, setting the pace for the others.

By the time they reached the next town, Eugène was less than a minute behind. The effort from sprinting had worn on the riders, and they slowed as they passed through the town. If nothing else, they had ensured that Eugène would have to work as hard as possible to reach the end of the stage. It was, some must have thought, their last chance to challenge his lead. Perhaps they weren't meant to beat Eugène, but they still did not let him pass.

The wind had picked up and was gusting against the cyclists' flanks. It blew across their path, not slowing them down significantly but forcing them to lean against it. They stayed tense through turns and straightaways to counter its force, which bent them from their natural route. Suddenly, near Thionville, Luigi hopped off his bike near a copse of trees. He leaned over his back tire to pull the wheel from the chain. The others cycled past. Perhaps he had a flat, they thought, but those closest to him hadn't noticed the familiar pop and wobble that normally accompanied a blown tube. If it was a loose rim or a stuck pedal, it would take him longer to recover. Whatever it was, they kept pace, refusing to let Eugène back among them. Behind them, Luigi swapped the bike's larger gear for the smaller one that would allow him to speed along into the final stretch. A few riders noticed his strategic play. The terrain had a few small climbs ahead, but the majority of the road was flat. If the riders continued under the power of the larger gear, they'd be forced to work harder for slower speeds on the remaining straight sections. They might make up some of it, but only if the climbs were long enough. If they swapped their gear for the smaller one, as Luigi had done, they would temporarily give up their position in the pack and forfeit their aerodynamic advantage, all the more important with the wind that still shoved them. One at a time, the cyclists banked for the roadside, deciding to risk losing their place to gain some later speed. Their staggered approach allowed those who remained to press on together and keep their formation tight. Those who turned their wheels first were able to rejoin quickest. Desgrange's wish, to have the race exist only between individuals, drove them. They had tried to unseat Eugène together and failed.

Like the others, Eugène pulled away to switch his gears with twenty or thirty kilometers of mostly flat ground until Metz. With so little road remaining, it would be difficult for any of the others to change their fortunes. They could only push themselves for a distance and hope that it would be enough to secure a prize at the end of the day. From the pack, Luigi and Honoré sprinted forward; the others picked up their pace in response. They passed two towns that had been spared by the war—Amanvillers and Châtel-Saint-Germain—whose residents had fought loyally for Germany, only to be folded into a different country.

Their destination was a temporary memorial in Metz. For now, the statue stood in plaster, a structure set up for the parade taking place later that month. It rested at the end of the town's esplanade. On the other side of the road the Moselle River rushed. The poilu memorial had been designed by the sculptor Henri Bouchard, who had joined the French military at the beginning of the war and had helped build false trees and other forms of camouflage for soldiers so they could more safely traverse the ground between trenches. The monument stood where a statue of Emperor William I had been taken down by French troops on November 17, 1918.

Horizon blue ran throughout the city that afternoon. The pack rode at a staggered sprint past a row of soldiers in formation. The cyclists entered the town along rue de Nancy before taking a series of lefts toward the poilu model. Eugène pushed against the frame of his bike, twisting it back and forth on the ground, a steel pestle, but Luigi and Honoré led the sprint well in front of him. The two leaders battled one another for the first-place position. The sidewalks were packed with spectators who leaned around and hung from tree limbs to catch sight of the cyclists as they passed. Luigi was barely half a length in front of Honoré as he began one last attempt to break away, edging in front of Honoré and reaching the line inches before the French cyclist. It had almost appeared that the finish line had caught Honoré off guard, as if he had been prepared to press on for another hundred meters. He rode in second, in front of Léon, who crossed the line two minutes later, in front of Eugène.

Those who stood around the journalists were overwhelmingly of military rank. Among them, a man in a full dress uniform stuck out. Braided epaulets rested on his shoulders, and he wore a bicorne hat, stitched with a wide brocade down its center. General Maud'huy had been the person who had suggested to Desgrange that the racers arrive at the statue's foot, that he and his soldiers should preside over the finish. Maud'huy was the military governor of Metz, a position he had held since the end of the war. A lifelong resident of the town before it was lost to the Germans in 1871, his father had been killed in the Battle of Magenta during the Napoleonic Wars, fighting against the Austrians. His entire life, his son had harbored a grudge only enflamed by the Great War. Then he had been put in charge of bringing order to the once-German town during its transition of loyalty.

Eugène had extended his lead over Firmin with his time. Firmin would have to make up twenty-eight minutes for the two to be neck and neck. Chipping away at Eugène's time became more difficult. Another twenty-one minutes separated Firmin from Jean, in third.

Despite their efforts to unseat him, Eugène had beaten the others. He held on to the yellow jersey for another stage. The crowd still called to him with the occasional jeer, but what had once felt like a small distance between him and Firmin now felt secure. And if he won? He'd be the oldest cyclist to ever place first in the Tour. In time, people wouldn't think of his performance as different from any other victor. He deserved to win. He had continued past injury and exhaustion and the point when so many others would have stopped—and had stopped. All he needed was to continue along the next two stages: first to Dunkerque, then to Paris. The following stage was long, 468 kilometers, the second longest since they set out from Paris, but he had performed well on the extreme distance between Les Sables and Bayonne. The damaged ground was becoming increasingly hostile to their bikes, but Desgrange had trusted him with mapping the route from Paris to Roubaix earlier that year. If anything, it was his ground to lose.

He just needed to rest. One of the *l'Auto* journalists came up to Eugène at the finish line and asked about the day's leg. "Luigi is the best among us," he responded simply. It was true, Luigi was the most athletic. Few would have denied it. The younger Italian even had something of a strategy, unlike Honoré, who was too young, too eager to speed along in the most difficult climbs at the cost of tiring before the stage was done. The finish that day had caught him by surprise. Maybe in a few years, things would be different. Honoré would better understand the race by then, and Luigi's athleticism would continue to develop alongside his instincts for Desgrange's Tour.

The day had taken the cyclists through battlefields different from the ones they had encountered in the war. The sites passed were smaller: the war's nature was clear but its scale was not. Hundreds of thousands of young men slung themselves against one another to the north, on the flat, muddy ground, but not here. The Alsace had been too valuable for that destruction. The ground between Metz and Dunkerque, their next ride, however, would be different. Desgrange had decided to take the race all the way to the Belgian border. They would cross the country's most devastated terrain. It had seen militaries clash against one another with their full force, with their new armaments and their desire to win at whatever cost. The ground had seen the concept of war change, extend to a fight that bore into the soil, to its silty bed, to its bedrock. In the following 468 kilometers, the racers would traverse it, all the way to the English Channel and the country's northern coast.

Joseph Caillaux

Joseph Caillaux only wished he had been better able to sway his colleagues in government. If he had, if the war's course had been up to him—the number of young men the French threw at the lines, a date when he decided enough was enough—the cyclists on that year's Tour would never have had to cross the inhuman place. The land to their north wouldn't have existed at all, or rather, it would have been someone else's responsibility. Germany still would have crossed the border and marched onto the land, but the two belligerents wouldn't have traded blows for quite so long. Some of the towns and structures and populations would have been spared when it became clear the opposing side was more stubborn than the French had once thought. Some of the land would have had to be given up, but was that such a terrible cost in exchange for the lives that could have been saved and the preservation of the country that did remain? Instead, France had kept the land and then some, but the territory could not do what it once did for the people who lived there.

Joseph had only wanted the war to end as soon as possible. He was everything up to what Prime Minister Georges Clemenceau accused him of in the senate earlier that year: a traitor, someone no longer allegiant to his own country but instead to another. There had been no need for Clemenceau to publicly accuse Joseph of anything—to bring forward evidence that Joseph could rebut, to plainly state his case against Joseph to parliament—it had been enough that Clemenceau had implied the transgression. Everyone in the senate committee room agreed that it was believable enough that Joseph would sell out his own country for the benefit of its enemies. *Of course Joseph wanted Germany to win the war,* the thinking went, *even if France would come out of it as a second-tier state. He holds his own convictions over those of anyone; just look at how many times he's switched his beliefs to whatever felt right in the moment.*

His colleagues' opinions of him were founded in truth. Though splashed with his own miscalculations and betrayals, each step in his political career had nevertheless miraculously landed him in ever higher offices, up to the premiership itself.

Now he sat in prison de la Santé in Paris's fourteenth arrondissement. The warden had placed him in the VIP section, away from the general population, but his cell was still cramped and dirty, a far cry from the quarters he had become used to over the years, first as a banker, then as a politician. If in a trial his prosecutors sought the death penalty—not out of the realm of possibility, even for a former prime minister—they would only have to cart him out front onto rue de la Santé, where a guillotine would have been erected to finish him right there, in front of a gathered crowd.

His accuser, Clemenceau, was the man who had helped Joseph reach his ever-loftier positions in the first place and gave Joseph the chance to reach the premiership. He was as wrong about Joseph now as he was then: he would never support Germany over France. If anything, Joseph was just concerned with what was best for himself.

In each season of his political advancement, Joseph had discarded something in his wake—a policy fought for in a preceding government, an interest group who thought him their savior—in order to reinvent himself depending on the balance of power in the national assembly. He'd done away with friends and allies frequently; to say he did the same with ideologies would require that one had a clear grasp on the core of Joseph's political philosophy, which was a tricky, if not impossible, thread to unspool. With each ideal and cause he shed, he managed to glide through another door that had once been too thinly opened for him. Most recently, before the war began, he had taken a final cautious step from right to left so that he might lead the Radical Party a year after the party split over mandating three years of military service, when Radical Party members discredited him. The left-leaning members of the party opposed the bill, as did Joseph, until the moment he changed his stance.

His rise in the Radical Party had just been his latest shift, the one that led to his prison sentence and perhaps the only place Joseph-Marie-Auguste Caillaux could not remove himself from, though if a bookmaker were to ask a betting Frenchman whether Joseph would leave public life permanently, violently or otherwise, only the reckless gambler would stake his money on Joseph's downfall.

Before Joseph's second rise in the Radical Party, before he was accused of acting against the country he had served for almost twenty years, Joseph had been known as a man who understood the intricacies of France's fiscal system. His first job, at twenty-six, had been in the office of the Inspector General of Finance. As soon as Joseph could, he stood for election as a Conservative Republican—a party membership he had decided upon just weeks before. He ran for the seat his father once held in the Chamber of Deputies, the lower parliament house. The seat was held by the Duke of Doudeauville at the time, a monarchist who had recently taken the extreme step of supporting the revision of the French constitution with the hope it would lead to another monarchy.

The duke had heard rumors that Joseph hoped to run for his seat. When the duke confronted Joseph about his plans, Joseph assured him that he had no intention to run, that the duke's seat would remain uncontested. When the duke left the city for a trip, however, Joseph began his campaign against the incumbent politician, eventually winning the election while the duke was away.

Certain traits were common in Joseph Caillaux's lineage: pride, a temper that rose alongside it, and with that a tendency for combat, no matter whether it was advantageous. Joseph's face flared when he encountered difficult coverage in the press or stubborn allies and rivals. More than anything, however, he had a desire and willingness to do what it took for his survival in politics.

Stories say the first Joseph Caillaux had made his fortunes by purchasing the assets of a failing Jacobin seminary. He then promptly resold the land and nearly everything the seminary owned, amassing a fortune that allowed him to spend 649,000 francs in a single day, at least according to rumors. That same Joseph had played both sides of the 1789 revolution. He'd ingratiated himself with the sansculottes and the bourgeois. On his death bed, he gave his family the advice to *never serve the nobility. They don't know gratitude.* His grandson, the Joseph who found himself in prison, had expanded that proverb to encompass the entire political class.

In 1899, just ten months after winning his first election, Joseph had been appointed minister of finance, called upon by Pierre Waldeck-Rousseau, the new prime minister, who had been putting together a coalition government. As the minister whose politics fell second closest to the right, Joseph carried out his service without achieving much. He'd failed to pursue any of the reforms he had once publicly supported. His one success had been the defeat of an income tax measure, a stance opposed by the Radicals, the Socialists, and treasury officials.

At the turn of the century, the public gaze had fixed on Alfred Dreyfus. In 1899, the president pardoned Dreyfus's case. In 1902, Waldeck-Rousseau pardoned Dreyfus. France broke along lines of support for and opposition to Dreyfus. In response, French politics and many of its cultural institutions, including sports, were upended. Before the pardon, Joseph's Conservative Republican party had held much of the power in parliament. The party, which had historically been aligned with the right, began to drift leftward. The center-left Radical Party instead formed the majority. Waldeck-Rousseau resigned following the pardon, and Joseph's Conservative Republican party split. Joseph read the winds and followed the left-leaning faction that favored popular anticlerical sentiment.

◆ ◆ ◆

Seven years later, in 1906, the newly elected president of the council, Georges Clemenceau, was leading a Radical Party whose platform brought together elements of both the traditional Radical Party and the conservatives who were in power at the time. Clemenceau hoped to remain as part of the left to attract working-class votes but also stop short of instituting a socialist agenda. Few members of parliament had made efforts to thread the needle between the groups. One of the few politicians who fit the bill was Joseph, who had voted for the separation of the church and state in 1905—a litmus test for the party—and had continued to make a name for himself by writing a second volume of his book on taxation in 1904 titled *Impôts en France*. Again, Joseph was named minister of finance, and, in accepting, shed his past convictions as a Conservative Republican.

Once in the cabinet, however, he became a needle in the side of Clemenceau, flanking him on the anticlerical movement within the country. When the Clemenceau government lost its support in 1909, it was replaced with the Monis-Caillaux cabinet. Joseph served as a de facto prime minister given that the premier himself, Ernest Monis, left most policy matters to three of his trusted ministers, one of whom was Joseph. All three men stood as potential heirs of the party leadership once Monis had retired.

Adin Dobkin

The matter of who would next lead the party was decided at the Issy-les-Moulineaux airfield on the morning of May 21, 1911. That day, the Paris to Madrid air race was to take place, a three-stage event where competitors flew from Paris to Angoulême, then to San Sebastián, and finally to Madrid. Joseph's fellow ministers, Ernest Monis and Henri Berteaux, attended the event and were involved in a tragic accident that occurred when a self-taught pilot crashed his plane into a crowd of spectators. Berteaux was killed and Monis was injured. In their absence, Joseph rose to leadership of the Radical Party and to the premiership. The somewhat unpopular Joseph, who had few allies in government, appointed himself head of the Ministry of the Interior, a traditional role for the prime minister, allowing him to oversee large swaths of government administration.

At the beginning of July, less than one month after Joseph had risen to the premiership, Germany sent a gunboat to the port of Agadir in Morocco. The people of Morocco had rebelled against the sultan; Germany wanted to actively protect their investments in the country, though the country was officially under French protection. The deployment was seen as an act of hostility to the French and enflamed tensions that had been building between Morocco, Germany, and France over the last decade. The sultan, Abdelhafid, an ally of the French, was under siege in his Fez palace. Joseph's diplomatic position had been weak. With a German cruiser in the port, the French ambassador to Germany, Jules Cambon, informed his government that Germany required the French to cede the French Congo to them. In exchange, Germany would not stand in the way of France declaring Morocco a full protectorate. The British prime minister, worried that France would agree to German requests at the cost of the Allies' security, responded in a public speech that honor was more important than peace. Tensions grew. French businessmen with money in Germany began to withdraw it. War between France and Germany appeared imminent. Joseph, however, didn't wish for war: he knew the French

226

people still blamed politicians and military leaders for the Franco-Prussian War, and—though the British and the French had become closer as Germany withdrew—he still distrusted the western neighbor and knew that members of the German government saw the allyship as a sticking point for peace in the region. Ignoring the call for aggression against Germany, Joseph began speaking to German officials and bankers through private channels, hoping to quietly resolve the matter.

In November, a resulting bill came before the Chamber of Deputies. In exchange for leaving Morocco and acknowledging French protection over the land, Germany would be given territory along the French Congo river. In hindsight, the deal was about as good as the French could have mustered short of war. While the accord was being debated in the senate, Joseph also brought forward an authorization for German securities on the French market. The combination of the two bills was too much for parliament to stomach. Despite passing both bills, they rejected Joseph's audacity. They forced him out of office by the middle of January, just six and a half months after he had risen to the premiership.

◆ ◆ ◆

His fellow politicians argued against his methods, but were they really willing to go to war? Had they seen a better outcome than the one Joseph had negotiated? Alfred von Kiderlen-Waechter, the German secretary of state who'd agreed to the deal, had practically been thrown out of the Reichstag when he informed his own government of the agreement. Friedrich von Lindequist, the man responsible for overseeing German colonies, had resigned in disgrace. If Germans saw the deal so poorly, surely Joseph's colleagues should have seen it in more positive terms, those who supported Joseph thought.

The Morocco Affair haunted him even after stepping down as prime minister. The right-leaning newspaper, Le Figaro, hounded him in the first few months of 1914. Documents collected by the newspaper, according to its editor, Gaston Calmette, proved Joseph had been duplicitous in political matters, publicly supporting bills while privately rejecting them. The newspaper also came upon letters between Joseph and his then mistress, now wife, Henriette, exchanged while he had been married to his previous wife. On the evening of March 16, 1914, Henriette walked into the office of Calmette and shot and killed the editor only to be acquitted on account of the violence being a crime passionnel.

Joseph kept his seat in the Chamber of Deputies and served another term as the minister of finance through it all. He accepted blow after blow, penetrating layer after layer of his armor. He had been weakened but hadn't fallen. When the Great War began, after he had left his position as the head of the Radical Party, he joined the French army as a paymaster, away from the front.

René Viviani's government recalled him to Paris after a few months to help convince South American countries that they should join the fight against the Central powers, or at least remain neutral for the duration of the war. At the same time, Joseph, who opposed the continued fighting and its cost to the French government and people, met with a Hungarian agent. The agent passed along peace proposals with the directive that Joseph should read them and consider sharing them with others in government. Eventually, Joseph did deliver one, revealing it to Aristide Briand, the prime minister at the time.

"Peace without victory" was what Joseph wanted, according to his opponents, and he was willing to go around the back of government to accomplish it. He hoped that public opinion would change with the realization that peace might be possible, that the French people would realize the folly of the war and demand its quick end. He believed that with what the people had already seen, they would agree peace was better than continued fighting, whatever conditions were required to achieve it.

In November 1917, Clemenceau, the man who had brought Joseph into national government, became the prime minister once more. He'd been selected by President Raymond Poincaré over Joseph, due to Joseph's too-eager sentiment to end the war. Georges Clemenceau ascended to the premiership as the Allies struggled in the east. Throughout the year, the French faced battlefield mutinies after losses in the Nivelle and the Chemin des Dames offensives. Unrestricted warfare resumed off the coast. US troops arrived in France that summer, as did Greek forces. The Battle of Passchendaele ended just one week before Clemenceau's entrance into office. The battle was an Allied victory that came at the cost of hundreds of thousands of men. Even if progress in the war continued, few knew whether their victory would be worth it or whether that progress would last at all.

Clemenceau had an even more hawkish stance on Allied conduct in the war than Poincaré. He saw the German attempts at peace as a trap and believed that the best end for France would be achieved through the war's continuation. He attacked Joseph and asked that his parliamentary immunity be revoked. Following the vote, Joseph was arrested on January 14th. In trial discovery, Joseph's papers were brought out. They showed that Joseph had kept a record of his plans for a second premiership that never came. Within them he'd outlined his desire to dismiss a number of government figures. A few politicians, including Clemenceau, were to be arrested.

The war continued for almost another year as Joseph sat in prison de la Santé. At the war's end, Clemenceau's efforts bore fruit; Germany was forced to concede territory and power that they would have kept under Joseph's plan. By the time he was arrested, much of the damage he had fretted over had been done to his country and to his people. Still, the Allies suffered more than one hundred thousand casualties in April on Flanders Fields. Ninety-five thousand Frenchmen alone suffered in the Second Battle of the Marne. If he'd had his way, they could have started to rebuild that year, families could have returned to one another, and factories could have started contributing once again to the French economy. Nothing could replace those months and souls in Joseph's mind.

A decimated town in Zone Rouge, with a sign that reads "This was Forges."

14.

The war had cleared the trees from the ground as if they were weeds, and flattened old ridgelines from the horizon. The war saw glades, meadows, ponds, parks, and fields as paint gobs not yet spread across a canvas. The war began and the ground bore the violence stoically. What remained in front of Eugène couldn't be erased, no matter how hard both sides may have tried.

The land accepted the changes to its composition: the trench stitches, the heavy press of craters covering the ground around them. It was a distant planet. On the ground, present but not visible, were the materials deposited by the shells and the violent movement of human bodies, the chemicals leaching slowly from shrapnel and casings. Brooks of blood and flesh and excrement sunk into the ground where it settled before being carried away by an underwater vein.

The land that was left after the soldiers returned home needed a name. It needed something to be put around it. Not a border, but a marker to separate it from those areas that had avoided most of the war's violence. A memorial, a sign that would stand once the land had regained whatever semblance of its past life could be found, a designation that the area would never be the same.

Parliament settled on Zone Rouge. Le ministère des Régions libérées gradated the areas based on how much of the war the ground had absorbed. On the lowest end, green zones were places the military only passed through, where armies perhaps stored rusted gasoline canisters that had been breached, lines of artillery shells unloaded from narrow gauge train tracks then lost or disturbed while moving them to the front. The ground soaked them up. Then there were sites that had seen occasional fighting. Trenches disrupted the ground, and artillery at times found its mark. The shells dug shallow craters and upset the temporary shelters that had been built. They were not the places where soldiers had marched back and forth across the ground, living in it and dying on it before being buried beneath its surface. The less damaged sites were at times fronts in the war's first years, when the German military attacked French forces in 1914, sending them into retreat, or where militaries had otherwise passed through with minimal resistance.

The most affected areas, circumscribed in red, were the later battlefields, the ones contested for years once the conflict ground to a halt and the militaries buried themselves alive. Most prewar infrastructure was damaged if not destroyed in those areas. The land between the trenches had been uprooted. Abandoned or unexploded artillery shells lay hidden among tangles of barbed wire and hastily dug graves. In places, the ground underfoot was the only thing left. A few walls might stand in the distance, the pond in the town's corner might still endure. In the distance, a scattered line of trees could still mark the horizon, but of the town itself, nothing remained. Zone Rouge occupied a narrow stretch: it curved down and cut along the border of the country from the coast on the north, digging deep like a trowel near Compiègne and lifting back up near Lille. In that swath, the land might not ever return.

The racers were to pass through Lille that day, and Armentières, and Charleville. Armentières was said to be destroyed, the once prosperous linen-making town damaged in the eponymous battle that erupted there in 1914 but whose survival seemed possible up until the war's last year. Three thousand houses were destroyed, and nearly as many were damaged almost beyond repair. The town hall, the church, countless workshops and factories were nothing more than ruins. For every building spared, nine were destroyed.

The hard-packed pebble roads that would lie underneath the cyclists' wheels had cropped up under Napoleon. Eventually, a railway system was more convenient for most travel purposes, particularly between regional hubs. Some roads continued to receive maintenance commensurate with their use, while less frequented paths found little support from the national government. The war didn't follow common routes, however, and the heavy trucks that rumbled across their surfaces in those years broke down the same byways the cyclists now rode over. The route would turn to cobbled streets after Hirson until they reached Dunkerque at the end of the day. The heavy stones stood up to wear better than dirt or pebbled surfaces, but when they wore down, the uneven surface strained whatever rode over them.

Desgrange had dubbed the fourteenth stage the "Stage of Hunger," which in the past had stretched from Roubaix to Metz, or Dunkerque to Longwy. The damage to those towns prevented the cyclists from spending the night in them. The upcoming stage had once forced Lucien Petit-Breton from the 1913 Tour after he fell on the stone path. In that same year and stage, Philippe Thys had been knocked unconscious after a similar accident. Philippe had been able to repair his bike once he regained consciousness and eventually won that year's Tour. Neither would face the route that year. One had died in the war; the other had already abandoned the race.

Between the thirteenth and fourteenth stages, a group of poilus came up to Eugène. They introduced themselves as from the Fourth Cyclist Group, a sister unit to his own in the war. The captain of the unit, Dupuis, and his two lieutenants offered to host Eugène for the day. Expressing their pride in the cyclist's strength so far, they were hardly surprised one of their own looked set to win the Tour. Eugène, as ever, was gracious. After eating and drinking together in the town, the poilus left the cyclist with a gift and a few parting words of encouragement for his last two rides.

The forecast anticipated rain and low temperatures. If it came, the water would fill the small gutters between cobblestones and slick their surfaces. Without noticeable wind, the racers hopefully wouldn't feel much of a chill, but if a breeze picked up, the sensation in their limbs would be lost to them in those early morning hours after they left Metz. Their reactions would be slowed on the unstable ground.

Eugène exited café Francais et des Halles at 34 place Saint-Louis late on the night of July 24th. He rode casually toward the Thionville Gate, where the eleven cyclists would take off for Dunkerque. On the side of the road, musicians from the Lorraine Sportive society played; their small movements cast flickering shadows on the ground. The cyclists lined up below the old stone archway. The pistol fired at 10:00 p.m. and their pedals turned. As Eugène rode from town, the sky was as dark as charcoal. It would not brighten. Large clouds hung heavily above him, barely moving. Then the rain came. It pattered as he rode along. He was slow, more plodding than he had been before.

Still, he rode in front of the ten others through Longwy, and into Sedan after that, 164 kilometers. In 1914, Germany had taken control of Sedan. Depots in the city stored ammunition and supplies for German soldiers; those who worked there routed them north and south along train lines at a constant pace. A line cut through the city itself, minimizing the effort needed to keep the battles going.

Charleville was much the same. A German military administration had governed the twenty-thousand-person town until the end of the war. As it went on, Charleville was the site of the German crown prince's headquarters while he served as the commander of the Fifth Army. About half the town had been razed in the war during artillery strikes and bombing runs. Mézières, just next door, was bombed on the morning of armistice, almost right up until the moment the document took effect. Towns like these had once provided one-third of France's industrial output. Only the German army's success in the first days of the war had prevented their total destruction.

The cyclists continued. As the stage wore on, they neared the upper band of Zone Rouge, the gravitational center of the two armies. Around noon, they passed through Valenciennes. On the first and second day of November 1918, a battle had taken place here. Allied forces recaptured the town from the Germans, who had occupied it from the war's first days. In the fighting, Valenciennes's cathedral had been destroyed, as had countless buildings. That March, the French government asked the damaged towns of more than ten thousand inhabitants, like Valenciennes, to assist them in the development of city plans the government would use to rebuild those towns in the coming years. Those larger towns' complexity, their history and the years of growth within their borders exposed the limitations of rebuilding, and with a labor shortage it was unclear how long it would take before the towns again resembled themselves, even if many of their central features could never be replicated.

Eugène left the town and set off on the cobbled path. The ground skittered underneath his tires where it hadn't turned to mud. Each time a bike wheel left a cobblestone, it fell into a crevice. The motion shook the bike's frame and wheels. Each fall stressed the welds between the bike's tubes and those screwed-together parts. Eugène's weight had decreased from the beginning of the Tour, and his bike had weathered thousands of kilometers already. The rain that streamed down coated his jacket and filled his thin leather shoes. He weaved a bit; his wound from the accident in Nice still pained him. The mud splashed up his shins. The bike's frame and its wheels made alien sounds, as if he were riding on a set of rusty springs flicked by a fingertip. The squeaking, the rain, and the din of the people who had still shown up in their small towns to watch the Tour de France leader ride past surrounded him.

His bike then made a different, more resolute sound. In an instant, his front fork broke. His machine no longer responded to his movements, as if the tether between the two had been cut. The front of his bike sagged closer to the ground; Eugène slowed and stopped between the cobblestones. Looking down at the frame, he could see that it was broken, unusable. His weight had caused the fork to bend from its position. The rest of the cyclists in the pack rode past him. He had seen a break like this before, in the 1913 race, down to the cracked sleeve between the bike's frame and its fork. He couldn't fix it on the side of the road; he'd need a shop with tools to weld the metal back into a functional shape. Even if he found the tools, he knew it would take him at least an hour to finish the repairs, and he wasn't sure his rushed job would stand up to the cobbled ground that he still had to travel.

Eugène dismounted his broken frame. The steel bike weighed him down as he picked it up and slung it across his back. The weight, his posture, it was all familiar to him, but he was slower than he'd been six years ago. His feet had left him this late in the race. He walked forward. His shoes rubbed his ankles; the water slopped up in the space between. He hoped the town ahead would have a metalworking shop and that the owner would let him in. Unsure whether the yellow jersey he still wore would help or hurt his cause, he pressed on. If the shop owner wasn't home, or if he refused Eugène's request—well within his rights—Eugène would wind up in last place. As it was, he knew he'd lost his title.

Eugène continued walking the few hundred meters to the next town. The cyclist labored into Raismes. A *l'Auto* correspondent watched him from the side of the road. Earlier, he had watched as the pack of cyclists came through without the leader's yellow jersey. He'd waited, checking his clock, thinking perhaps he had missed the first-place cyclist, that the mud coating all their jerseys had disguised even Eugène's. In the town, Eugène found a small bicycle factory that supplied the surrounding region with hand-built machines. The owner granted him access. The last time Eugène had repaired a bike like this one wasn't far from his mind: the steps he'd taken then, the feeling he'd put behind him once he'd finished the repair and set out on the remainder of the Tour. Then there were those times he'd done the same not so far from there, after the 1913 Tour, when the repairs were for his fellow soldiers, who'd relied on him for far more than their performance in a race.

Eugène entered the shop and set to work on the bellows, heating the furnace that would allow him to bend the fork back into shape and weld the bike together again. He worked alone under the watchful eye of the owner and the *l'Auto* correspondent. He heated the steel, then carefully bent it while it was still pliable. He then quenched the fork in a bath. A few curious neighborhood children had followed him into the shop. The *l'Auto* correspondent kept a careful record, waiting to telegram ahead and report on Eugène's progress, making sure the cyclist didn't break any rules while he repaired his bike. Once Eugène had bent the frame back into a shape that would hold to the road, he welded the fork's break, tracing a path along the cracked steel, making it whole. He was one of the few racers who knew how to complete this work. Had the same happened to Honoré or Luigi, they wouldn't have been able to go on. If they had even attempted to fix their bikes, they would have needed the owner's assistance, and their times would have slipped further with the resulting penalty.

A little over an hour later, he took the fork from its last bath and slotted it back through the bike's empty socket. He secured it to the bike and replaced the wheel below. Testing its sturdiness, he again placed the bike on the cobbled path. He was satisfied. After thanking the owner of the shop one last time, he mounted the bike and rode out toward the road. He had one hundred more kilometers to go before resting. In that distance the road wouldn't become safer for the stressed frame. He hoped it would hold. If the bike broke again, if his repair failed, fixing it would be more difficult, and then, even if he could accomplish it, his bike would be more fragile, less likely that the fork could hold its shape. He picked up his pace. The correspondent watched him leave beside the spectators who had looked over his shoulder in the small shop. A cheer grew as he left, as the people watched him reach the end of the town and continue on alone.

The people who saw Eugène from the side of the road had witnessed a foreign occupation, days, weeks, months of artillery strikes. They had lived with the constant thought that the war would simply wipe their town from the country's map, that they would be gone like so many others not so far from them and that, whenever new maps were written, they would be nothing more than a stretch of green where their town had once been. Otherwise, structures would replace them, but wouldn't recognize their onetime existence.

Those who saw Eugène near the town's edge had a difficult time catching a glimpse of his face between the rain and the mud and whatever speed he had mustered to catch up to the other cyclists, now more than an hour in front of him. If they could have seen his face, if they could have made out his features in the brief moment before he rode past, they would have seen his fixed gaze, his strained face, the tears that ran down it as he heard them cheer even after he had left the town behind.

They watched him grow smaller until he was swallowed up by countryside. Still they called out for him. The correspondent sent a telegram ahead: "Eugène has repaired his bike but will lose his first place in the general classification."

◆ ◆ ◆

Lille had been marked as an open city at the war's start, one not to be defended by French troops but instead left unguarded so the soldiers once garrisoned there could be sent to another, more critical part of the front. Perhaps, the thinking went, the lack of military forces would help the town avoid the war's worst damage. Then plans changed. The French army returned to the town in October 1914 once German offensive movements around the area had become apparent.

The siege started shortly after the French soldiers arrived. Germans began shelling the town, then entered it on vehicles and by foot on the twelfth of October. The following occupation would last four years. Policy governing the occupied land shifted from year to year. First, the Germans promised that no damage would occur; they were only occupying the town to prevent the people and the factories in Lille from working against them. In time, however, the policy became harsher. Soldiers stripped machine parts from the factories. Then, the machines themselves were broken so they could not be used by the French.

Lille families were singled out. The German military wanted to keep the morale of the occupied people low to prevent them from mobilizing against German forces. They split up and deported family members, sent them to labor camps. Soldiers printed and circulated the *Gazette des Ardennes*, a French-language newspaper. Its articles detailed the destruction in the surrounding area and the French military's unwillingness to take back the region. The reports were false, but their vision succeeded. The population of 217,000 fell to 88,000—many moved away or were forcibly sent from the town; others had already fled when the war broke out. Tuberculosis spread, and the population was shaken further.

When armistice was declared, people began to move back to their homes. Oftentimes they didn't bother to visit a passport office to ensure their papers were up to date and that they could pass through the countryside without encountering trouble from soldiers stationed at checkpoints along most roads. They returned without knowing what they would find, without knowing what work would be available for them. Some heard that their towns had been leveled, others heard no news at all. In either instance, it didn't dissuade them. Once they arrived back in their towns, they remained. The buildings and homes were damaged and destroyed, but the people built shelters in the intact cellars underneath decimated houses. More arrived. They began cobbling together an existence. Few provisions had been made by the French government. The ministère des Régions libérées had been established in 1917, but it had only taken limited proactive measures before the end of the war. It handed out contracts to private companies to begin the rebuilding process, starting with towns' most essential functions. The ministère paid people to reconstruct their old homes. Like birds scavenging for a nest, citizens pulled material from their old homes and from abandoned wartime structures in order to build anew.

Eugène entered Lille at 5:19 in the evening. Firmin, riding in first, had passed through the town a little after 3:30 p.m. The Belgian cyclist had seen Eugène's accident for what it was and accelerated to the front of the pack. The city they entered was a product of these still limited efforts at rebuilding. The town's bishop had described Lille as "a grave-yard." Rubble had been cleared from a corridor in the street, and remnants of buildings had been stripped of their remaining walls to build other, temporary structures. Bricks had been pulled from mortar like loose teeth.

Through these streets, Eugène rode. After his crash he had fallen again on an exposed set of railroad tracks and reopened a gash on his knee that bled down his shin, slicked his ankle, and caused the joint to rub against his shoe. The grit he rode over lifted in his wake, clung to his wound. He continued.

The cyclist made his way across the cobblestone streets. The entire stage was a thread connecting a patchwork of recovering towns in various states of disrepair. After witnessing the damage in Lille, he continued to Armentières. Germans had entered the town on October 10th of 1914 but, ten days later, it had been retaken by British soldiers who then controlled it until April 1918. The soldiers ran drills on la Grand Place and at l'Ecole Nationale Professionnelle, marching in columns across the dirt courtyard. The front was just four kilometers away, and so their training only lasted until the units had been deemed ready enough to fight. They marched out from the relative safety of the courtyards and onto the fields, toward the nearby trenches. The soldiers who remained inside the town, and the town's factories, were targeted. Even buildings without strategic value were targeted: l'église Saint Joseph du Bizet had been reduced to a few discontinuous standing walls. High-explosive shells had caused the most damage. The shells flattened structures and destroyed roads and bridges, but incendiary and poisonous gas had also been used, especially in the summer of 1918, when tens of thousands of shells were dropped onto the city, eventually triggering the evacuation of civilians who had, until that point, remained.

Eugène passed through the towns of Zone Rouge alone. He rode by Mont Cassel, where Marshal Ferdinand Foch kept his headquarters. The crowds came and went, but when they saw him, without fail they yelled and cheered as if he were the cyclist they had been waiting for all those hours.

◆ ◆ ◆

At 6:30 p.m., the first car rolled into Dunkerque. No racers followed. The crowd grew more anxious and pressed against the barriers along the flat stretch of road. They jostled for better views on both sides of the canal and in boats floating on the water, though rain beat down on its surface. Still no racers were in sight. The officials in the car got out to inform those waiting that they were half an hour in front of the cyclists, who were then between Wormhout and the coastal city.

A few minutes after seven, the first pack was spotted entering the town. The weather didn't seem to bother the audience. Nor did the labored pace at which the cyclists rode. They cheered for Firmin, Léon, Joseph, Luigi, and Jean, who came in one after another with some distance separating each rider. After the cyclists passed through, the audience waited, again growing quiet. Two and a half hours later, Eugène rode in. The timekeeper had left the finish line; he could no longer see the marks on his watch. Eugène rode through the finish line and continued straight to café des Arcades. Those who had waited broke into applause, though the night had grown dark and cold. They crowded around him, the cyclist who still wore the yellow jersey as he signed into the logbook.

The Tour riders were in their rooms asleep by 11:00 p.m., exhausted by that day's efforts but at least glad the haphazard accommodations in Dunkerque would be their last. Earlier, when a journalist from *l'Auto* asked him his thoughts on how the stage turned out, Eugène had remained composed, with the same simple attitude that had endeared him to Desgrange and the others. "I didn't deserve it," he said of the accident, "but the fates saw otherwise." Firmin had been less circumspect. He would have preferred to lead the race on account of his own actions, not due to Eugène's misfortune. Taking his yellow jersey wasn't a Pyrrhic victory, if such a thing could exist between two individuals, but it was unsatisfying. Firmin's performance hadn't been better than Eugène's. He had known shortly after Eugène fell that the accident would be enough to change their positions. Eugène and the course had accomplished what Firmin could not. The jersey would be passed to him for the first time. It was late. Eugène couldn't beat him back or even come close to challenging him unless the Belgian suffered some similar calamity. In time, maybe people would forget how Firmin had won the race, how he had only survived and that had been enough. Instead, they might recognize him as the Tour's thirteenth winner and only that, but it was hard to set aside the thought that he was—more than anything else—the cyclist who prevented Eugène from taking his rightful place, and the others would only remember him as that.

Eugene Bullard

July 27, 1919—rue Navarin, Paris

Paris would arrive to watch the Tour's end that day, even if Eugène Christophe, the Frenchman that so many had set their hopes on, had taken off the yellow jersey and handed it over to a Belgian. It had been eight years since a Frenchman had won the race that wrapped around their country, that beat the bounds and showed no small number what their border looked like. Eugène's misfortune wouldn't dim that Sunday's celebrations, not for Eugene Bullard nor the thousands who left their homes that morning to watch the cyclists arrive again at Parc des Princes.

Eugene knew what it was like to be cautiously celebrated, to find himself at a party someone begrudgingly hosted on his behalf. He had been in that position not so long ago after winning the Croix de Guerre, then becoming a fighter pilot, a war hero in his adoptive country if not in his actual one. He'd earned more than party toasts and newspaper mentions, as anyone who fought in the first days of Verdun had. "We were in hell for sure," he said of his weeks there, when he'd lost all but four of his fellow legionnaires from the 170th Infantry Regiment.

He'd had to use his issued close-quarters carbine to fend off a German soldier who dropped into the crater where he was sheltering.

At least the public recognition was better than what he'd find waiting for him back in the US. When he'd fled his home in Columbus, Georgia, at the age of eight, following the attempted lynching of his father, maybe his life could have shifted tracks without much further trouble. Instead, he wanted more than to escape the oppressive South and the life he stood to inherit there. After three years, he left the US entirely, bound for Aberdeen, Scotland, a sixteen-year-old stowaway on the *Marta Russ*. Perhaps life could have then seen fit to reward his perseverance. Or certainly after the Great War had ended, after he had volunteered for the French Foreign Legion in those early halcyon days of the war, after he'd received positive marks from his commanders and ascended to become the first African American aviator in history, certainly then he should be allowed some earned respect. But no, Eugene's life wound and weaved, at times seeming like the charisma so many had recognized would set him on a comfortable path, but that route hadn't yet appeared.

◆ ◆ ◆

Eugene had rented a place on rue Navarin in Montmartre, an apartment that looked onto a small courtyard where, if he liked, he could wake up and greet his neighbors who had walked out with their cups of coffee and that morning's edition of *l'Humanité* or *l'Auto* on warm summer mornings. He could be forgiven, however, if he chose to avoid them and instead woke up late. His social life, busier in recent months, had been constant enough. On any given week, invitations arrived at Eugene's apartment for dinners and parties, hosted by distinguished members of Parisian society.

Groups of temporary transplants from London and Beijing had been meeting at Versailles, discussing what sort of world would be built in the wake of the war. Between those meetings, the visitors hoped to take in the culture and society that Paris had to offer. Eugene—a war hero, a former champion boxer, and an American who had chosen to serve as a regular poilu for the country he now called his home—was a desired dinner companion. It helped that he was a natural storyteller. The dinners weren't as far removed from his professional life as he'd like, however. Eugene formally tutored the son of Wellington Koo, one of the representatives from China, on cultural matters and on Parisian society. It was just one of the odd jobs he'd picked up after he realized he wouldn't be able to competitively box again without months of training. He found the work agreeable enough, well-paying and suited to his personality, a demeanor that allowed him to just as easily slip between distinguished Versailles crowds to clubs in Montparnasse or Montmartre, down the street from his apartment, where gilded dining rooms and hushed conversations between pairs of guests gave way to smoky parlors and a cacophony of roiling laughter, trombone slides, and shouts of young men trying to get the attention of a passing waitress.

If Eugene had his way, he'd have preferred to spend all his time roaming the clubs that had sprung up in his neighborhood. Jazz filled the vacuum in Montmartre that the cafés and cabarets of the Belle Époque had left behind after closing. The music's import had begun with the end of the war. The French first heard jazz last year, when James Reese Europe performed alongside his bandmates from the 369th Infantry Regiment. *The World* magazine had reported on a sound that "might be called liquefied harmony. It runs and ripples, then has a sort of choking sensation; next it takes on the musical color of Niagara Falls at a distance, and subsides to a trout brook nearby." In recent months, Eugene had started to spend time with Louis Mitchell's Seven Spades Band. Mitchell had been the drummer with James Reese Europe's regimental band, but following Europe's death just a couple months ago—when he'd been stabbed by one of his drummers—the

Seven Spades Band had been in high demand. Seth Jones, one of the band's percussionists, had taken Eugene under his wing, teaching him the drums in the odd hours before the band's live sets.

The music had its critics. Even those who supported its rise often didn't know how to put words to jazz musicians' flair. "A jazz band is a unique organization of which it may be said the worse it is, the better it is," the 1918 Victor record catalog said. Whether one liked or disliked the music itself, jazz was the US financial institutions—Morgan and others—who established branches on Paris's right bank to support the flow of foreign goods into the city; it was bakelite pipe stems and fake amber necklaces; it was short skirts and short hair on women who wore men's jackets; it was Marcel Duchamp's *L.H.O.O.Q.*, where found objects were, through intent and vision alone, turned into art; just as it was Wyndham Lewis's *A Battery Shelled* and Mack Beckmann's *The Night* that made the familiar unfamiliar. It was the fear that those things that had existed before would be replaced by these new ones—had been replaced. Just look at the ball following the Treaty of Versailles's signing; it had not been an orchestra but the Original Dixieland Jass Band who played. Jazz was the modern era, an art crafted by African Americans. It was as if the war's barren fields had made way for shallow cultural roots to take hold just as it had for plants of that same variety.

The French were taken by jazz but wary of its origins. The American soldiers who remained in their country, the diplomats, politicians, and businessmen, too, didn't seem to care about much except money—its creation and its disposal. The American jazz musicians weren't above French scrutiny.

For their part, Americans didn't like everything about Paris, or the people who chose to live there. The country where Eugene was born, and all that came along with it, still hadn't given up its hold on him.

On May 28th, just two months earlier, Eugene had been visiting with some friends on the balcony of café de Paris. He had been at the café for an hour or two, drinking and growing boisterous. The café itself was busy, filled with the eclectic crowd common to postwar Paris: the sedate green drab of US doughboys, the glistening fabrics of women who surrounded them, the plain suits of Parisian men who observed the rollicking scene. Eugene, a bit unsteady after a few drinks, stood up and bumped into an American officer who'd been seated behind him. The officer turned to look up and saw the Black man who'd knocked into him. The American officer had almost surely known that Paris was unlike the US. It's not to say France was free of racism: Parisians eroticized Eugene's jazz; they viewed the music as emotional and somber, qualities they thought were inherent to Black people, instead of jazz being a response to their circumstances in the United States. For most Frenchmen, the extent of their interactions with Black people were with the country's colonial subjects, who were read about but not seen until the years they fought alongside Frenchmen. Still, in Paris, the law saw white and Black men as equal in day-to-day matters. Perhaps the officer recognized the lilt of American English as Eugene brushed off the accident as a joke, or apologized—reports were conflicting. In any case, the American soldier's response had been unambiguous. He stood and punched Eugene, who fell into the arms of a nearby newspaper salesman. Despite the drinks, Eugene got back up. The officer came over and punched Eugene again, knocking him out.

Eugene had been taken to Beaujon Hospital, a stone-faced building that served as a military hospital during the war. Doctors examined him for internal injuries following the assault but found none. Eugene was released the following morning. By that point, however, local journalists had filed their stories reporting on the incident. In the immediate haze, a few details were mistaken. Eugene hadn't died, as some outlets had reported, and he wasn't Aaron Lister Brown, a welterweight world champion, as others had claimed. Maybe they had seen Eugene and Brown, the "Dixie Kid," years before. The two were barely separable before the war.

By late July, the incident had receded. Americans in their dark-green uniforms could still be found in cafés around the city, including Eugene's haunt, the Bal Tabarin, where he went to see the city's latest jazz acts. Fresh singers and bands arrived regularly. Eugene's life continued without much trouble from the soldiers, except for cutting eyes, hushed jeers present in the American crowds.

It was a foggy Sunday morning. The night before, Harry Pilcer, an American dancer, had headlined at the Bal Apollo alongside three orchestras. The Bal Tabarin had hosted a French cancan performance.

Despite the late festivities, Parisians and visitors to the city woke up early. They made breakfast and drank coffee to shake the spirits of the night before. They read the latest edition of *l'Auto* and were informed that the doors to Parc des Princes would open early, at 12:45 p.m., in order to handle the crowds who would undoubtedly line up outside the velodrome. *L'Auto* was hosting a series of track races, with a few of the competitors who weren't racing in the Tour's final stage. Francis Pélissier was among those who would ride around the oval track. For those who weren't interested in joining the crowds at the stadium, the newspaper mentioned that the cyclists would enter the city from the northeast, where they'd perform a timed loop around rue du Chalet for a separate prize. Then they'd cut across the city and dip down through its center before making their way across the Seine toward Parc des Princes. Two hundred fifty mounted police officers would line their path, keeping order. The Parisians who wanted to watch the finish at Parc des Princes, the paper noted, could arrive at Porte d'Auteuil metro stop, just a quick five hundred meters from the stadium's entrance.

Eugene woke up with the city. He took in the morning air and the haze that would soon give way to sun. He left his apartment and walked down rue Saint-Georges among the scattered crowds that milled about in the soft light.

Belgian soldiers inspect the remains of a villa near Dunkerque, destroyed in the fall of 1914.

15.

Three hundred forty kilometers separated Firmin from one final lap around Parc des Princes, the arena where the sixty-seven cyclists, now eleven, had started one month ago. It didn't feel like a victory. He'd finish the race, that much seemed likely, though there was plenty of time for him to suffer an accident. The Belgian who had been given the leader's yellow jersey hadn't performed better than Eugène, he'd only been luckier. Both of them knew as much, as did every person who had followed the race. He'd sign his name into *l'Auto*'s log at Parc des Princes, he would leave his bike at rest to collect the money from a first-place finish, and that would be it. He had wanted to win, of course, had rode as best as he was able and fought to tip Eugène from his first-place position while Eugène held it for so many days after Henri left the race, but in the end it was the roads, not Firmin or Eugène, that had placed the jersey on Firmin's back.

"GLORIA VICTIS," Desgrange wrote in that morning's *l'Auto*, calling to mind Antonin Mercié's sculpture designed after the Franco-Prussian War. The statue's bronze features showed a winged woman holding a broken French soldier. Eugène was the moral winner of the Tour if not the actual one, the editor wrote.

Firmin had never seen the war so close. The stretches they had crossed, the mud-slicked paths and the alpine climbs hadn't been shaken from the cyclists' bones, but they were nothing compared to that strip of Zone Rouge. The war was scarcely over—was still raging—in those untended places. The people who'd just returned hadn't realized what it would take for the towns to reappear: years, hard labor, francs, the national government guiding them, and then what?

Firmin's supporters had crossed the Belgian border to watch the cyclist ride through the harbor city of Dunkerque all the same. They and so many others like them turned out, despite the two countries' losses, in numbers as great as in the Tours prior to the war. Their towns' rebuilding had barely begun. Twenty-four hundred of the three thousand buildings that made up Dunkerque had been damaged in the bombings. Its Allied logistics base had been targeted. Four hundred of the twenty-four hundred buildings were destroyed completely. Legislation that would determine compensation for wartime damage had only passed parliament in April, and so on that day, those buildings were rubble and their old plans were elsewhere, if not destroyed in another one of the bombings.

The fans had gathered on the Dunkerque streets to watch Firmin ride past. They stood between stacks of rubble with more of the same on the road's opposite side—others sat on larger chunks—the cyclists in a corridor, or a sea of bricks parted for a time.

They were to leave that Sunday morning. The crowds had again preempted them, gathering around place Jean-Bart. Men stood underneath a statue of the privateer in that cobbled courtyard where the town hosted its winter carnival, where local fishermen were celebrated one last time before leaving for the cod season in the Atlantic. They sat at tables outside cafés. They drank from bottles of wine and greeted each other as if they knew every inhabitant of the city—one that had been home to thirty-nine thousand people before the war and had only begun to recover from its population of seven thousand toward the war's end.

The newspaper's sign-in booth, staffed by local cyclists, would open at midnight, but given that it was a weekend, people showed up well in advance of the competitors. The streets had been lit earlier in the evening, as had many of the shops, whose windows still glowed though no one shopped at that hour. The city lights and the energy that wended through the crowd gave the impression it was barely dinnertime when the racers arrived at the café, one after another. Jules Nempon signed in first, just after the station had opened. As the final B classification cyclist remaining, he received a higher esteem than some of the lower-ranking A classification racers. In recent days, after the second-to-last B classification cyclist, Aloïs Verstraeten, had been disqualified following the eighth stage, Jules collected the prize money many towns had set aside for his perseverance. He had not arrived first, but he had arrived. He'd gathered 1,300 francs in total, more than Eugène, whose strategy seemed to deliberately avoid first-place finishes on individual stages.

Despite his bike's failing, Eugène sat in third. It was not impossible that he could pull ahead of Firmin and Jean if they both crashed, but those who argued that Eugène hadn't deserved his first-place standing felt vindicated. Better to be a B classification racer no one expected to last than the onetime first-place rider who lost his position and had never been aggressive enough for some people's taste anyway.

The final racers signed in at 1:30 a.m. They left from the square and trudged to quai de Saint-Omer, along the Bourbourg Canal. Behind and around them, the crowd followed their movements. Many were on foot, others were on bikes, pedaling slowly next to the cyclists, as if they'd decided to enter the race themselves, outfitted with water bottles and caps and protective goggles and only lacking the gray and blue of La Sportive. Desgrange knew the race couldn't ignore the fans entirely; without them the race was nothing. He had still felt compelled to publish a notice in *l'Auto*: those who wanted to join the racers on bikes or in cars should avoid the front of the pack so as not to kick up dirt ahead of the cyclists and to avoid collisions. Those first Tour years of brawls and nail-strewn roads were not so distant after all.

The final distance was longer than most amateurs would ride on any other occasion, but with 340 kilometers of more or less straight ground, it was possible for fans to follow the cyclists much of the way without exhausting their fresh legs. The weather wasn't predicted to cause much trouble, either: the rain had cleared up around much of the country, though it remained cloudy that morning, and the temperature was supposed to hold in the midfifties.

At 2:00 a.m., Firmin and the others set off, as they had done in fourteen other towns. There was no difference between those times and this one, and yet there was every difference. Few fans had paid attention to Firmin in the earlier starts—Eugène had led the race, and other cyclists had performed better than the Belgian on individual stages. Now he led the general classification. It was his gray-and-blue La Sportive jersey that had been replaced by *l'Auto*'s yellow. He had become the canary the other racers would attempt to beat, and, to those who watched from the side of the road, he was the one who had unseated Eugène. Few looked to him now as their hero; Eugène still held that title, and Firmin's accomplishment over him bred as much resentment as it did acclaim.

Almost immediately after the cyclists pushed off, Paul Duboc crashed, dropping from the pack of eleven. The cyclists left him behind and began following the English Channel. Less than forty kilometers separated the two countries at the Strait of Dover. The white cliffs of England were so close they could have been seen from their path, though the early morning light and their accelerated pace prevented them from noticing the Allied country. If they'd kept riding, they'd have reached Dover far sooner than they could Paris. The ocean was black; the moon was more than waning, it was extinguished from the sky. There were few features on the roads to distinguish one from another. The front soon retreated. The war was not absent from the port towns they passed through, with their recently built loading docks and hospitals still crowded around each small town's structures, but the ground no longer regularly bore its scars.

The excitement of the crowds reflected the racers' proximity to the Tour's end. They lined the streets of Calais, forty-two kilometers into the stage. Lamps had been lit, and along boulevard d'Egalité, business lights had remained on through the night. Jules Nempon entered the town where he lived at 4:22 a.m., the first competitor but almost a full hour after Desgrange had told viewers to expect them. As with tradition, the other cyclists allowed him that moment. He rode through to the cheers of those who lined the boulevard. They recognized the 151 on his jersey, unobscured by mud or rain. A group of locals approached the Brasier and passed along a collection of eight hundred francs for the cyclist. Others gave Desgrange the sums they had collected for Eugène. He had not yet ridden through the town, but they had followed his fortunes in the paper; they had seen what he had gone through, how his progress had been halted as it had been in 1913, right when it appeared like his fortunes might turn out differently this time.

Though the stage was shorter than others and had few features to strain the cyclists' abilities, man-made or otherwise, the path to Paris was slow. The roads were still cobbled. They moved together, but just after passing through Calais, a nail punctured Eugène's tire, dropping him behind the others, including Paul Duboc, who had managed to catch up to the pack after his crash. The crowd who watched Eugène cheered for him as if he were still wearing the yellow jersey, as if he had only just earned it and there was nothing that could prevent him from winning the entire race. Desgrange saw people's response, too. Beyond his performance, Eugène had come to symbolize something slightly different for each person he rode by, a reflection of themselves and their country as they had experienced it in those past five years.

He arrived twelve minutes after the others in Boulogne-sur-Mer, at 6:38 a.m., behind Honoré, Paul, Jean, Luigi, Jules, Firmin, Joseph,

Alfred, and Léon, who all rode into the town together. The journalists who watched him pass by saw the crowd perk up. They shouted "Cri-cri!" They raced onto the street behind him with a fervor, as if they might just strip him off his bike and carry him away as a souvenir. Instead, they kept pace with him, just behind his bike, still cheering.

Eugène continued, hoping to avoid any more punctures from the cobbled path. He soon passed Paul Duboc, unseated along the side of the road. The Rouen cyclist's crank had broken; his bike was unusable. Eugène entered Étaples at 8:05 a.m., fifteen minutes after the leading racers. Five minutes after Eugène, Paul arrived, carrying his bike. A car that held a group of fans had picked him up from the side of the road. They had seen his state and drove him to the outskirts of the town, where he leapt out and started walking, far enough away that the transgression had eluded the race officials' eyes, he'd hoped.

A short while later, Jules fell from his bike but got up quickly enough that a brief sprint brought him back to the pack. The road continued trying to tear the cyclists from their vehicles.

By the time the first riders reached Abbeville, 163 kilometers into the stage, they were more than an hour and a half behind Desgrange's estimates. The crowd's impatience died once the cyclists were spotted. The clouds had broken away to sunlight, and the temperature had remained mild, if slightly brisk, which kept the racers and the viewers attentive. They recognized Luigi first, followed by Jacques, Firmin, Honoré, Joseph, Alfred, Jules, and Léon. As Desgrange pulled the Brasier to a stop and let out the officials so they could check the cyclists, a group of townspeople came up to the editor and thrust 210 francs into his hand. "For Eugène," they said.

Abbeville had been spared in the war, but around its edges, farmers could reach into the sodden earth and pull up the sharp-tipped noses and blunt backs of artillery shells. The instruments had been fired in a long arc toward those opposite points where soldiers refilled their ammunition pouches and where they sheltered briefly between stays in the trenches. Civilians who understood the danger reported such discoveries to local officials or to the soldiers who remained posted at an Australian hospital nearby. Those who didn't moved the shells themselves, or brought them into their homes as souvenirs, like death mask mementos. In a day or a week or sometimes—if the villagers were lucky—never, the shells would tip over or were too closely inspected, and the weapon would find its mark, blindly.

◆ ◆ ◆

The cyclists were less than halfway into the stage, 177 kilometers from Parc des Princes. The crowds no longer ended at towns' edges. Along the farmland between Abbeville and Beauvais they lined the road. They left the towns, looking to avoid the more populated areas, hoping to stand at the road's edge, with no one interrupting their view of the cyclists as they passed. Between the two checkpoints, near Achy, Honoré hit an imperfection in the road and fell with his bike. He got up and examined the machine, but nothing appeared out of place. Sprinting, he caught up to the cyclists who followed behind the pack.

All but three of the racers appeared together in Beauvais at 1:33 p.m. The crowds had waited for almost two and a half hours, not sure when the racers would arrive or whether their preferred rider had given up somewhere along the way. Honoré had rejoined the pack and led through the small cross of the town. Alfred followed six minutes later, then Eugène and Paul ten minutes behind him. Eugène was too far behind to make up the ground that separated him from Firmin and Jean. The 1919 Tour would have a winner in Firmin, but the race had created another. Once, it would have been unacceptable. Better to have one remaining competitor win by default than two competitors claim the title. It would have undermined the integrity of the race and Desgrange's desire to have an unequivocal winner, but that year the fans would have a Tour cyclist who won and one who survived; it only seemed right.

The cyclists passed into a forest. The lane tightened and trees pressed in on them. Fans still crowded the claustrophobic stretch. It appeared, at moments, as though there would be no silent ground from there to Paris, about sixty kilometers away. The spectators jammed onto the side of the road to avoid tree branches. They narrowed the lane further as the cyclists jockeyed for their positions, not quite close enough to Paris that they could sprint. Still, they kept their quickened pace. They neared a hill. Luigi led the others up it, followed by Jean, then Honoré, Léon, Jacques, Joseph, Jules, and Firmin. None of them was content; each waited for the moment they could jut out with enough energy to carry them through to Parc des Princes. Near the top of the hill, Jean, Honoré, Luigi, and Léon all accelerated, leaving the others behind. Jacques watched them gain ground and sped up to catch them. The others receded into the distance behind the five as they exited the hill and the forest.

The pack rode through Poissy, the industrial city just up the Seine, at 3:56 p.m. They were surrounded by supporters on bikes to the front and the back and on both sides, not caring for Desgrange's rules about riding some distance away, though they managed to not interfere with the racers. The cyclists rode through Poissy, where rows of people stood along the road's edges, almost no ground visible between their feet. Jules rode in four minutes after the first group, followed by Firmin and Joseph. Eugène entered Poissy at 4:30 p.m., just behind Paul, the last of the remaining cyclists. No group received as much applause as Eugène. He passed through the site of royal hunting grounds, forested and lush, then Château de Saint-Germain-en-Laye. Louis XIV had been born in a now-demolished portion of the palace. It had housed the Stuart family and their followers after the Glorious Revolution in England. It was a house where old wars had been led. During the Hundred Years' War, the château was sacked by Edward the Black Prince, though he took pains to leave the chapel standing. Eugène followed the tramway tracks out of town, which led all the way to Paris. He was almost at the race's end, he just needed to ride on, past the crowds who stood waiting. He could no longer see the others in front of him. He determined his resolute pace alone. Just beyond the horizon he could envision Parc des Princes, the end of this interminable month.

The American Red Cross Canteen and Enlisted Men's Hotel #13, at Champ de Mar, made of salvaged tents to accommodate the soldiers moving through Paris.

16.

The doors to Parc des Princes opened at 12:45 p.m. on July 27th. The crowd immediately flowed through, hoping to claim one of the ten thousand seats that skirted the straightaway sections of the cement track. There were more people than the stadium's bleachers could comfortably accommodate, that much was apparent from the number of people who lingered in Boulogne-sur-Seine on the southwestern edge of Paris. They had come early; the first race around the stadium's 666-meter-long oval wasn't scheduled until 2:15 that afternoon. Several cyclists who had given up along the Tour route and others who had decided not to enter the race would ride against one another in a two-lap sprint as well as a Grand Prix—an hour-long race around the track. Whoever passed through the start and finish line the most times would be named the winner. Francis Pélissier had entered the Grand Prix, but Henri refused to join the competition. Desgrange's words following the brothers' abandonment had not left his mind.

Desgrange hoped the races would turn the Tour's finish at 2:45 p.m. into an all-day event, rounded out by a four-hundred-meter foot race and a single-lap tandem bicycle race. The fans who filtered into the stadium later that afternoon were impatient. They crowded around the dirt path where the cyclists would enter Parc des Princes. Others jammed themselves between the front row of stadium seats and the thin wooden barrier that had been erected around the track. More ambitious Parisians climbed onto the awnings that shaded the back rows. Wherever there was room, people filled the gaps and then some, like surging water. They could see the Eiffel Tower in the distance, backlit by the sun.

The races began. A Tunisian cyclist, Ali Neffati, the first African to compete in the Tour in 1913, led the Grand Prix, completing sixty-two laps over the hour-long trial at an average pace of 41.29 kilometers per hour. He scored seventy-four total points, twenty-three points more than the second-place cyclist. Francis, trailing in seventh, received only nine. The crowd watched and cheered as the solo and tandem cyclists and the runners raced past them, but they were distracted; 2:45 p.m. came and went with no sign of the Tour competitors. The crowd grew restless. The sun beat down on the cement track and the spectators' dark clothes in the stands. The fans talked among themselves, turning from the events in front of them.

At that point, the leading pack rode along parc de Saint-Cloud, past the same greenery they had seen on their way out of Paris one month before. They briefly crossed into the capital before again arriving at pont de Saint-Cloud. Jean, Luigi, Honoré, Léon, and Jacques rode together over the bridge. It was 4:40 p.m.; they had been clustered together for over an hour. Now they reentered Paris and began their approach to the stadium. On either side of the road, the crowd was ten or twenty people deep, not counting those who had joined the riders on their own bikes, pedaling along at a sometimes respectful, other times intrusive, distance. Those who were able had climbed into the trees that lined the road so they might see the cyclists as they biked past. The Brasier, once closely leading them, pulled away to prepare for their arrival. At 4:45 p.m. the automobile arrived on the track. The crowd began to churn— those who hadn't found seats or whose view had been blocked jostled for position along the edge of the track, their bodies pressed together.

Then, at 5:00 p.m., the bugle sounded. Those who had been listening carefully, however, heard an earlier change in the cadence from those outside Parc des Princes. What had been a low static hum had pitched higher and became more animated. The spectators who leaned against the dirt path leading from the street to the track saw a racer, his blue-and-gray jersey bent over the bull-horned handlebars of his bike. He careened along the stretch of ground in front of him. His protective eyeglasses were lifted up, resting against his forehead, and he wore a white cap. Loops of flat bicycle tubes were strung around his arms like the straps of a backpack and cinched around his sternum with a leather belt. Another racer followed just behind him, less than a full bicycle's length separating them. His head was bare, and his dark hair whipped back as he chased the rider in first. One, two, three more followed, each as close as the one before. When they hit the clean, gray cement of the track, they accelerated. Desgrange had promised an additional one hundred francs to the racer who made it around Parc des Princes the fastest.

Jean, Luigi, Honoré, Léon, and Jacques raced around the track in a sprint. Three hundred meters and the cranks on their bikes groaned under the men's weight, each of them lighter than when they had set out on the Tour one month before, some downright wiry after hundreds of hours of cycling. Two hundred meters. They'd raced for more than nine days to get to where they now were. Fifty meters. No strategy was left to their movements; there was only whatever energy they had left to give. Less than a minute later, they would be done with the race. With ten meters to go, they gave one final burst. Five meters. Jean held his lead and passed through the finish line. It was 5:00 p.m., 54 seconds after the minute.

Five minutes later, almost to the second, Jules arrived alone, the only remaining B classification cyclist. Firmin followed him after another six minutes. The winner of the Tour de France rode through the finish line and was handed a wreath for one last leisurely lap around the track. "The Tour has never been harder. I'm just glad it's over," he told the journalists who crowded around him after the victory lap, his mind unable to conjure anything more in that moment. If there was any resentment in his finish, in how he unseated their Eugène, it was overcome by the crowd's excitement as one after another of the eleven remaining cyclists passed onto the track. Fans and race officials calculated the cyclists' times as quick as they were able in order to determine their positions. Had Desgrange kept the Tour's earlier scoring method and not changed the race to one judged on time, Jean would have placed first, followed by Honoré. Firmin would have come in fourth, followed by Eugène. Both groups knew there was little use in dwelling on how the race might have otherwise occurred. They knew Desgrange's vision had always superseded anything else.

Firmin Lambot, winner of the general classification prize, at the 1919 finish line.

Eugène arrived later, at 5:36 p.m. He sprinted around the track as if only seconds separated him from the others, as if Firmin and Jean were less than a length away. He rode along the outer width of Parc des Princes. His hearing was muffled by the wind against his ears; it softened the sounds of the crowd. He saw the people who lined the wooden fence: the teenagers and young children whose necks were bent and whose toes pushed into the ground to see over the shoulders of those in front of them; the men in civilian clothes who carried some remaining scrap of horizon blue—a side cap no longer neatly saddled on their heads, a jacket, lapels folded down to their breastplate. Women in sun hats shouted alongside the men, their hands raised around their mouths in the hope that Eugène would hear them, that he would turn his head in response.

He slowed minutely along the curve of the oval track, able to see almost its entire circumference. Just that day, he had cycled through the battle that had engulfed his country. Even in the capital, the war had left its mark. L'Église Saint-Gervais, in the fourth arrondissement, hadn't been rebuilt since a shell fell on it during the 1918 Good Friday service, but, in that moment, with the crowd packed into every corner of the stadium, with the men who had already started to surround the end of the straightaway, that devastation was briefly forgotten. Eugène accelerated out from the curve and rode toward the finish, still at speed. He sprinted slower than he had in past years. They were old, he and Firmin and Jean. Just five years since he had last competed, but it felt much longer than that.

As he rode through the finish, Eugène could see a country that existed beyond the war. Of course, it had always been true, but it had been out of focus for so long—so distant from those moments in the east when he worked on others' bikes and then when he had worked on his own, over those last four weeks—it might as well have not existed. His life and the country that remained weren't so different from those that had existed before. He still had his neighborhood in Malakoff, the races that would be run year after year for as long as he was able to compete. The war hadn't ended the sport—the competition, the appetite for glory; they would continue even after he left them behind. He was racing under a different banner, but perhaps the individual companies would again find their footing before he left. The race paths had changed; they ran along a new countryside, through altered land-scapes. The people were the same, though fewer in number, but they hadn't forgotten their towns and had continued to watch the cyclists from their doorsteps, to make their own, more productive dents in the countryside.

He passed the finish line, and the border between the track and the stands disappeared. People leapt over the wooden fence and ran onto the cement, surrounding him. The faces he saw as he'd circled the track joined him—retired soldiers and the men in uniform who attempted to control the crowd but forgot themselves for a moment. There were men and boys in suits and ties, families who had walked over to the stadium together; they all collapsed in on him. He was calm, gracious, but his eyes teared up as they approached, as he had found himself doing at countless points after his accident. The journalists who approached began asking questions, taking photographs before he had a chance to rise from the bike's seat. It was a weight underneath him, only more noticeable now since his legs had stopped moving. Desgrange and Firmin looked on, both part of and separate from the crowd that lifted Eugène up and ushered him toward *l'Auto*'s logbook. He signed in one last time. Without support, he was scarcely able to walk, but the crowd buoyed him, carried him. They held him in those late afternoon hours, even after they had left the stadium and returned to their homes.

◆ ◆ ◆

Eugène left Parc des Princes surrounded by fans. In the next few days and weeks, bundles of francs and personal checks, addressed to him, arrived in *l'Auto* offices on rue du Faubourg Montmartre. More than 1,705 francs had been collected by the next day, including the 1,000 that Henri Desgrange and *l'Auto* contributed on top of the 1,000 he had earned for his third-place finish. One franc, 50 francs, 2,000 franc sums continued to arrive. On the morning of August 6th, the amount had reached 8,613 francs and continued to grow. People Eugène had passed along the road sent in small sums, as well as fans in Italy and the outer French provinces. A ten-year-old future cyclist sent in a few francs, as did the innkeepers who'd watched him from their porch. The money eventually exceeded Firmin's first-place award and the town prizes earned by all the others who had competed in the race.

The Tour cyclists who lived in and around Paris retreated to be with their friends and families, who had come out to Parc des Princes to see them after a month away from home. A few family members joined the cyclists on the track; they didn't wish to be apart from them a second longer. Before that, it had been months if not years.

The cyclists, for their part, wanted little to do with the race as soon as it was over. "Where can we shower?" was all that Joseph offered in his postrace interview. "We were all on our knees," Léon said of its last stages. Those who lived farther from Paris would have to make their way home, too. Luigi decided to return to Italy as soon as he was able rather than spend weeks racing in Paris; he had little more to give. Firmin left just after the race was over, as if he couldn't leave the Tour's finish fast enough.

The evening of July 27th, l'Étoile Sportive Saffile de Malakoff, Eugène's local sporting club, hosted a reception in his honor. He was received as the moral winner of the Tour if not the actual one. On Monday, the day after the race ended, a formal dinner was scheduled, once he'd had more time to rest. Before then, he was due to sit down with *l'Auto* to give a longer postrace interview. He was still tired; he could barely walk on his own. He brought a cane to steady himself during the interview. He was not defeated, but he was worn down, disappointed.

The journalist consoled Eugène, though the cyclist didn't seem to need it. He joked that he was thinking about retiring from racing; the factory owner where he repaired his bike had offered him a job as a foreman. Then, he grew quiet. After some time, the cyclist and the journalist agreed that a competition like that year's race, "that most terrible event," as the editor of *l'Auto* had described it, could never happen again.

A NOTE ON METHODOLOGY

Each story's particularities require decisions relating to structure and form that emphasize what makes that story worth telling. Some of these are apparent at first read: the use of multiple perspectives to follow the leaders of the 1919 Tour, one after another, who rose and fell, locations and memories as inroads to a cyclist's story before setting out on that year's race. I wanted to keep the race's momentum while also ensuring that you, the reader, were aware of the surrounding landscape—perhaps the most important part of this race—and how it came to be that way. Other decisions exist at levels beneath words on the page. You haven't been told why they exist; you may not have noticed they exist at all. Instead, they reflect the nature of my research, the Tour's history, and how I approached these characters' stories. Other times, they were simply my decision to make. As a broad disclaimer, any mistakes or disagreements you might have with the text are my responsibility alone.

First, the matter of what is said or written by others as it exists on these pages. Quotations were, for the most part, first written down or said in French, recorded by someone, then translated by me. This is a more tenuous strand than if I had been there at the time of the race, or if the language they spoke is the language I'm now writing in. Overall, I've done my best to accurately convey the experience of the 1919 Tour as it felt at that time. I first tried to keep the voice of the characters as consistent as possible. Desgrange's proclamations should read as if they came from the self-important Father of the Tour, even if they're at times stilted to today's ear. I did not, however, translate the writing and speech as directly as I could. Some translators may consider that admission unnecessary: no word, passing between languages, holds a perfectly equivalent meaning. I tend to agree, but plenty of nonfiction writers would then say at least the most direct translation—rapid to rapide—prevents the writer from saying something that the subject, who lived and said those words at one time, didn't say. For this particular work, I held the experience of feeling as though one were there more important than an exact fidelity to words that held different meanings then than they do now.

You likely noticed points at which the narrative, already close to the experience of the cyclists, closes in even further, peers through their eyes, inhabits their thoughts or memories. One hundred and one years separate me from these characters; I unsurprisingly didn't have the chance to sit down with them to ask directly what they thought in that particular moment. Instead, I've relied on an accumulation of sources that spoke to these characters' mindsets at the time. I recognize, however, that sources of any sort are imperfect: even those once written with the thought that no one else would ever read them. Other times, I've contextualized information in a way that connects one moment with another. At some point, at least given my own philosophy, a writer has to feel comfortable inhabiting the characters they've studied if they want to have any hope of accurately and meaningfully describing them when those characters can't do so themselves.

I relied on a combination of contemporaneous sources and modern ones, in 2020 (or 2019, when I wrote much of this book). *L'Auto*'s pages, helpfully digitized by Bibliothèque nationale de France (BnF), provided the turn-by-turn itineraries of the cyclists. The newspaper also covered moments before, during, and after each stage. These pages built the foundation of the race action, which I expanded upon with details that were less important to the immediate action of the race but that added to the setting and history of the cyclists. I located contemporary photos of the towns the cyclists rode through and city plans so that their paths could be traced down to the block and business, and maps that described the sites of artillery craters. Recollections and reporting from the cyclists, Desgrange, and others informed my general understanding of the race and its history and provided color when the original race reports did not. Finally, I followed much of the cyclists' path in a Peugeot around France. Where I didn't have time to drive their same route, I input the itinerary into Google Earth and traced the routes they took as best as I was able, seeing which turn allowed them to first glimpse the mountain peak on the other side of a valley, when the grade of an ascent took an abrupt lift. My understanding of the race events came from a synthesis of these sources, and at times I had to rely on conjecture about moments that were not directly referenced (e.g., if a report said that a cyclist caught up to the pack, they must have fallen behind at an earlier point).

The story of the Tour de France is a mythology. Desgrange's self-mythology, France's mythology before and after the Great War, the mythology of the Tour itself, helped along by Desgrange but surpassing his own first tempered expectations. The race described the country's boundaries and made them appear whole for the average, otherwise uninterested person for arguably the first time. Myths are by their nature, however, slanted and incomplete. In an attempt to articulate the myth-making occurring in the 1919 Tour and the experience of being there, I'm inevitably drawn into that same process, forgoing a distant and complete view for one within a particular moment in time.

I've accepted this, that my desire to tell a story of rebuilding and of this race existing despite the hurdles prevents me from telling the cold history of where the world or France would go after this point in time, into a period of economic and political turmoil that would give way to another world war. I just think it's important to talk about the particular moment that exists after a war is through, when those emotional, psychological, logistical, and political gears are turning.

SOURCES

My desire to re-create a moment rather than a broad history of the Great War's lingering effects, failed promises, and so on, directed much of my research, though I did not deliberately obfuscate information when a cyclist like Eugène might not have had direct knowledge of it. I relied on newspapers (*l'Auto*, *Le Temps*, *Le Figaro*, etc.) for daily news reports and weather. Characters' backstories were collected through a variety of sources, including local government, national government, and military documents, personal recollections, and reporting. Scenes were triangulated through city plans, contemporary photographs, *l'Auto*'s route itinerary, and contextual research. I also drove and walked what I could of the cyclists' route. A few other texts more generally shaped my thinking on the experience of the war and its effects on the people and the land. Included among these were *The Missing of the Somme* by Geoff Dyer; *The First World War: Unseen Glass Plate Photographs of the Western Front* by Carl de Keyzer and David Van Reybrouck; and *The Great War and Modern Memory* by Paul Fussell.

These sources list the documents as they were first used in my writing. Later chapters build on sources first referenced in earlier chapters, particularly those that relate to the backstories of individual characters. I haven't included each reference to these sources, but only as they first appear.

Chapter 1

For accounts of the armistice celebrations, I turned to photographs and videos housed at the Bibliothèque nationale de France, the Imperial War Museums, and the Library of Congress. For the details of the armistice signing itself, I looked to Hugh Cecil and Peter H. Liddle's edited volume, *At the Eleventh Hour*. I also considered the Twenty-ninth Infantry Regiment's history of the war for these moments.

The details of *l'Auto*'s offices were gathered from the pages of *l'Auto* itself along with official records at the Paris Archives. I consulted maps and contemporary photographs, as well as Pierre Pinon's *Atlas Historique des Rues de Paris* for further details about the nature and history of rue du Faubourg Montmartre, the neighborhood of Faubourg Montmartre, and the surrounding area.

Desgrange's story relied on official government and military documents, collected when Desgrange was due to receive the Legion of Honor, now housed at the grande chancellerie de la Légion d'honneur. Additionally, for both his original primary source research as well as his deep study of Desgrange's life, I have Jacques Lablaine's *Desgrange Intime* to thank, a copy of which the author helpfully furnished.

I also referred to Lablaine's book when considering *l'Auto*'s founding, within the context of French sporting as well as through the lens of the Dreyfus Affair. One could study the latter for a number of years, which I couldn't hope to fully explain in these pages, but I did look to Eric Cahm's *The Dreyfus Affair in French Society and Politics* and Louis Begley's *Why the Dreyfus Affair Matters*. Throughout this process, I turned to Desgrange's own words in the pages of *l'Auto* for his public-facing views of domestic politics and sport, even if he had to amend himself on occasion, as with the date of the 1919 Tour, which would have coincided with the 1919 French Track Championship, also to be held at Parc des Princes on June 22nd.

Chapter 2

Prerace updates were located in *l'Auto*'s pages, most drawn from June 6th up to the race's start on June 29th. Details of newspaper production at the time were collected from *The International Encyclopedia of the First World War*, among other contemporary encyclopedia records. For the psychology of Desgrange's vision and its place within the postwar landscape, I relied on a synthesis of sources, and in many ways the entirety of those I've collected for this book. I read his regular columns in *l'Auto* as well as *Desgrange Intime*. Desgrange wrote introductions for those involved with the Tour, including Lucien Petit-Breton, *Comment je cours sur route*, and Alphonse Baugé, the La Sportive manager, *Messieurs les Coureurs: vérités, anecdotes et réflexions sur les courses cyclistes et les coureurs*. I once again considered what others wrote about him in his citation for the Legion of Honor, too.

Eugène's military records were found at the Grand Mémorial. Additionally, I considered Eugène's memoirs of his cycling experience, serialized in *Le Miroir des sports* from November 1922 to April 1923.

That year's details of Paris–Roubaix were found in *l'Auto*'s pages. I consulted Hugh Clout's "The Great Reconstruction of Towns and Cities in France 1918–35" to better understand the state of the area, the papers of le ministère des Régions libérées as stored at the BnF, as well as photographs from town archives along the route, lined up with Paris–Roubaix itineraries before and after the war, as they appeared in *l'Auto*.

Details of Henri Pélissier's experiences in the war and in early life were similarly pulled from his military records. For the cyclists' performance in races, I turned to *l'Auto*'s pages and at other times to *Pro Cycling Stats*' records, correlating them with newspaper reports from the time whenever possible. Photos of the cyclists were used for their physical descriptions, most notably those they used when registering for the 1919 race as well as those from *La Vie au grand air*'s photos of the race.

Details regarding La Sportive were collected from advertisements, from *l'Auto* coverage, and from Jacques Goddet, Victor Goddet's son's, *L'équipée belle*.

Chapter 3

The geography of the race relied on a synthesis of material that included the first stage itinerary, published in *l'Auto* on June 28th, coverage of the stage on June 29th, June 30th, and July 1st, contemporaneous maps from regional archives, as well as research conducted on Google Earth and through local histories for sites like Saint-Cloud. This general model of synthesis was used on each stage, though the nature of successive landscapes changed the weight and accessibility of each source type. I also consulted a range of more contemporary books on the Tour's history, but I found that details varied minutely between these sources and thus avoided using them except when they included references to original source texts that could be consulted.

Details of the Pélissiers' lives were compiled through official Paris documents, military records, recollections of the brothers as found in sporting newspapers, and coverage of races they competed in. I also considered André Leducq's *La légende des Pélissier*.

Further details of the Paris Peace Conference and the signing of the Treaty of Versailles were found in Margaret MacMillan's *Paris 1919*. The social dynamics of Paris at the time were found in articles like "The Strike Fever in France," from the July 12, 1919, edition of *The Living Age* and in Tyler Stovall's *Paris and the Spirit of 1919*.

Montdidier's state was found in contemporaneous photo postcards, as well as in a number of reports about the town and the surrounding area, including "1914–1918, L'Oise au coeur de la Grande Guerre" from the Oise Archives, "Images de la reconstruction: Arras 1918–1934" from the Pas-de-Calais Council, "La victoire triste?: espérances, déceptions et commémorations de la victoire dans le département du Puy-de-Dôme en sortie de guerre (1918–1924)" by Aline Fryszman.

813th Pioneer Infantry Regiment

For accounts of the Black experience in World War I, I turned to Kelly Miller's contemporaneous *History of the World War for Human Rights*. For a more modern view on the Black experience in the war, I looked at Chad L. Williams's *Torchbearers of Democracy*. I also referenced Addie W. Hunton and Kathryn M. Johnson's *Two Colored Women with the American Expeditionary Forces*.

The operations of Camp Pontanezen, as well as camp leadership, were found in the letters of General Smedley Butler, located at the US Marine Corps History Division library as well as collected by Anne Cipriano Venzon's *General Smedley Darlington Butler: The Letters of a Leatherneck, 1898–1931*. More about Butler was found in Hans Schmidt's *Maverick Marine*. Volume 46 (Jan–June 1920) of *Military Surgeon: Journal of the Association of Military Surgeons of the United States* was also considered, as were photographs of the camp, now stored at the Library of Congress.

The particular activities of the 813th Pioneer Infantry Regiment were found in the official narrative reports of Lieutenant Kenneth Knowlton as well as with the US Army Transport Service Passenger Lists.

Chapter 4

Details on the stage between Le Havre and Cherbourg were found in the June 30th, July 1st, July 2nd, and July 3rd editions of *l'Auto*. For the stage between Cherbourg and Brest, I looked to the July 2nd, July 3rd, July 4th, and July 5th editions of the newspaper.

Details of Le Havre were found in contemporary plans of the city as well as in local archives. I consulted Claire Etienne's *Le Havre – un port* – *des villes neuves* and the records within for a closer look at the movement of goods through the town.

Earlier details about the cyclists' conduct in the race were gathered from the prerace columns mentioned in chapter 2, as well as in the race rules, listed in the November 20, 1918, edition of *l'Auto*.

Weather details from the second stage were found in *Le Temps* and in historical calendars and moon cycles.

Contemporary photographs and official sites of the Gendarmerie nationale were used to establish the uniforms of gendarmes.

Local histories and drives were used to establish some of the locations along the Cotentin.

Chapter 5

Details of the stage between Brest and Les Sables were found in the July 4th, July 5th, July 6th, and July 7th *l'Auto* editions.

I continued to rely on the sources listed above for details of the Pélissiers' progress on the stage between Cherbourg and Brest, specifically the July 5th edition of *l'Auto* for the activities of the cyclists in Brest itself. Baugé's role with the cyclists was confirmed in these pages and others as the race continued.

I also considered what the brothers said to Albert Londres of *Petit Parisian*, the newspaper, after withdrawing from the Tour de France one final time in 1924, as well as the letter Henri sent to *l'Humanité* after the fact. I used these when considering Henri's state of mind, though I recognize these sources were directed toward particular audiences. I also used these sources when considering details of the brothers' drug use in the race.

The differences between the Tour's scoring system and its timed system were collected from records of the race through its inception, focusing on the performance of particular cyclists and how their performances translated to their standings on individual stages and overall. The implications of these models were confirmed with cycling colleagues.

Chapter 6

Details of the stage between Brest and Les Sables can be found in the preceding chapter source list. I also looked to *l'Auto* editions from the surrounding stages to confirm the accuracy of Desgrange's time predictions.

Details of Strasbourg's dancing plague were found in John Waller's "A forgotten plague: making sense of dancing mania," in *The Lancet*.

I looked to the US Bureau of Public Roads records for an understanding of some of the French road features at the time, contemporary Michelin maps, and in articles like Anne Conchon's "Road Construction in Eighteenth Century France," from the Proceedings of the Second International Congress on Construction History, for a history of the road system.

Firmin's success in the Tour de France to that point was put into context by turning to earlier years of the newspaper. Records in the State Archives of Namur detailed his early life, as well as that of Léon. Selections of Dries Vanysacker's *Le cyclisme en Wallonie jusqu'à la Seconde Guerre mondiale* also assisted in establishing Firmin's life as did the archives of the website Memoire du cyclisme.

Alice Milliat

I turned to the *New York World* and the *New York Tribune* for coverage of the women's cycling movement, as well as Nellie Bly's interview with Susan B. Anthony.

Coverage of Alice's public events came from *La Femme Sportive*, the publication of FSFSF, as well as *l'Auto* and *L'Echo de Paris*. I also considered journal articles like Thierry Terret's "From Alice Milliat to Marie Thérèse Eyquem: Revisiting Women's Sport in France (1920s–1960s)," published in *The International Journal of the History of Sport*, "The Pioneering Role of Madame Alice Milliat and the FSFI in Establishing

International Trade and Field Competition for Women," by Mary H. Leigh and Thérèse M. Bonin in *Journal of Sport History*, and "Alice Milliat et le premier « sport féminin » dans l'entre-deux-guerres," by Florence Carpentier in *Revue d'histoire*.

For more on Pierre de Coubertin, I looked to Yves-Pierre Boulongne's "Pierre de Coubertin and Womens Sport," from *Olympic Review*.

Details on conscription and volunteering in the First World War, and the role of women, came from the British Library's series on the war as well as from Susan R. Grayzel's *Women's Identities at War: Gender, Motherhood, and Politics in Britain and France during the First World War*.

Chapter 7

Details of the Aubisque climb were found in *l'Auto* editions from its initial inclusion in the 1910 Tour, the topographical map of the 1919 Tour, and in Pierre Chany's *La Fabuleuse Histoire du Tour de France*. I also considered regional topographical maps.

The stage between Bayonne and Luchon was described in *l'Auto* on July 8th, July 9th, July 10th, and July 11th.

I considered Euskal Kultur Erakundea Institut Culturel Basque's history when summarizing the region's past and contemporaneous photographs, postcards, and plans for towns along the road.

For details on the strikes and the strikers' demands, I looked to articles such as "The Miners' Strike," from *The Spectator*'s July 26, 1919, issue, "All French Miners Strike Tomorrow," from the *New York Times* on June 15, 1919, "The Eight-Hour Law: a Social Europe Project? (1918-1932)," by Najib Souamaa in *Travail et Emploi*, among others.

Chapter 8

In addition to the sources mentioned above, I looked to *l'Auto*'s pages on July 10th, July 11th, July 12th, and July 13th for coverage of the stage to Perpignan and July 11th, July 12th, July 13th, July 14th, and July 15th for the stage to Marseille. July 13th, July 14th, July 15th, July 16th, and July 17th were referenced for the stage to Nice.

I also examined plans for each of the towns in order to detail the cyclists' paths through them.

I turned to Rosemonde Sanson's *Les 14 juillet: fête et conscience nationale (1789-1975)* as well as contemporary photographs and coverage in the local newspaper for how la fête nationale, Bastille Day, was treated that year in Marseille.

Drives through the region supplemented this archival research.

Marguerite Alibert

As an eventual (then abdicated) king, much has been written about Edward VIII. For Edward VIII's military record, as well as his movements in the wartime years, I looked to his own *A King's Story*, a memoir written by the then Duke of Windsor. For a more complete picture of Edward, details were confirmed and filled in by *Edward VIII* written by Frances Donaldson, and *King Edward VIII* by Philip Ziegler.

These narratives, particularly the duke's own, do not spend much if any time on Marguerite's story. *The Woman Before Wallis*, by Andrew Rose, looks at the relationship between the two through Marguerite's own backstory. *Le Figaro* on May 2, 1919, reported on Marguerite's marriage to Charles Laurent and their subsequent honeymoon. Details regarding Marguerite's and Raymonde's births were found in the Paris Archives and confirmed municipal letters and police reports kindly furnished by Andrew Rose.

French sex work has been described by Alain Corbin in *Women for Hire: Prostitution and Sexuality in France after 1850*, "A Brief History of the Regulation of Prostitution in France," by Thiphaine Besnard-Santini in *Journal of the International Network for Sexual Ethics & Politics*, and Jill Harsin's *Policing Prostitution in Nineteenth-Century Paris*.

Chapter 9

The cyclists' tenth stage itinerary between Nice and Grenoble can be found in the July 16th edition of *l'Auto*. The July 17th, 18th, and 19th editions of the newspaper provided coverage of the stage. Sections of the route were confirmed with city plans found at local archives along with contemporary photographs found on BnF's digital library (Gallica), and in local archives. Google Earth was used to re-create sections between towns.

Details regarding the concept of the French hexagon were located in Nathaniel B. Smith's "The Idea of the French Hexagon," in *French Historical Studies*.

For contemporary views on the Alsace-Lorraine, I considered David Starr Jordan's "The Future of Alsace-Lorraine," from *The Journal of Race Development*. I also looked at Sam Henze's "France, Germany, and the Struggle for the War-Making Natural Resources of the Rhineland," and newspaper accounts, such as "Remaking the Map of Europe; Jean Finot's Views on How Parts of Germany and Austria-Hungary Should Be Redistributed in Case the Allies Win," by Jean Finot in the May 30, 1915, issue of the *New York Times*.

I looked to Thomas Nelson Page's *Italy and the World War* and Mark Thompson's *The White War: Life and Death on the Italian Front, 1915-1919* for accounts of fighting in the Alps, as well as contemporaneous photographs.

Like those of the other cyclists, Jean Alavoine's and Henri Alavoine's military records were located at the Grand Mémorial.

I looked at A. P. Padley's "Gas: The Greatest Terror of the Great War," from *Anesthesia and Intensive Care* for details on the effects of gas, as well as contemporaneous newspaper accounts for responses to its use.

Chapter 10

Stage eleven's itinerary was found in the July 18th edition of *l'Auto*. Coverage of the stage itself was found on July 20th, July 21st, and July 22nd.

Details of Pont Charles-Albert were found in *A Handbook for Travellers in Switzerland, and the Alps of Savoy and Piedmont*, by John Murray. Postcards and photographs from the time confirmed details about the bridge's setting and features.

The organization's "World War I and the American Red Cross" confirmed some details about its activities at the time, as did "The Internment of Civilians by Belligerent States during the First World War and the Response of the International Committee the Red Cross," by Matthew Stibbe in the *Journal of Contemporary History*.

Chapter 11

Geoff Dyer's *The Missing of the Somme*, in particular, was considered when detailing the experience of soldiers in the trenches, as were contemporary maps of wartime devastation. I looked to *Three Days in Reconquered Alsace*, by Jean Breton, as well as "The Mortality of Allied Prisoners of War and Belgian Civilian Deportees in German Custody during the First World War: A Reappraisal of the Effects of Forced Labour," by Mark Spoerer in *Population Studies*. *Historique du 6ème régiment de dragons pendant la guerre de 1914–1919* and *Plan der Stadt Mülhausen in Elsass 1911* added to my understanding of the route they rode through, as did postcards from the Alsace region, stored at BnF. John Ellis's *Eye-Deep in Hell: Trench Warfare in World War I* and *Poilu: The World War I Notebooks of Corporal Louis Barthas, Barrelmaker, 1914-1918* helped me understand the trench experience.

The July 20th, July 21st, July 22nd, and July 23rd editions of *l'Auto* were consulted when tracing the riders' routes. Michelin maps from the time helped determine the relative state of the roads.

Chapter 12

For details of the battle at Joncherey, I turned to the *New York Times*, which translated an article from *Le Temps* originally published on February 25, 1916, "First to Fall for France."

Details of the Alsace experience were collected from David Allen Harvey's "Lost Children or Enemy Aliens? Classifying the Population of Alsace after the First World War," published in *Journal of Contemporary History*.

Details on *l'Auto*'s circulation were found in *The Tour de France: A Cultural History*, by Christopher S. Thompson.

Chapter 13

For some of the tactics used at the time, I considered sections of Hall Gardner's *The Failure to Prevent World War I: The Unexpected Armageddon*, contemporaneous posters of the flooding of the Belgian plains, Tait Keller's "Destruction of the Ecosystem," in the *International Encyclopedia of the First World War*, and Zdzislaw Pucek's "European Bison: Status Survey and Conservation Action Plan," among others.

I also looked at Manuel Martin Meersmans, et al.'s "A High Resolution Map of French Soil Organic Carbon" from *Agronomy for Sustainable Development* and Joseph P. Hupy and Randall J. Schaetzl's "Introducing 'Bombturbation,' A Singular Type of Soil Disturbance and Mixing," for more on the effects of artillery strikes on the ground.

Joseph Caillaux

Two book-length narrative accounts I considered were Edward Berenson's *The Trial of Madame Caillaux* and John N. Raphael's *The Caillaux Drama*. I also read selections from Caillaux's translated books, specifically *Whither France? Whither Europe?*

A number of shorter accounts, scholarly and contemporaneous opinion and reported pieces, also went into my understanding of views on Caillaux. Included among these were "Joseph Caillaux: A French Statesman Who Serves Both God and Mammon," from the September 1, 1924, edition of *Current Opinion*; Louis Latzarus's "Joseph Caillaux: A Character Sketch" from the October 1, 1919, *Living Age*; Arthur Julius Nelson's "Joseph Caillaux on Responsibility for the War," from Volume 18, Issue 11 of *The American Monthly*; Arthur Singer's "Caillaux's Defense," from April 1, 1921's *Living Age*; Major T. H. Thomas's "Caillaux" from the June 1925 *Atlantic Monthly*; and Donald G. Wileman's "Caillaux and the Alliance, 1901–1912: The Evolution of Disillusioned Conservative," from *The Canadian Journal of History*.

I turned to the *New York Times* and *New York Times Magazine* for other reported pieces about Caillaux's trial as it was ongoing and for accounts of la Santé Prison, as well as the geopolitical clashes existing during his time in politics.

Jonathan Mercer's *Reputation and International Politics* included a helpful account of the Agadir Crisis and how the diplomatic dynamics of the crisis acted as a prelude to the First World War.

Chapter 14

I looked to le ministère des Régions libérées documents and maps at the BnF for markers and borders of the devastated regions. I also consulted Hugh Clout's "The Great Reconstruction of Towns and Cities in France 1918–35," published in *Planning Perspectives*, for further details about damage to particular towns on the cyclists' route and for the trajectory of those towns' rebuilding.

The July 24th, July 25th, July 26th, and July 27th editions of *l'Auto* provided details about the stage from Metz to Dunkerque.

Eugene Bullard

I turned to Craig Lloyd's *Eugene Bullard: Black Expatriate in the Jazz Age* for a scholarly account of Bullard's life that included selections of his unpublished memoir, *All My Blood Runs Red: My Adventurous Life in Search of Freedom*. I turned to the papers of Louise Fox Connell, a journalist and Eugene's friend, editor, and sometimes agent, at Radcliffe College for more insight into the manuscript's creation.

Margaret MacMillan's *Paris 1919* discussed the ongoing proceedings of the Paris Peace Conference, which Eugene was involved with due to his role as an occasional tutor for conference attendees' children.

I also looked to Jeffrey H. Jackson's *Making Jazz French* for insight into the growing jazz movement in the city and the underlying cultural dynamics that went alongside the movement as well as *Experiencing Jazz* by Richard J. Lawn for contemporary responses to early jazz performances.

Chapter 15

Both this chapter and the following one draw heavily from *l'Auto* on July 26th, July 27th, July 28th, and July 29th for details of the cyclists' route from Dunkerque to Paris. I also consulted BnF and local archives for photographs, postcards, and maps of the surrounding areas.

I referred to Structurae's site for information on Château de Saint-Germain-en-Laye, as well as le ministère de la Culture's site and that of le musée Archéologie nationale, located at the château.

Chapter 16

I consulted *l'Auto*'s newspapers up through the first two weeks of August and onward to understand the response to Eugène's and Firmin's standings at the end of the Tour.

ACKNOWLEDGMENTS

I'd like to thank those who've helped me grapple with the sometimes monstrous task of collecting a one-hundred-year-old story and placing it into the world. Becky, my agent, who first saw the proposal for this project and helped shape its scope and vision, answering emails and phone calls and buying lunches along the way. Laura, my editor, who lent her keen eyes and pen once I had wrestled with a draft as much as I could and who guided me through the weeks where I couldn't look at anything else. Célia, who expanded my amateur knowledge of French with her translations and knowledge about the world at the time of this story. Finally, my fact-checker, copyeditor, cover designer, publicists, and all the others at Little A who shepherded this book.

I'd also like to thank my friends, who, in general, give life meaning that writing cannot. Among that wider group, Allison, David, J. D., Matt, Rachel, and Tom read some or all of the book in its earlier, more haphazard form and offered up kind critiques that helped define early revisions. They forfeited a clean first read for one with more TKs than I can count, and for that, they've gained my unending appreciation.

I'd also like to thank my family: my parents, Julie and Jeff, as well as my brother, Finn, who supported me endlessly—financially and emotionally—as I moved from student to public policy staffer to writer, each step more tenuous than the last. Then, there are my grandparents: Stan, Arleen, John, and Germaine who—throughout their lives—have given me an appreciation for the intimate and far-reaching ripples that pass through generations.

INDEX

A

Abbeville, 256–57
Abdelhafid, sultan of Morocco, 226
Alavoine, Henri, 167–168
Alavoine, Jean, xiii, 38, 92, 96, 101, 104, 108, 112, 113, 131, 133, 135, 142, 144–45, 146, 147, 167–68, 168, 169, 173, 177, 184, 199, 203, 205, 206, 207, 209, 216, 219, 241, 253, 255, 257, 258, 262, 263, 264, 265
Albert I, Prince of Monaco, 149
Alcyon, 35, 73, 91, 170
Alibert, Firmin, 154
Alibert, Marguerite, xiii, 153–60
Alibert, Raymonde, 156, 159, 160
Alsace, 54, 186, 192–93, 196, 206, 207, 208, 220
Alsace-Lorraine, 164, 193
American Red Cross canteen in Bordeaux (1918), *102*; at Champs de Mars, Paris, *260*
Amiens, 51, 52
Anthony, Susan B., 117–18
antisemitism, 9
Antwerp, 194
Argelès, 133

Armentières, 232–33, 240
Armistice after WWI, *xvi*, 3, 7–8, 17, 239
Arras, 30–31
Aubisque, 125, 131, 133–134, 280
Aucouturier, Hippolyte, 191
Aurand, Marie, 154

B

Bal Tabarin, Paris, 248
Barbusse, Henri, 215
Barthélémy, Honoré, xiii, 33–34, 38, 92, 104, 108, 134, 135, 138, 142, 143–44, 146, 147, 148, 149, 150, 151, 163–64, 165, 167, 173, 177, 178, 179–80, 185, 203, 207, 208–9, 209, 216, 218, 220, 255, 256, 257, 258, 262, 263, 264
Basque region, 129
Battery Shelled, A (Lewis), 246
Battle of Arras (1914, 1917), 31
Battle of Passchendaele (1917), 229
Battle of the Frontiers, Donon, 180
Battle of the Marne (1914), 131, 180
Battle of the Somme, *188*, 189–90
Baugé, Alphonse, 89, 90, 115
Bayonne, 104, 113, 128, 219

Beckmann, Mack, 246

Belfort, 23, 185–186, 193, 196, 197, 198

Belgian soldiers near Dunkerque, *230*

Berlin, 62

Berteaux, Henri, 226

Bly, Nellie, 117

Bordeaux, 104, 111, 112

Borel, Maurice, 37

Bouchard, Henri, 218

Brasier, the, 177, 178, 262

Brasserie Schmitt, Bayonne, 114

Braunstein, Jacques, 11

Brest, 59, 61, 65, 68, 80, 86, 89, 91, 92, 94

Breteuil, Francis de, 157

Breteuil, Marquis Henri de, 157

Breyer, Victor, 28, 30, 31

Bricon, 65

Brown, Aaron Lister, 247

Bullard, Eugene, xiii, 243–48

Butler, Brigadier General Smedley, 68–69

C

Café Central, Luchon, 137

café de la Couronne, Lake Geneva, 184

café Riviera Palace, Marseille, 149

Caillaux, Henriette, 228

Caillaux, Joseph, xiii, 194, 267

Caillaux, Joseph (the first), 224

Caillaux, Joseph-Marie-Auguste, 221–30

Calais, 255

Calmette, Gaston, 228

Cambon, Jules, 226

Camp Pontanezen, 61, 62, 68, 69, *88*

Camp Sherman, 64, 65

Cavan, Major General Lord, 158

Champ de Mars, Paris, *260*

Charleville, 232, 234

Chassot, René, 113

Château de Saint-Germain-en-Laye, 258–59

cheating, 191

Cherbourg, 59, 79, 80, 91

chlorine gas, 171–72

Christophe, Eugène, xiv, 25–30, 39, 52–53, 56, 57, 77, 89, 92, 93, 101, 104–5, 106, 108, 111, 112, 128–29, 130–37, 139, 165, 168–69, 173–75, 177, 178, 180, 181, 184, 185, 197, 199, 203, 205, 207, 213–20, 231, 233–38, 240–43, 251, 253, 255, 256, 257, 259, 264–68

Circuit des Champs de Bataille, 22, 92

Clemenceau, Prime Minister Georges, 221–22, 225, 228–29

Clément-Bayard, Adolphe, 9–10

col du Galibier, 175, 177, 180, 181

Colle Saint-Michel, 165

Conseil National des Femmes Françaises, 122

Conservative Republican party, 223, 225

Coomans, Jacques, xiv, 113, 147, 194, 196, 206, 207, 256, 258, 262, 263

Cotentin, 77–78

Coubertin, Baron Pierre de, 4, 119, 120–21, 123

Coutances, 83

D

Defraye, Odile, 26, 93

Deley, Jeanne, 6

Desgrange, Denise, 6

Desgrange, Henri, xiv, 2–7, 8–17, 21–25, 25, 28–30, 34, 37, 38, 39, 71–82, 91, 93, 94, 95, 96, 98, 100–101, 104, 105, 106, 111, 115–16, 117, 123, 126–28, 130, 138, 142–43, 144, 151, 163, 164, 169, 173, 174, 177, 183, 185, 186, 190, 191, 196, 208, 209–10, 214, 215–16, 219, 220, 233, 242, 251, 253–54, 255, 256, 258, 261, 263, 264, 266, 268

Desgrenier, H. (Henri Desgrange), 14, 18

Desmarets, 151

Dieppe, 55, 56

Dieudonné, Robert, 17–18

Dinan, 81

Dompierre, 65, 66, 68

Doudeauville, Duke of, 223–24

Drac River, 169, 170, 171

Dreyfus, Alfred, 9, 203, 224

Dreyfus Affair, 10, 224–25

Duboc, Paul, xiv, 112, 128, 145, 194, 196, 207, 254, 255, 256, 257, 258

Duchamp, Marcel, 246

Dulaurens, Marie, 6

Dunkerque, 220, 233, 234, 241, 242, 250, 252

Dusseiller, Victor, 185

E

Edward, Prince of Wales, 153, 155–56, 157, 159

Edward the Black Prince, 258–59

813th Pioneer Infantry Regiment, 61–69

Engel, Louis, 44

Erzberger, Matthias, 7

Eugénie, Empress, 125

F

Faber, François, 97

Farman, Henry, 17

Fauré, Antoine, 191

Ferdinand, Franz, 14, 201, 202

Fête nationale, la, 146–47

Foch, Ferdinand, 7, 241

Forges, decimated town in Zone Rouge, 230

Fort de Joux, 195

Forty-ninth Infantry Regiment, 113–14

Fourth Cyclist Group, 233–34

France, 213, 221, 222, 226–27, 229, 235, 238–40; borders of, 164; infantry regiment marching in 1918, 40; map of, xi

Franco-Dutch War, 192

Franco-Prussian War, 24, 192, 196, 205, 213, 227, 251

Fréjus, 147

French orphans delegation in Marseilles, 140

FSFSF (Fédération des sociétés féminines sportives de France), 117, 118–19

G

Gambetta Square monument, Le Havre, 70

Garin, Maurice, 20, 25, 174, 191

Gazette des Ardennes newspaper, 239

Geneva, 184, 185, 186, 192

Germany, 164, 204–5, 213, 221, 222, 226–27, 229, 235, 238–40

Giffard, Pierre, 9, 10

Goddet, Victor, 13

Godivier, Marcel, 27

Goethals, Félix, 112

Grand Café de la République, 207

Grand Café du Commerce, Brest, 89, 94

Grand Prix, 261, 262

Great War. *See* World War I

Grenoble, 170–71, 172

Grignard, Victor, 172

Guernsey, 82

H

Hartmannsweilerkopf after Alsace-Lorraine evacuation, *200*

Heusghem, Louis, 38, 104, 128

Honfleur, 77

Hundred Days Offensive, 50

I

Impôts en France, 225

International Olympic Committee (IOC), 123

Italy, 166

J

James Reese Europe regimental band, 245

jazz, 245–46, 248

Jenin, Léonie, 46

Jersey, 82

Jones, Seth, 246

K

Kiderlen-Waechter, Alfred von, 227

Kitchener, Lord, 157–58

Knights of Columbus, 65–66

Knowlton, Lieutenant, 63, 64, 65, 66, 67, 69

Koo, Wellington, 245

L

La Grave, 177

La Rochelle, 109

La Sportive, 35, 36, 49, 80, 89, 92, 93, 174

Lambot, Firmin, xiv, 42, 105–7, 110–11, 112, 128, 135, 137, 141–42, 144, 145, 147, 165, 168, 171, 172–73, 177, 178, 180–81, 182, 184, 192, 193, 194–95, 197, 199, 207, 209, 215, 216, 219, 241, 242, 251–52, 253, 254, 255, 256, 257, 258, 263, *264*, 264, 265, 267

Langois family, 156

Lapize, Octave, 15, 128

Laurent, Charles, 154, 159

l'Auto magazine, 2, 3, 4, 9, 11, 21–23, 24, 28, 30, 51–52, 54, 73, 89, 91, 105, 114, 115, 119, 126, 143, 144, 146, 191, 208, 220, 237, 238, 242, 248, 253, 266

Le Havre, 48, 55, 57, 59, 71, 80; monument to war dead in Gambetta Square, *70*

Le Petit Journal, 22

Le Tour de France par deux enfants (book), 12

Le Vélo magazine, 9, 10, 11, 12, 13, 59

Lefèvre, Géo, 12, 13–14, 190–91

l'Eglise Saint-Gervais, Paris, 265

Les Sables, 100, 104, 108, 115, 128, 219

Lessay, 82

l'Etoile Sportive Saffile de Malakoff, Paris, 267

Lewis, Wyndham, 246

L.H.O.O.Q. (Duchamp), 246

l'Hospice de France, Port de Vénasque, *124*

Ligues François pour le Droit des Femmes, 122

Lille, 232, 238–40

Lindequist, Friedrich von, 227

Lorient, 95, 100

Louis Mitchell's Seven Spades Band, 245–46

Louis XIV, 192, 258

Luchon, 137, 138, 139

Luçon, 108

Lucotti, Luigi, xiv, 42, 44, 113, 131, 132, 134, 135, 141–42, 144, 145, 147, 148, 149, 151, 167, 177, 178, 181, 182, 203, 205, 207, 209, 217, 218, 220, 241, 255, 256, 258, 262, 263, 267

Luz-Saint-Sauveur, 134

M

map of France, xi

Marais Poitevin, 108–9

Marseille, 140, 145, 146, 147

Martinvast, 78

Masselis, Jules, 55, 56, 72, 74, 84

Masson, Émile, 37–38, 39, 44, 84, 104, 105, 106, 134, 141, 146

Maud'huy, General, 219

Meller, Andre, 155

Menton, 148

Mercié, Antonin, 251

Metz, 217, 218, 219, 220, 233, 234

Mézières, 234–35

Michiels, Alexis, 38

Milliat, Alice, xiv, 117–20, 123

ministère des Régions libérées, 239–40

Misme, Jane, 122, 123

Monis, Ernest, 225, 226

Mont Blanc, 162, 182

Montdidier, 50–51

Morlaix, 83

Morocco Affair (1911), 226–28

Mottiat, Louis, 131

Mulhouse, 197, 198, 203–6

N

Nantes, 99, 100, 115

Napoleon III, 125

Neffati, Ali, 262

Nempon, Jules, xiv, 42, 71–72, 111, 134, 146, 196, 206, 207, 215, 253, 255, 256, 258, 263

Nice, 148, 149–50, 163, 235

Night, The (Beckmann), 246

O

Oberndorff, Count Alfred von, 7

Ocean Parkway bicycle path, New York City, 118

Olympic Games, women's participation in, 119–20

Original Dixieland Jass Band, 246

P

Parc des Princes, Paris, 248, 251, 257, 259, 261, 263, 264–65, 266

Paris, 146–47, 157, 167, 219, 262; American Red Cross canteen, 260; on Armistice Day (1918), xvi

Paris Commune, 213

Paris Peace Conference, 184–85

Paris–Roubaix bicycle race, 28, 30–32, 33, 35, 101, 128, 180, 210

Paris to Madrid air race (1911), 226

Parmentier, Antoine-Augustin, 50

Pélissier, Francis, xv, 38, 39, 46–47, 53–55, 72, 75, 76–77, 79, 80, 85,

86, 89, 90, 93, 94, 95, 96–97, 97, 98, 99, 100, 104, 115, 165, 216, 248, 261, 262

Pélissier, Henri, xv, 32–33, 36, 38, 39, 43–47, 48–50, 53–55, 56, 57–59, 80, 82–86, 89, 90–92, 93, 94, 95–96, 97, 98–99, 100–101, 103–4, 115, 116, 117, 174, 216, 261

Pélissier, Jean and Elisa-Augustine, 45

Pélissier, Jean, Jr., 44, 46

Perpignan, 144, 146

Perrin, Georges, 25

Petit-Breton, Lucien, 15, 116, 233

Peugeot, 35, 73, 170

Peugeot, Corporal Jules-André, 202–3

Peugeot-Wolber, 110

Pilcer, Harry, 248

poilu memorial (Bouchard), 218

Poincaré, President Raymond, 229

pont Charles-Albert, 182–83

Port de Vénasque, *124*

Pothier, Lucien, 191

Pottier, René, 126–27

Princip, Gavrilo, 14

Q

Quimper, 95, 97

Quimperlé, 97–98

R

racial discrimination, and the 813th Pioneer Infantry Regiment, 65–66

Radical Party, 223, 225, 226, 228

Rauvaud, Charles, 39, 44

Raymond family of Grenoble, 172

recreational cycling, 118

Red Cross, *102*, 184

Retinne, 57

Richepin, Jean, 17

Riviera-Glacier, 164

Rossius, Jean, 55, 56, 57–58, 71, 72, 74, 80, 82–83, 89, 92

Rostand, Edmund, 115

Roubaix, 31–32, 233

Rouvier, Alphonse, 138

rowing, 119

S

Saint-Cloud, 43

Saint Sava Blessing Serbian Children's Orphanage, Nice, 150

Scieur, Léon, xv, 42, 107–8, 112, 113, 131, 132, 134, 144, 145, 178, 181, 184, 207, 218, 241, 256, 258, 262, 267

Second Battle of the Marne (1917), 180, 229

Second Battle of the Somme (1918), 31

Sedan, 234

Seine river, 43

Sibille, Louis and Alphonsine, 107

Six Days of New York bicycle race, 17

Soppe-le-Bas, 197

Steinès, Alphonse, 126, 127

Steux, Alfred, xv, 144, 194, 215, 256, 257

Strait of Dover, 254

Strasbourg, 151, 185, 193, 202, 207

Strasbourg's dancing plague, 103

Switzerland, 183–84

T

Théval, Sonia de, 158

Thys, Philippe, xv, 14, 27, 33, 38, 39, 42, 56–57, 72, 74–75, 104, 110, 135, 136, 137, 233

Tiberghien, Hector, 38

tires, bicycle, 51–52, 83–84, 206–7

Tour de Belgique, 91, 93, 107

Tour de France, 12–17, 18, 21, 24–25, 32–33, 36–39, 121, 126, 127, 129, 142–43, 178–79, 190–91, 191, 237, 257; 1919 finish line, *264*; 1939 peloton ascending col du Galibier, *176*; sponsors, 34–36; winner Firmin Lambot in 1919, *264*; winner Maurice Garin in 1903, *20*

Treaty of Versailles, 164, 246

Triple Alliance, the, 166

U

UFSF (l'Union française pour le suffrage des femmes), 122

USS *Cap Finisterre*, 69

USS *Pocahontas*, 64, 65

V

Van Daele, Joseph, xv, 113, 241, 255, 256, 258

Vannes, 99

Vanselow, Captain Ernst, 7

Verdun, 97, 243

Verstraeten, Aloïs, 113, 146, 253

Viviani, René, 228

Vizille, 170–71

Vosges Mountains, site of battle, *212*

W

Waldeck-Rousseau, Pierre, 224, 225

Ward, Winifred "Fredie" Dudley, 159

Wemyss, Rosslyn, 7

William I, Emperor, 218

Winterfeldt, Major General Detlof von, 7

Wissembourg, 214

World War I: in Alsace, 208; and Belfort, 197; and Dunkerque, *250*; end of, 1–9; in Lille, 238–41; start of, 193, 201–3; Vosges Mountains, site of battle, *212*; and Zone Rouge, 231–32, 235, 241, 252

Z

Zone Rouge, *230*, 231–32, 235, 241, 252

ABOUT THE AUTHOR

Adin Dobkin is a writer and journalist whose work has appeared in the *New York Times Magazine*, *The Atlantic*, the *Paris Review*, and the *Los Angeles Review of Books*, among others. Born in Santa Barbara, California, Adin received his MFA from Columbia University. For more information about the author and his works, please visit www.adindobkin.com.

IMAGE CREDITS

Chapter 1: Photo 12/Alamy Stock Photo

Chapter 2: Keith Corrigan/Alamy Stock Photo

Chapter 3: Photo 12/Alamy Stock Photo

Chapter 4: ND/Roger Viollet/Getty Images

Chapter 5: adoc-photos/Getty Images

Chapter 6: Interim Archives/Getty Images

Chapter 7: ART Collection/Alamy Stock Photo

Chapter 8: Branger/Roger Viollet/Getty Images

Chapter 9: Sueddeutsche Zeitung Photo/Alamy Stock Photo

Chapter 10: AFP/Getty Images

Chapter 11: Trinity Mirror/Mirrorpix/Alamy Stock Photo

Chapter 12: akg-images/Alamy Stock Photo

Chapter 13: Sueddeutsche Zeitung Photo/Alamy Stock Photo

Chapter 14: Science History Images/Alamy Stock Photo

Chapter 15: WATFORD/Mirrorpix Getty Images

Chapter 16: Niday Picture Library/Alamy Stock Photo; Albert Harlingue/Roger Viollet/Getty Images